Enda McDonagh

DOING THE TRUTH

The Quest for Moral Theology

UNIVERSITY OF NOTRE DAME PRESS

Notre Dame, Indiana

Copyright © 1979 by Enda McDonagh
This edition published by arrangement with
Gill and Macmillan, Dublin

Library of Congress Cataloging in Publication Data

McDonagh, Enda.
 Doing the truth.

 1. Christian ethics—Catholic authors—Collected
works. I. Title.
BJ1249.M155   241'.04'2   79-63361
ISBN 0-268-00844-2
ISBN 0-268-00845-0 pbk.

Printed in the United States of America

Contents

Introduction:
Theology as Autobiography

GIVEN that the man Jesus Christ and his story have always formed
the basis and centre of Christian theologising, it is surprising that
theology has been predominantly schematic and systematic rather
than narrative in approach; philosophical and 'scientific' rather
than personal and literary in character. Recent attempts to amend
through discussions of theology as story or biography[1] have not
yet really affected the dominant method and tone of theology.
Future developments along these lines should be enriching and
draw some theologians more closely to the ranks of the literary
critics and away from the philosophers or even the historians.
Not that theology can afford to jettison its philosophical and
historical modes, but that some aspects of the Christian message
may be more fruitfully pursued and understood in the literary
mode.

This will still be a second order intellectual pursuit, at a remove
from the disorderly sequence of occurrences and decisions (the
given, the achieved and the failed) which constitute the faith
life of the believer. As he receives his faith life and its professional
expression in theological work over a period of years, a Christian
theologian may find that the professional and scientific efforts,
in their philosophical, historical and even literary modes, reflect
more of the involvement and the escape, the triumph and the
failure, the joy and the sorrow, the excitement and the boredom,
the order and the chaos which have characterised his life as human
and Christian than he had realised on the particular occasions
of theological composition and exposition. Drawing together a
series of papers composed even over the relatively short period
of three to four years, as this book does, provides the author at
least with opportunity for insight into the history of his own
struggles, personal and social, intellectual and spiritual. It reveals

how far his theological writings are autobiographical and raises
the question of how far autobiography may be another valid way
of theological exploration.

The Issues

The issues which are treated in this book may seem the surest
guide to the author's recent involvements. Yet certain reservations
are in order. The treatment of an issue presented here had a previous history, perhaps a previous and different presentation. It
may—almost certainly will—recur and require different treatment
in the future. And the issues were (very) occasionally dictated by
the needs of the moment, at a conference or for a periodical, and
not the fruit of a long-standing interest and study. It is a matter
of autobiographical record that such occasional responses become
more and more infrequent and that my choice of themes for
lectures or articles is now much more determined by my own
preoccupations and much less by the requirements of organisers
and editors. It is the history and value of these preoccupations
that determine the autobiographical significance of the issues
discussed in this book.

The preoccupations took on a certain intellectual dynamic of
their own within the academic context. They were, however, born
of personal concern and engagement and constantly nourished
by return to the concrete experience and need. Obvious examples
of this are the chapters on marriage and violence. Despite or
perhaps because of my celibacy, I have been privileged to share
quite closely in other people's marital success and failure. The
paper published here, one of many lectures delivered on the topic
in recent years, ultimately derives from that shared experience.
The insight into friendship as at once a vital mode of husband-
wife relationship and one frequently extended to include outsiders
like myself, summarises more autobiographical material than this
volume could effectively express. Such friendship, within and
without marriage, incorporates and reveals the saving presence
of the God of Jesus Christ in a manner that is central to the
sacramental understanding of Christianity.

As an Irishman I find it impossible to distance myself from
the relationship between violence and political change. The paper
reprinted here focuses the experiences and reflections of years.

It reinforces the growing conviction that the theologian of morality must somehow have the 'insider' feel to be able to analyse effectively the moral components of a particular human problem. The methodological significance of 'insider' analysis lays fresh emphasis on the autobiographical quality of effective theological work.

The personal and social preoccupations which marriage and political violence illustrate, stimulate the need for more general and deeper discussion of ethical questions in their social context, personal intensity and Christian significance. Most of the other chapters in this book concentrate on the interaction between the personal and social and its ultimate Christian meaning. What has increasingly influenced my own moral experience and analysis in recent years is the primacy of the social in relation to which the personal finds its true and irreducible place. The opening chapter, which was written after all the others, offers some elaboration and justification of this. But all the chapters and particularly chapters 5–11 (including therefore marriage) return in one way or another to this dipolarity of society and person and endeavour to provide a more comprehensive ethical approach, context and analysis than were allowed by previous distinctions between personal and social ethics or particular, practically unrelated divisions of ethical material. Perhaps it is only at a certain stage of one's personal and intellectual development that one feels sufficiently liberated to recognise more fully one's independence in interdependence. Only then can one find one's personal identity within a comprehensive social context. Autobiographical data have here undoubtedly contributed to theological stance.

The emerging social context of moral analysis and the social engagement which underlies it find a further counterpoint in prayer-experience, communal and personal, and its analysis (chapter 2). The surface dichotomy between social service and worship could not be adequately overcome for the Christian by a 'morning offering' spirituality which referred extrinsically all one's activities to the glory of God. Prayer and moral behaviour turn out to be two sides of the same coin or two phases in the single dynamic response to God and the neighbour. This intrinsic connection, observed experientially and confirmed in reflection, protects the unity of Christian community and activity while it challenges and enables Christians to transcend their present moral and spiritual condition. The summons and power of moral self-transcendence and the expression which that finds in genuine prayer illuminate the contemplative element at the heart of human activity. Such an approach offers guidance on the asceticism apt for our times (chapter 3). It helps to unravel some of the tangled difficulties relating human and Christian freedom. It may well be that the real answer to the possibly misconceived question about a specifically Christian ethic lies in the capacity of the Christian to appreciate the inner if transcending relationship between morality and prayer. Chapters 2, 3 and 4 distil some of the experiences of and reflection on these issues as they have become inextricably entangled with my life, personal, social, professional, human and Christian.

The eccentric and unclassifiable piece in this slice of life and reflection appears to be chapter 12 on Scandal. This is in part because it was, unlike almost all the others, specifically requested by editors and on a topic to which I would not naturally have gravitated at the time. Yet its writing proved for me at least a rewarding struggle as I endeavoured to come to grips once again with the scandal of Jesus, the Cross and the gospel message on the one hand, and that of the evil in the world on the other. The natural law tradition of morality and the recent optimistic view of the world by the Church (cf. *Gaudium et Spes,* Vatican II) have tended to obscure for moralists the inherent evil in the world. This can lead to an unrealistic presentation of moral problems, moral analysis and moral response. The triumph over the evil which has been achieved in Jesus Christ does not automatically liberate us. We do not live simply by the light and power of the Resurrection. A genuine account of our moral lives will see us as candidates for crucifixion as well as for glory. I was pleased to be reminded so forcibly of that in confronting the topic of scandal.

The Life

The collection of issues treated in this book and the accumulation of events and experiences which lay behind them indicate, however fitfully, something of the author's preoccupations and course of life in recent years. Such a relationship between theological issues and concrete experiences reveals at most a very simple, first-stage understanding of theology as autobiography. The further understandings depend on the interaction between these experiences, theological reflection on them and the transforming (or other) effects on the author's further living and thinking, acting and praying, on the whole, integrated life or *bios* of which the *graphe* must be composed.

This is very intimate and dangerous territory. The difficulties of getting an adequate grip on the shifting sands of one's total life experience, even or perhaps especially over a short period, are enormous. The opportunities for self-deception are boundless. The risks of embarrassment for self and others are incalculable. The difficulties if not the dangers may be reduced by recognising that the theological significance of autobiography does not rest on any Sunday paper type 'confessions' involving detailed self-exposure or betrayal of other people's confidences. A theology of what these events, experiences and reflections have made of me arises at a level of abstraction or, as I would prefer to put it, intensification and concentration that leaves the particularities of the living sources for the most part anonymous. Other-protection and a certain measure of self-protection are thereby ensured. The self-protection is necessarily limited. All authentic writing and teaching, at least in the theology of morality, involves a measure of self-revelation. The good teacher is continually giving himself away, in all the positive and negative senses of that phrase. In the more self-conscious treatment of theology as autobiography, the giving away is deliberately accepted as essential to the method. The self-protection is directed to saving the reader from the self-indulgent exhibitionism of the author and to saving the author from the prurient curiosity of the reader.

Autobiography and Conversion

Although it would be a gross simplification to redescribe the classic of theological autobiographies, Saint Augustine's *Confessions,* as the story of his conversion to Christianity, the theme of conversion taken in all its richness dominates the work and provides an important insight into all our lives, in their change and development. The change of heart, *metanoia,* to which Jesus summoned his followers and the centring of that heart (Matt. 6 : 21) by which he indicated they were to be judged, enable us to plot the graph of our Christian and human lives. Conversion is not just a Christian or religious phenomenon. It may, without betraying its Hebrew and Christian origins, be applied to the significant movements, changes in all human living, by which we are deeply engaged or committed. Such conversion may not last. Like the seed on shallow ground or among the thorns (Mark 4), engagement may die from lack of sustenance or be choked by other cares and distractions. It may be that the movement of life is merely drift without any serious engagement. And even the most serious engagement may yield to greater needs or just greater pressures in difficult circumstances. The ebb and flow of one's deepest engagements provide the material for autobiography as theology, even if they only indirectly find expression in one's professional writings and use for that expression issues of professional as well as those of more intimate concern.

In the choice of themes presented in this book, that ebb and flow of conversion, engagement and perhaps disengagement find expression, however indirectly. More direct acknowledgment is required if any further insight into the relation between autobiography and theology is to be attained.

The easiest place to start in many ways is with a kind of 'professional conversion'. It is not one which began with this book; explosions of conversion are often the result of very slow-burning fuses. This particular fuse reached its climax in many ways in my earlier book, *Gift and Call*, which attempted a theology of morality rather than a moral theology, by taking as its starting-point human experience of morality rather than the moral teaching of the Judaeo-Christian revelation and tradition. That fuse has set off some further explosions in my mind, leaving intact the conviction that the dialectic between moral experience and Christian faith must continue along the earlier lines but making me much more chary of any overall system of theology of morality comparable to the systems of the past, medieval, manual or modern. This combines paradoxically with a deeper conviction about the unity of the moral life, although it is no longer so clearly the moral life of an individual but of a person-in-community and a community-of-persons. That is another aspect of the conversion.

Without a unified system of morality, how can one maintain unity of moral living or offer a unified moral guidance? And surely that guidance is the only justification of the moral theologian's work. There are a number of helpful if not entirely satis-

fying answers to this objection: what the theologian is trying
to do is to decipher a style of life for the contemporary Christian
based on his reflection on the interaction between present-day
moral demands and Christian belief. The theologian might offer
an approach to all these problems and to Christian living as a
whole that derives from that reflection and dialectic. He may
provide a method or methods whereby the Christian can make
his own moral decisions and establish his own pattern of life.
It is along these lines that the theologian can help the Christian
to do his own theological reflection rather than offering him
prepackaged answers elaborated in the study and in the text-
book.

This 'conversion', if such it be, was not born of other theologians' published analyses, but of the daily experience of my own
life and of the lives of those who sought my support or advice.
As I found the 'prepackaged' answers less effective or relevant,
I began to recognise the inadequacies of the existing systems and
the difficulties of discovering any new, satisfactory and comprehensive system. A significant part of the conversion-discovery
was the realisation of how community-dependent the individual
moral agent is in his awareness of moral tasks, his decision-making,
his implementing of these decisions. For Christians the Christian
community is or ideally should be the most sensitive witness to
the moral tasks of the day, the most perceptive guide in decision-
making and the strongest support in implementation. A thousand
recent experiences have proclaimed how inadequately we, the
Christian community, fulfil these roles. Fortunately other people
and communities are sometimes at hand to supplement or replace
our feeble efforts.

Conversion, Values and Praxis

The conversion to 'experience' as the spring-board of moral
analysis demands further explication. In intellectual but also
deeply personal terms the conversion could be elaborated in terms
of growing commitment to such virtues or values as truth, justice,
chastity, or globally and climactically to charity. Such commit-
ments enter into one's life and have their effect on one's living,
if not always as challenge and achievement at least as judgment
on one's failure. The value of truth-seeking and truth-expressing

binds the person with an academic vocation, and so the theologian, in a particular way. The judgment upon him for failing to seek and speak the truth as fully as possible constitutes the most serious sign of his failure to live the project of conversion in fidelity to his vocation. The judgment which he may occasionally encounter for seeking and speaking the truth as fully as possible, while it may be painful and frustrating for him, is more revealing of others' failure to live their own project of conversion. Between these two kinds of failure, which every serious theologian encounters, lies the humbling and purifying process which every serious theologian requires.

More humbling and purifying still is to undergo the test of how far one does the truth one is perhaps busily seeking and expressing. The use of moral experience as a starting-point for moral understanding, which proved a significant stage of conversion earlier, is now yielding to the test of implementing or doing the truth. This provides a more searching test of theology and the theologian. It leads to a deeper understanding of both. Indeed, doing the truth of which he has already attained some understanding constitutes a summons to his further conversion and a source of his fuller understanding. His failure to do the truth, inevitable over a period, or, more damning, his failure to recognise that doing the truth is test and source of genuine understanding, constitutes a judgment on himself and his theology. The growing awareness of this judgment and the attempts to meet its demands will change the theological insight and Christian living of the theologian. It is not an easy change or conversion to accept.

With the privileged circumstances of the clerical and academic life which so many theologians including this one enjoy, it is difficult to take fully seriously some of their moral comments and conclusions on the need for justice, the evils of discrimination, the horrors of violence, solidarity with the poor and oppressed and generally the summons to do and live the truth of their Christian vocation. Because the theologian's personal conversion has not been fully realised, neither has his theology's. His evasion of the more painful implications of that conversion will render his theology less penetrating as well as less persuasive. Autobiography reveals the limitation of his theological understanding as well as the source of it.

Conversion as Personal

Conversion, continuing as it ought to be, does not affect the Christian or theologian in a vacuum. It is not simply or primarily an intellectual or moral conversion to intellectual systems, moral values and patterns of living. The conversion of a person finds its appropriate and ultimate term only in another personal reality. Conversions in consciousness (pre-reflective or reflective), in commitment and in action find their true meaning and fulfilment in relationships of conversion to other personal realities whether through face-to-face or structural relationships, whether to human or divine personal realities. Such a personally grounded understanding of conversion defines the true autobiographical structure of growth in theological understanding and of the final limitations to that growth.

Theology and Friendship

The face-to-face conversion to the other person as constituting another world, different from, irreducible to and finally beyond one's own, has played a long-standing role in my life and theology. It is easy to flatter oneself that one has been lucky in one's friends. That luck may refer to a superficial social smoothness or to deeper feelings of support and consolation in times of difficulty. The friendship that is critical but not exclusive, that serves as a stimulus and standard for other face-to-face relationships, has more tangled roots, a more fragile history and must sometimes issue in real pain as well as joy. The historical, time-laden conversions, to a human other and to a range of human others, which constitute one's most intimate autobiography, may move through stages of exciting discovery and reassuring familiarity and predictability, of disintegration and reintegration, of life, death and resurrection. Not all these terms and stages will be appropriate to every developing relationship. Perhaps it is only in the intimacy, exclusiveness and permanence of marriage that these stages may be experienced in all their complexity and depth. At any rate marriage and friendship are related, as I suggested earlier, in a fashion not always sufficiently recognised. Friendship provides for marriage a goal and standard of independence and separateness of identity in intimacy of relationship; while marriage provides for friendship a standard of intimacy and interdependence in independence and separateness of identity. The powerful sexual intimacy of marriage should not obscure the need to respect the continuing strangeness of husband and wife or their separate identity. The lack of such intimacy in unmarried friends should not obscure the bonds of interdependence which may develop between them.

The friendships I have directly experienced and the marriages in which I have indirectly shared have undoubtedly shaped my life and my theology to a considerable degree. Indeed it would be impossible to separate out aspects of life and theology which have not been at least deeply influenced, if not actually formed, by these deep personal relationships. As the location of theological understanding, the deeper, more developed, longer-standing ones form one end of a spectrum that stretches to relationships which amount to little more than long-term coexistence or fleeting, if warming, contact. And the inconsistencies, pain and frustrations of even the deepest and most permanent of relationships add their own twists to theological understanding.

Human relationship, friendship and marriage as theological sources are clearly suggested in the history of God's relationship with his people as portrayed in the old and new covenants. The sharing and intimacy on offer from God, the permanency and fidelity required of mankind, the breaches which actually occurred and were repaired, not only parallel the history of human relationships; these human relationships are invoked as illustrations and realisations of the divine-human relationship so dramatically inaugurated in the Exodus story and definitively completed in Jesus Christ. To suggest such parallels for human friendship does not exhaust its theological potential. Experiencing human friendship is a gateway or a channel, as the sacraments used to be called, to encountering God. Not just *like* relating to God; human friendship *is* relating to God. In one's loving relationship with the friend one is opened up to the mystery of the human other, a mystery that derives from and embodies the ultimate mystery of God. To respond to the other as other is to discern and experience something of his or her mystery and so of the ultimate mystery. To know one's neighbour in this way is to know one's God, as to love one's neighbour as the New Testament insists is to love

God. That knowing and loving, the sensitive awareness and alertness to the value or worthship of the other involved, move by an inherent dynamism into awareness of the value and worthship of the ultimate other. Human response to the human other tends to transcend itself in response to the ultimate other in what is called worship or prayer. Perhaps what is distinctive for Christians about moral response (rather than what is a distinctively Christian morality) is the way moral response can transcend itself into prayer. And as the recognition and acceptance of the others as others opens the self to increasing understanding and acceptance of the self, the sense of the transcendence of the ultimate other achieved in other-awareness is complemented by the sense of immanence achieved in the awareness and acceptance of the self.

The chequered history of human relationships which form the heart of one's autobiography provide a continuing source for awareness of and reflection on the divine. The deliberate or negligent exclusion of certain people, or the concentration on one's own kind in race or class or sex or interest or temperament, reduces the opportunity for understanding the diversity of God in all the profusion of his images. And while one's time and energies and opportunities limit the range and depth of one's relationships, they should retain a sense of the continuing strangeness and diversity of the others which will evoke our awe, mediate the mystery and provoke theological reflection.

The most threatening and rewarding aspect in human relationship is the constant re-emergence of the stranger. Someone as close as husband, wife, parent, child, life-long friend, suddenly appears in an unexpected and unfamiliar guise. Growth in relationship depends on the capacity to evoke and to cope with the loved one as recurring stranger who, while at times appearing so close and so familiar, remains elusive, unpredictable and irreducibly strange. The strangeness, the difference, may prove painful to the point of disruption and yet it provides the fresh soil for nurturing new and deeper bonds. The stranger-friend is the model as well as the gateway to the totally transcendent God who is yet more intimate to me than I am to myself. Without the ability to rediscover the strangeness of God, faith languishes and theology is trivialised into the constant polishing of a petrified and domesticated idol. Autobiography as theology is about the search for the Perfect Stranger who comes to meet one in the imperfect strangers of daily life.

Autobiography and Conversion as Social

The thrust of this discussion has so far tended to focus on face-to-face if not one-to-one relationships. Yet, so much of our relating is not face-to-face but through the structures and institutions of society. And such relating constitutes a critical part of one's autobiography—for some theorists the critical part. In any event, the theological significance of autobiography and its conversion dynamism are inextricable from the social context in which the autobiographer exists and develops. The web of face-to-face relationships which may provide his immediately conscious human environment is shaped and developed by the underlying social environment, ethnic, linguistic, cultural, economic and political. The scope and direction of his life, of his continuing conversion, depend on the freedom, support or push which the social environment provides. And if he is not simply reducible to the play of social forces but retains some ability and freedom to shape that environment in turn, as I believe, the relationship of person and society involves theologically not just personal change or conversion but social conversion also if the Christian call is to receive adequate recognition and response.

The further implications of this emerge in some of the later chapters and are given explicit treatment in chapter 13. Here it should be noted that the role of engagement or praxis in moral understanding must include social engagement not simply as one's own individual response to the problems of society but as part of society's response, a response involving the conversion of society as well as the self.

In theological terms the direction of that conversion is towards the establishment or emergence of the ultimate Christian social reality, the kingdom of God. No historical social achievements may be identified with the ultimate kingdom but the summons of the final kingdom provides in Christian terms a dynamism and critique for the struggle to transform society. In the course of that transformation the God of the kingdom becomes more accessible and discernible. The society-transforming process in which one is engaged is also one of encountering and recognising the God who lies ahead of us, who is calling us to him and who comes to meet us. The conversion of society in which one participates includes one's own conversion to the neighbour in more human structures and relationships and to the God whose ruling presence is reflected and partially realised in these structures and relationships. Access to that God and critical understanding of mankind's relationship to him in faith and hope and love, also depend on commitment to and engagement in the transformation of society. The value of theology as critical understanding of faith, hope and charity is clearly related to the story of engagement. Autobiography as theology must combine social engagement with critical reflection on its faith-significance.

The Continuing and Unfinished Task

In so far as autobiography in its personal and social dimensions enters into theological work, it underlines theology's incompleteness and provisionalness. As the autobiography can never be finished by the autobiographer, neither can his theology by the theologian. The life which the autobiography seeks to chart goes on. The conversion which for the Christian provides the dynamism and direction of that life must continue. The critical reflection on that life of conversion which shapes his theology remains a continuing and unfinished task for the theologian. His every completed work has the provisionalness of an introduction to the rest of his life, conversion and theological reflection. His last theological word prepares the way for the first word of the rest of his theology. In this incomplete and provisional condition he will always come before his readers.

I

The Quest for Moral Theology

No longer free to reach for his manual to find the answer to a particular problem, the Catholic student of moral theology finds himself confronted with a bewildering range of information, analysis and opinion on an increasing range of problems. If he has time and inclination to work through the information, analysis and opinions available on even one problem, he may sometimes find a convergence of views on the practical conclusion. He will almost always find a divergence of approach, method and argumentation in reaching that conclusion. The traditional manual has not been replaced—not by a single answer-all volume nor even by an agreed method of approach and analysis of contemporary moral problems. The search for a replacement continues. After some twenty years of intensive activity by the professionals, the quest for a renewed moral theology remains unfinished and confused.

I. The Range of Issues:
From Slobland to Barricade to Prie-dieu

The incompleteness and confusion characteristic of the present state of moral theology derive in part from the extension of its brief and the emergence of new issues. The range of individualist issues to which the manuals with their focus on the confessor mainly confined themselves, has long been seen to be inadequate. Problems which were formerly and safely confined within the social teaching of the Church have begun to escape their imprisonment and demand serious and systematic moral analysis. Industrial conflict has appeared far more in need of and far more resistant to moral analysis and moral resolution than the anger, quarrels and frauds of friends, neighbours or business associates. Even the traditional concern with the social moral problem of the just war has been overtaken by the new possibilities of nuclear war, the thrust towards violent revolution in face of tyranny, the spread of international terrorism, the reaction to institutionalised violence, the development of non-violent philosophies and strategies of radical change, and the extended recognition of the right to conscientious objection and to a pacifist vocation. The increasing consciousness of peace and war, population and starvation, racial and sexual discrimination, economic and political exploitation as constituting great moral challenges in our time, has altered the perspectives of moral analysis dramatically, profoundly and irreversibly. While the first stage of alteration, that of the destruction of purely individualist or personalist perspectives is almost complete, the further constructive stage has barely begun. Social issues are receiving increasing and systematic attention from moral theologians to the point of overshadowing individual issues in some instances. However, no critical presentation of moral theology has effectively attempted to combine the whole range of social and individual issues within new and unified perspectives.

To add the social to the individual does not do justice to the current range of issues. A morality of the people and for the people must come down to earth in a way unnoticed by previous generations. The ambiguity of technical progress, the gradual disappearance of some of the earth's critical resources and the destruction by pollution of others, have all combined to awaken a new moral sensitivity to planet earth. If our biosphere is not to become a thanatosphere for future generations, critical moral decisions have to be made and implemented now. Moral responsibility for stewardship of natural resources must replace the profligate and exploitative attitudes of the past. In analysing such responsibility, promoting attitudes and facilitating decisions, moral analysts, philosophical and theological, have an essential if modest role. The moral theologian's task is complicated more than ever by having to add to his brief such problems as those of the preservation of sloblands in the cause of ecological balance and the defence of the barricades in the cause of social justice. And that is not all.

One of the gains of moral theology presently has been the realisation that the call to perfection applies to all Christians. A two-stage morality of the perfect and imperfect, the religious and the laity, through counsels and commandments, is no longer defended or defensible. The theological background to this need not detain us here. And it is not the place, either, to linger over the complexities of the relationship between religion and morality or between human and Christian morality. A related issue is however very pertinent to this stage of the discussion. The disappearance of the two-stage morality or way of life among Christians has had the effect of requiring from moral theologians in their analysis a discussion of the means and stages of perfection in that life, including prayer. The questions hitherto treated in 'Ascetical and Spiritual Theology' have become in theory at least the province of the moral theologian. Some of the difficulties and possibilities of this requirement are discussed in later chapters. Here it is sufficient to note that the sudden expansion of issues from mainly individualist to predominantly social and thence to the earthiness of diminishing oil supplies and destructive fertilisers and back again to the stages of ascent to God in prayer, was bound to induce a sense of vertigo in the moral theologian. In that somewhat unbalanced condition he must continue his quest for a critical and systematic moral theology.

II. Questions of Perspective and Strategy

The diversity and confusion of moral theology today is at least in part due to the different starting-points, frameworks, methods of argumentation and overall goals which characterise the work of moral theologians around the world. I choose to discuss some of these differences under the headings of perspective and strategy as at once indicating the broad scope of pursuit and the particular methods employed. Some more fundamental questions will be reserved for my third and final section on questions of theology.

For Confession or Christian Living?

The well-defined purpose of the manuals which emerged in the seventeenth century was the training of confessors in discerning the kind, number and seriousness of sins. For almost four hundred years moral theology was dominated by the pursuit of the nice distinction of sins within a basically legal framework which had a rational philosophical background and deferred to Scripture for token confirmation of its analysis. The other strand in moral theology which understood it as a theology of Christian living never entirely disappeared. However, it was only in the last twenty years that it began to dominate moral theology. So emerged a critical change in the purpose of moral theology with the broader and more positive understanding of Christian behaviour and life for all Christians replacing the sophisticated discernment of sins for confessors. The expansion of the range of issues described in the previous section was stimulated and reinforced by this change of purpose.

More immediately the shift from the confessor to the Christian and from the sin to Christian living had some effect on the role and consciousness of sin in moral thinking, teaching and so practice.[1] And this was later accompanied by an effect on confessional practice itself. Indeed one of the main complaints of the critics of recent moral theology is that it has tended to abolish sin or at least unduly reduce its importance in the life of Christians and so undermine the practice of confession. Some superficial and naïvely optimistic moralists may have been guilty of this failure to take sin seriously. But there were other far more powerful influences at work. Many of these from the secularised and consumerist Western world had no direct connections with moral theology at all. Indirectly the forces trivialising sin received more support from the legalistic sin-inflation of the traditional manuals than from the fresh search for a morality of love and virtue. The inflationary tendencies of the manuals with their multiplications of laws and rules which could be violated and of occasions which might lead to their violation, inevitably devalued the currency to a point where it was unacceptable to an increasing number of people. The hopping in and out of sin which a certain praxis based on manual training suggested, led to sin's trivialisation and obscured its true meaning and importance. The restoration of its significance involved a number of new approaches and perspectives which, although they still resist synthesis and may do so for a long time, illustrate progress made by moral theologians in their quest.

The legal model of morality focused on the individual action as fulfilment or violation of the law. Sin was an individual violation of the law in so far as it was a human act, based on knowledge and freedom. Psychological and environmental influences could and did affect the agent's knowledge and freedom but the particular action was the focus for moral assessment of good and evil. Fresh advertence to the unity and integrity of the person as moral agent and his development in history suggested a different perspective. Actions are expressive of and creative of personal character. To be properly understood and morally assessed they must be set in the context of the developing person. Morality in these terms applies to the person in act not to the act isolated from the person. That person, as he matures, acquires a dominant stance or basic orientation which develops out of his patterns of action and in turn determines these patterns. For many moralists some version of that dominant stance as basic orientation or fundamental option or formed character provides new insight into moral behaviour and development.[2] Where that basic orientation is assessed as predominantly good it will normally find expression in good actions and be reinforced and developed by these in turn. Because it is a predominant stance and not an exhaustive one, because ambiguity persists and no man possesses the whole of himself at a particular time but must risk it anew in the future, contrary or bad actions can take place. As they increase in frequency and depth of involvement the basic orientation may be changed from good to bad, from virtue to vice, in religious terms from a state of grace and God's friendship to a state of sin and God's rejection.

There are many obscurities and uncertainties in this analysis of man's moral life as to how and when such a basic orientation develops and occurs; what is its more precise relationship to individual acts: how and when it is fundamentally changed. Yet it does seem to many theologians more securely founded in the experience of the moral life and its faith-understanding as illustrated in Scripture than the rather atomistic discontinuous sequence of discrete human acts analysed in the manuals. And it demands a much more serious view of both sin and conversion involving the person at the centre of his life rather than the periphery and over a significant period of time rather than a momentary aberration towards evil or good.

The practical and pastoral implications for moral education are enormous. The sin-list will no longer do as an outline of the moral demands to be prescribed to young Christians or as the basis for an examination of their lives by penitents seeking forgiveness, reconciliation and renewal in the sacrament of Penance.

But it opens up exciting possibilities for revitalising both moral education and the sacrament which in turn will deepen and clarify the present provisional understanding of the moral agent, his basic orientation and moral activity. The interaction between 'confessional practice' new style and developments in moral theology may recur at a more profound level and in a more searching and sensitive fashion.

The Search for Absolutes

Rules and Exceptions. Hard on the heels of the accusation that moral theologians are abolishing sin, comes the charge that they are abandoning 'moral absolutes'. The precise nature of this charge does not seem always clear to the 'chargers' or to the 'charged'. But it is a persistent and serious charge and has yielded a number of plausible interpretations and responses. While it is necessary to review some of these interpretations and responses briefly, it is impossible here to discuss adequately what seems to me a highly technical, frequently confusing and certainly unfinished chapter on the strategies of moral theology.

It may be useful to draw attention to some of the semantic difficulties which affect the debate. When some people rather emotionally and accusingly demand 'Are there no absolutes left in moral theology any more?' they frequently mean 'Are there no longer any moral rules which do not admit of exceptions like "You should not tell a lie—(at whatever cost)"?' This interpretation is frequently accepted by the accused but I believe that the cause of language and debate would be better served by speaking of moral rules as universal (not admitting any exceptions) or general (admitting some) or particular (applying to a particular set of instances) rather than absolute or non-absolute.

In the theological, philosophical and linguistic moral tradition in which Catholic moral theologians work, this would set the time for a more intelligible and realistic debate. That tradition as represented by its most creative and authoritative spokesman, Thomas Aquinas, saw rules of this order as applying *ut in pluribus* or generally.[3] The later manual tradition did not hesitate to admit of exceptions to that most fundamental of moral rules 'Thou shalt not kill'. And it was only in the sexual area and some narrowly defined areas like abortion that exceptions to rules were totally excluded. Such universality might be open to reasonable justification but as an exceptional universality it requires special justification.

Another part of the difficulty arises, as many contemporary authors emphasise, from the confusing interchange of value and non-value terms, of prescriptive and descriptive language, of moral and pre-moral realities. The rule 'Thou shalt not lie' already includes its value-term and so can according to these authors be regarded as universal. (Many say absolute but this recalls the earlier confusion and anticipates a later clarification.) 'Thou shalt not tell a falsehood' like 'Thou shalt not kill' is not yet a morally determined statement. 'Telling falsehood' and 'killing' are in this analysis pre-moral realities, pre-moral evils which only become moral evils or goods when some further specification is given which in general terms is described as the absence (or presence) of a proportionate reason.

The theoretical sophistication and practical applicability of this analysis together with its prestigious support among moral theologians in Europe and the United States, make it a very formidable piece of moral theory.[4] Whether it involves the purely teleological understanding of morality which some of its defenders claim, is not entirely clear to me. It may be that the terrain to be explored between one's primitive and general perception of moral demand or good and the actual decision about whether a given piece of behaviour is good is teleological in character and in case of conflict may be best helped at present by a comparison of pre-moral values at stake and the invocation of proportionate reason. And yet that underlying moral capacity and awareness as well as the particular decision may be deontological and share a certain unconditioned or absolute character. Some of the more confused interchanges may then be due to the introduction of deontological absoluteness into terrain appropriate to teleological analysis or the extension of teleological 'relativity' to the terrain of the deontological. In any event a finally satisfactory presentation of moral analysis which does justice to man's primary moral capacity and his reasonable decision-making procedures has not yet appeared. When it does it may take justifying account of the circularity which seems to be built into the condition of man as moral subject.

Needs, Values and Virtues. Another strand of the debate recognises rules, positive and negative, as derivative but generally safe guides to the making of moral decisions. The wisdom of communities, ecclesial and civil, drawing on the moral experience and moral reflection of their heritages, arrived at a particular formulation as 'do' and 'don't' which has proven worth in protecting a particular good or value of and for the human person. Because such formulations could not cover all conceivable circumstances even in one man's life-time and because critical shifts in society and culture occur, the rules are approximate rather than exhaustively precise and in principle open to revision. Capital punishment was morally permissible as an exception which became a rule in particular societies in the past. It may well be that capital punishment has become morally obsolescent in the same societies with the development of a different understanding of communal responsibility, fresh insight into the meaning of retribution (and its consequent rejection), awareness of the possibility and demand for rehabilitation and the availability of other means of protecting society from further killing. Slavery, to which St Paul apparently raised no moral objections, was finally excluded as immoral.[5] Religious liberty was finally accepted as moral. Racist and sexist discrimination are increasingly rejected as immoral. War may yet be. Such earlier moral insights were frequently expressed in rules such as 'Murderers (and many lesser criminals) shall be put to death' or 'Governments may not permit religious liberty in their jurisdiction'. These rules did, even then, frequently admit of exceptions. The *thesis* and *hypothesis* device, made famous by Mgr Dupanloup after Pius IX's Syllabus of Errors in 1864 and subsequently widely applied to the problem of religious freedom, was an example of using proportionate reason to justify the (pre-moral?) evil of tolerating 'false' religions for the sake of a greater good, e.g. the peace and unity of a state or freedom of Church in that state.[6] More basically, changing conditions and changing moral insights demanded not just increasing exceptions but a total revision of the rule(s) in protecting and promoting the human values at stake. John T. Noonan's classic studies of usury and contraception abundantly illustrate this.[7] Similar historical studies on other aspects of marriage, on slavery and on war expose the developing relation between moral rule and changing insight into the moral value from which it derives. In that sense rules are not absolute but relative, relative to values.

The applicability of particular rules would of course be much more readily discernible if there were a clear and agreed understanding of the meaning, origin and interrelationship of the values from which they derived. No such comprehensive or even intelligible, if incomplete, map of values is available.

An uneasy and frequently obscure alliance exists between needs considered to be essential to the human person, such values discerned in moral analysis as responding to these needs, and virtues cherished in moral tradition as seeking these values. As the needs range from the basically physical to the psychological and intellectual, the social and religious, the values from health and work to freedom and truth, and the virtues from humility to fortitude, any overall and systematic outline of the needs, values and virtues with their derivative rules is simply not possible.

For all the intellectual dissatisfaction which such untidiness and obscurity provokes, moral life remains liveable and even intelligibly so. Needs, values and virtues are recognised and lived before they are reflected upon and given theoretical foundations and an overall context. Analysis goes on as required and with considerable effect in particular areas and in response to particular demands. The absence of a comprehensive framework makes that work sometimes more difficult and may easily bring its results into conflict with findings in other areas or with what is taken by other workers to be the one true system of morality. Yet the particularity and the conflict may prevent the totalitarianism and destructiveness of a single false system. While making moral decisions possible in so many areas the particularity also induces a healthy sense of humility in regard to the provisionalness of the present state of moral theory and practice; it also leads to openness to the possibility of further development and to the need for it. And the one true system may in the historical nature of the case never be achieved. Even the most formal expression of such a system, if it goes beyond the primary distinction of good and evil (*bonum est faciendum, malum est vitandum*), shares the historical condition of its formulators in the intellectual resources they employ and the range of moral concerns on which they employ them. Both resources and concerns may look and be very different in one hundred, one thousand, five thousand years hence. The moral for moral analysts is to accept their historical condition and seek the best and most coherent, if necessarily incomplete and provisional, understanding of morality possible for them today. If it is all they can achieve, it must be graded adequate.

Persons as Absolutes. A more convincing case for use of the word absolute in moral discourse turns on the increasing recognition of the centrality of person. Such recognition has already altered perspective on individual moral actions, good and bad, and the possibility of critical change in moral stance through serious sin or conversion. The discussion of rules, values and virtues as conventional criteria for distinguishing morally good and bad actions, finds its way ineluctably back to the person. Values must be defined in personal terms if they are to have any moral significance. The virtues which pursue them are clearly personal realities and the rules which protect them find their ultimate root in persons. In the historical world of the moral, actions, rules, values and virtues are all relative to and derived from persons. Of persons only may one properly use the word absolute, that to which all else in this discourse is relative. A critical appreciation of the person provides the primary protection against the frequently lamented relativism of moral theology today.

The person must always be seen in community and in history, in essential relationship with other persons and becoming a reality in and through time. Some of the implications of these dimensions of the person are explored more fully elsewhere in this book. It is important to keep them in mind here because they could be and are frequently ignored in the 'personalist' approach so dominant among contemporary moral theologians. The irreducible, inviolable and non-relative character of person essential to moral analysis is of person-in-community-in-history not of person *in vacuo* or on a desert island or in 'this moment of time'. Yet the irreducibility and inviolability into which social and temporal relationships enter, signal the source of moral value and moral call to which all our exploring must return. The moral experience is generated and born in awareness of the person commanding and demanding recognition, respect and response. The first aspect of person as moral absolute is revealed.

Personal awareness again, with its necessary social and historical dimensions, is the way of moral insight. That of which one is unaware cannot properly influence one's personal and moral activity. More profoundly, personal capacity for moral awareness and understanding, exercised in history and community, provide the way to moral understanding. If the source of moral value is the person, the understanding of it must be personal. What is proclaimed as moral value or asserted as moral rule must be in principle accessible to the collective and historical personal understanding and capable of explanation and justification by and to reasoning human beings. To deny this is to remove moral insight from its proper human context and destroy its genuine moral character. That much the Judaeo-Christian tradition, particularly in its Catholic form, has long insisted.

At the concrete level of moral decision and response, personal awareness and appreciation of the moral value to be realised, of the response to be made to the personal source(s), is essential to authentic moral activity. To act exclusively out of somebody else's moral understanding, however exalted and admirable he be, is to live by proxy. It reduces moral living to obedience to another—a practice as indefensible in principle as it is dangerous in practice. This age has seen too much of the destructive results of blind obedience and of the treatment of dissidents from Auschwitz to Kampala not to recognise the inherent and limitless dangers of evading personal moral evaluation and decision. In principle, even if the danger should be removed or reduced by some benevolent dictatorship, surrendering critical appropriation of moral insight and personal formulation of moral decision cuts the moral response off from its creative centre in the heart of man. Response becomes an empty shell incapable of expressing true personal involvement because it does not incarnate personal understanding and decision. Previous separation of intellect and will carried the suggestion that action was the fruit of the will under the direction of the intellect instead of being the dynamic completion and expression of a unified person with intellect, will, imagination and feeling all at work. In the final and concrete stage of moral decision and response, the absoluteness of the person (in no sense to be interpreted as arbitrariness) is reflected in the freedom and integrity of conscience.[8]

Anthropological and Theological Perspectives

The debates reviewed in the preceding pages are conducted within a framework of morality as a human phenomenon based on mankind as personal, and discernible by mankind as reasonable. In the current jargon they adopt an anthropological perspective. However, all moral theologians would reject such a perspective as exclusive or exhaustive for their work. The very term theologian commits them to giving some account of the relationship between faith and morality. Their manner of doing so varies enormously. And it is very difficult to find a single consistent theory of the relationship. In that fundamental respect moral theology is undoubtedly a continuing quest.

Perhaps the most obvious and banal of truths may need to be recorded once again to prevent the issue from becoming hopelessly tangled. In history, we find that where people actually believe and behave morally, Christian belief implies moral behaviour and Christians are committed to it if they are to be truly Christian. Yet people who are not Christians do not recognise the need for Christianity to behave morally. So the fact and the problem, in so far as it is a problem, of the relationship between Christian faith and morality are a fact and problem for Christians only. The repetition is intended to emphasise the obligation of the Christian theologian to investigate the relation between faith and morality in his tradition, community and life. It is the investigation of this relationship rather than the search for a specifically Christian ethic that seems the more profitable approach for moral theologians just now.

The renewed moral theology over the past few decades has been expressed in fruitful re-examination of a host of particular questions, some important extended work on the fundamentals of moral theology and the (very) occasional attempt at complete synthesis. All of these have combined in varying degrees and fashions both theological and anthropological perspectives. They have recognised Christian faith as the horizon of moral discussion, the ultimate basis of moral commitment and frequent source of moral insight. Yet many of the particular questions, discussed independently or in more synthetic works, from contraception to trade relations, have been analysed in terms that seem to make perfect sense irrespective of faith commitment and perspective. Even in the work on fundamental moral theology where the relationship between faith and morality is most frequently, directly and systematically addressed, a good deal of the discussion on deontological or teleological models of morality for example, bears little relation to and derives little light from the faith-reflection of the participants. The diversity of relationship between faith and morality can appear even in the same author dealing with different topics, indicating a widespread weakness in method in moral theology which has still to be overcome. The seminal work of Bernard Häring, for example in his *Law of Christ* and in subsequent numerous particular writings, adopts as starting point a predominantly theological perspective but is inevitably forced to analyse many particular issues in almost exclusively anthropological terms. At least, it is difficult to perceive in his work or that of so many other competent moral theologians a consistent and satisfactory method of relating the theological and anthropological. This emerges in uncertain or inconsistent handling of the Bible as source of moral understanding, in divergent views about the relationship of the concepts of nature, sin and grace to moral understanding, in the discussion of the rationality and autonomy of ethics and its relation to divine revelation and the Church's teaching authority, in attempts to integrate biblical teaching, philosophical ethics and empirical sciences. These and other difficulties that moral theologians face are shared to some extent by other theologians and other moralists as they seek to discover and justify a hermeneutic and method for their own disciplines. In moral theology the cumulative effect is to create a crisis of identity for the discipline itself.[9]

Part of moral theology's consolation in this crisis derives from its recognition of its dual character as theological and anthropological and of the inevitable tension that this involves, if it is to be fair to both dimensions. Some of the more theological sources of tension I will discuss in the next section. The anthropological dimension offers the further mainly cold but essential comfort that in morality, moral philosophy and moral theology, life and praxis are antecedent to and finally critical of theory. Moral theory for Christians and others, as critical reflection upon moral behaviour, derives from practical behaviour and must return to be judged by it.[10] Moral theologians have a limited role in helping Christians to understand their moral lives so that they may more consciously appropriate and develop them but all their theory and theology has to be tested anew in the moral life of the Christian community. Because of this interaction between theory and praxis in the morals, life and thought of the Christian Church there can in the nature of the case be no finally satisfactory theoretical exposition of the relationship between theory and practice. This limitation the moral theologian shares, for his limited consolation, with many other theoreticians. And while it should not weaken his resolve to find an ever more satisfactory theoretical method, it will provide a note of critical realism for his expectations and his achievements.

III. Some Fundamental Theological Questions

Morality and God

For the believer and theologian the first and last question is that of God. 'And the end of all our exploring/ will be to arrive where we started/ and know the place for the first time!' For the moral theologian, as already noted, the exploring carries its own obscurities and risks, risks to his commitment to morality and to God and obscurities in his understanding of both.

The Divine Threat to Morality. I was once asked to give a lecture to a Christian student audience with the title 'Do we need a morality without God?' The deliberately provocative character of the title was no doubt something of a publicity gimmick to attract an audience. I do not recall very much about the lecture now but it reflected then a worry that still persists—that for many Christians belief in God constitutes a threat to a true concept and practice of morality.

The popular overtones if not the more sophisticated understanding of morality as divine law clash with the growing appreciation of morality as a human phenomenon. Deriving from the human condition, it is developed, even created, discerned and implemented in human history. In this view it is an integral and autonomous human reality which has no need of attribution to an extrinsic, transcendent law-giver and can only suffer from such attribution. To argue for the origin of morality from outside the human violates the integrity of the human itself. To argue for it in historical interventionist terms compounds the attack on the integrity of the human and creates insuperable problems of discerning and interpreting such interventions. And to present that divinely caused morality as the law of the supreme being betrays the best understanding of morality today which transcends the legal model. It reduces moral living to obedience rather than personal development or growth. The obedience is no more enriching for the human because it is demanded by and directed to the extrinsic authority of a supreme being. It may even be less enriching, more destructive, because of the fear which acceptance of such a supreme authority might inspire.

This may seem to exaggerate any claims of morality as human and to distort any presentation of the divine as source of morality. Yet it is important for the moral theologian to feel to the full the tension between the understanding of morality as human and autonomous and his Christian acceptance of God as origin, guarantor and end of all our moral exploring and acting.

The tension is heightened still further by a consideration of the most modest claim to divine authority and human obedience involving divine sovereignty and human freedom. Freedom is indisputably central to an understanding of men as moral. What can that freedom betoken in the face of divine sovereign claims? In more philosophical and theological terms, the problem translates into one of divine and human causality, and of the paradoxically dependent freedom of the creature. Christian tradition raises any number of difficulties about the relation of grace and freedom, divine election (predestination?) and human achievement, sin, redemption and the possibility of any truly moral life.

No less threatening for the moral enterprise is the concept of divine reward and punishment with which it has been so intimately connected in Christian teaching. Apart from the unfair pressure on human freedom which such ideas might seem to embody, to relate performance of good or avoidance of evil to extrinsic rewards or punishments seems to deprive moral activity of its inherent value. If good is to be done not for its own sake or value but as a means to achieving a reward here or hereafter, the whole enterprise is impoverished and distorted. Many non-Christians dismiss the morality of Christians as long-term self-seeking. Where the long term transcends history, there is the added danger that moral challenges such as oppression and poverty will be accepted in resignation or ignored in comfort in expectation of celestial 'pie' for all. Such religious impoverishment of morality offers a basis for Marx's charge of providing opium instead of accepting the moral challenge to change the oppressive and destructive situation.

An adequate response to these difficulties would cover a very wide theological area. Because the questions are age-old, the answers cannot be entirely new. But because fundamental problems recur in new circumstances and receive new formulations, they have to be appreciated, assessed and answered anew. At the present stage of their work of renewal, moral theologians should appropriate to themselves the real and searching difficulties which many people experience in seeking to reconcile their best understanding of morality with their traditional belief in God.

Some of the surface difficulty would be removed if the term 'divine law' were dropped altogether and the legal model of morality relegated to a very subordinate place in discussion and teaching. The more critical difficulties remain and will never be totally removed for the very good reason that the basic relationship between the human and divine in morality as in all other domains, can never be adequately conceptualised and understood.[11] To pretend that it could would be to deny that God was God and ultimately beyond human comprehension. Yet easy resort to ultimate mystery will not suffice. A great deal of penultimate clarification is necessary and possible. Mystery may exceed human powers of understanding; it should not blatantly outrage them.

The Christian doctrines of creation and covenant, sin and redemption, resurrection and kingdom shed some light both individually and as a unity on the difficulties already encountered. The more exact exploration of these doctrines in illuminating the God–morality relationship involves some of the hermeneutical and methodological problems which were mentioned in the previous section and which constitute a continuing challenge to moral theologians. Without meeting that challenge immediately it is possible to indicate some lines of possible progress in regard to the difficulties in hand.

The integrity and autonomy of humankind and so of morality are partly a matter of experience, partly a matter of aspiration and still partly a matter of frustration. The theological understanding of the experience, the aspiration and the frustration while still in the searching and the making, can appeal to the consistent Judaeo-Christian tradition of man's distinctive position within creation as a knowing and free being who then enjoys a knowing and free relationship with the Creator. The distinctiveness within creation and the distinction from the Creator (necessary to a real relationship) suggest a human integrity and an independence of mind experienced and aspired to in moral life and its analysis. The more intransigent difficulty of combining such independence/integrity with a continuing dependence on a creator God can be partly illuminated by theological reflection on the biblical description of man, as God's image and covenanted friend, which reaches its climax in Jesus as son of God sharing that divine sonship, the nature and life of God with all men. In this vision the distinction between God and man is not total. God enters into the definition of man as well as providing the critical other pole for man's relational condition as creature, friend and son. The integrity and autonomy of man is respected by the transcendent God while it is founded in the immanent God. Man as moral agent takes his distance from and develops his moral life in distinction from the creator God who is also partner. The moral life is his own, expressive of the resources which constitute his endowment as a man, and realising them. These resources find a guaranteed origin, continuity and significance in the creating, preserving and ultimately significant being called God. The circle or spiral whereby man, in the light of the Christian tradition, defines himself in relation to and in independence of God, can, if developed in a coherent way, provide some insight into the threshold stages of the finally mysterious relationship between man and God. And so it may release man from the distorting influence of morality as law and as divine law or at least as imposed will of a mastering and enslaving God. As the flowering of resources integral to and deployed freely by himself, man's authentic moral life is no longer undermined by extrinsic reward and punishment. The reward is in the good itself which is done and in the ultimate flowering to which it leads, a flowering that is truly ultimate because for Christians it triumphs over the critical threat to all human and moral development, historical death. The punishment is historically mediated, if not always consciously experienced, in the distortion of development that may render one finally unable to rise above the threat of death by sharing in the fulfilment of resurrection.

The fragility and frustration of moral development are only too evident in moral experience and too often ignored in the analysis of that experience. The problems they pose for the moral theologian in his understanding of both morality and God should not, just because they are such permanent and obvious problems, be sidestepped in his overall vision or discussion of particular problems. The theological understanding of sin has too often, as noted earlier, been reduced to a concept of individual actions of weakness or malice while the pervasive and permanent destructive tendencies of persons and institutions have been ignored or regarded as having only secondary importance. This has been particularly true of Catholic moral theology in its use of an abstract type of natural law derived from some pure and metaphysical nature. The tension in Catholic theology as a whole between the goodness affirmed in creation and finally triumphant in redemption and resurrection and the universal evil of sinfulness in person and institution with implications even for the cosmos, must play a more significant role in the area of moral theology. This may lead to a more realistic understanding of the actual fragile and frustrating conditions in which men seek to be moral and a more persistent commitment to overcome the evil. For the Christian the good, no less problematic than evil in origin and meaning, beckons in hope to the eventual triumph of resurrection but only when evil has been given its due by the personal acceptance of crucifixion. Moral theology must be pursued in both the light of the resurrection and the shadow of the cross if it is to do justice to its human authenticity, autonomy and fragility and its divine origin, significance and fulfilment.

Morality's Impact on God. The theologian, even of the moral variety, turns and returns to the central reality of God. Little enough attention has been paid in moral or other theology to the impact of moral development and analysis on the understanding of God. If God constitutes a threat to the integrity and authenticity of morality, morality in experience and understanding may also constitute a threat to one's concept and understanding of God.

This could be illustrated by examining for example the interaction between Israelite moral sensibilities and their concepts of God. More readily accessible is one's own selectivity in confining oneself to those moral instructions, insights and examples in the Old Testament which harmonise with one's current concept of God. The discrimination used in relation to the Book of Exodus accounts of the events formative of Israel as Yahweh's elect people reveal how far current moral presuppositions influence concepts of God. The Exodus story itself, the Covenant and the Decalogue as Covenant charter are, in various stages of purification and demythologisation, perfectly acceptable to Christians as an understanding of divine concern and human task. The more detailed legal requirements are more easily dismissed as historically and culturally relative and so irrelevant to current ideas of morality or God. The destruction of three thousand Israelites by the sons of Levi at the divine command (*Exod.* 32 : 27-28) or the divine promise and power involved in the destruction of the Canaanites and others so that the Israelites might finally enjoy the freedom of their promised land (cf. *Exod.* 33 : 1-3; *Josh. passim*), are ignored in contemporary thinking about God because the moral implications are uncongenial. Liberation theology, together with the God of liberation theology, with all its Exodus background does not now include a theology of conquest and a conqueror God as the dynamic of the original story might suggest. Moral sensibilities influence the interpretation of the relevant texts and the particular formulation of ideas about God.[12]

It would be possible to invoke various scholarly achievements in the hermeneutics of the texts to justify some of this discrimination. Yet the hermeneutics themselves rest on presuppositions about God as good and the meaning of goodness which do not finally break the circle.[13] The relation between morality and religion, the recognition and understanding of moral good and of God as supreme good, have exemplified mutual influence. Theologians who concern themselves with morality have to attend to this in the hope of breaking the viciousness of the circle and providing an illuminating and justifiable spiral of growing understanding of both God and morality.

Jesus Christ in Moral Theology

For many moral theologians the relation between God and morality has been finally and clearly defined in the person, life and teaching of Jesus Christ. Where the manuals of almost four centuries treated Jesus as at best an authority for the occasional moral pronouncement such as that on divorce, recent works of renewal sought to establish him at the source and centre of moral life and thought for Christians. The resurgence of a more strictly anthropological perspective, particularly in discussion of particular questions, which was recorded earlier, does not necessarily exclude a central role for the man Jesus or invalidate the insights which were so perceptively and hopefully recovered in the past decades.

Jesus Christ as Norm of Morality. Considerable attention was given to defending and explicating the view that Jesus Christ constituted the criterion or norm of moral behaviour for Christians. While this idea may be less fashionable just now, the seeker after moral theology may not easily dismiss an idea with such obvious claims to centrality in Christian theology and such apparent potential for clarifying the relationship between human and divine in moral living.

Discipleship or following of Jesus Christ provides one key description of moral life for Christians which has at least a secure basis in the New Testament. Its value as an inspiring vision depends on the faith commitment and scriptural awareness of the believer. Its potential for resolving difficulties in concrete situations is more problematic. Yet one's basic commitment and overall vision provide the context for all authentic solutions to moral problems and the following of Christ may give more precise indications in actual situations than one's reluctance for moral effort may admit. How far discipleship exercises a more comprehensive theoretical role in moral theology depends on how one expands the more concrete biblical idea in theological terms.

Following Jesus Christ is readily translated in the synoptic writers into sharing his life and his death. Theologians John and Paul envisage sharing the life and death of Jesus Christ in terms that exceed conventional discipleship even unto sharing life and destiny. For them the sharing is intrinsic to the sharer and the shared. The Christian lives in Christ as a branch in the vine or an organ in the body. 'In Christ' is Paul's dominant description of the condition of the Christian and of the basis for his moral activity. Activity is the sign, expression and further realisation of life for the Christian, of the life of Christ in whom he lives and moves and has his being (*Acts* 17 : 28).

The being of Christ in which Christians share is the being of sonship, sonship of the Father. The divine enters into the definition of the human in a new way. Participation in divine sonship introduces them to the very life of God himself. The transcendent, totally other is more intimate to them than they

are to themselves. A morality of sonship is of course a morality
of brotherhood. The two great commandments are indissolubly
connected and grounded in the status of Christian as member of
Christ and son of the Father. In a more metaphysical idiom the
being or *esse* of the Christian from which his behaviour or action
is to flow (*actio sequitur esse*) is the human being transformed
by participation in divine sonship. Traditional natural law understanding of morality must be reconsidered in the setting of the
redemptive transformation involved for mankind as sons of the
Father.[14]

Such theological systematisation and its further specification
does not exhaust the task of the moral theologian in interpreting
for contemporary Christians the concept of Jesus Christ as norm
of morality. The particular moral teaching of Jesus and the New
Testament writers did not attempt a comprehensive treatment of
the whole moral life of Christians even then. And of course it
does not deal with many contemporary problems, of ecology or
population for example. On other issues the New Testament
teaching seems inadequate or unacceptable to present-day requirements. The treatment of slavery and of the role of women provide
outstanding examples. How does one proceed critically as disciples
of Jesus Christ in discriminating within the existing New Testament teaching and in developing responses to questions which
had not occurred in that society or to those teachers? The question
of Jesus Christ as norm of morality is clearly bound up with, if
not reducible to the question of the normative character of Scripture and in particular of the New Testament for moral understanding. How both questions are posed, pursued and eventually
answered will depend among other things on how one views
the relationship and the tension between faith and morality.
Taking morality as included in and deducible from faith and its
explicit truths, or the two as independent and parallel realities
or somehow as (semi-) independent yet mutually interacting, all
offer different starting-points and the prospect of different answers
to the morally normative role of Jesus and the New Testament.

Which Jesus Christ? The tendency of every generation or
school of theologians to recreate the picture of Jesus Christ if
not in their own image at least in the image of their own insights
and interests has been sufficiently noticed, from the liberal Protes-

tant image of nineteenth-century Europe to the revolutionary
(Catholic) image of twentieth-century South America. The tendency is not entirely dishonourable or without respectable prece-
dent. The evangelists clearly reflected different insights and
interests in their accounts of the events, words and personality
of Jesus whose diversity was frequently glossed over by believers
until modern Scripture scholarship offered a way of understanding
them. The best of that scholarship cannot explain or reconcile
the differences in a totally satisfactory way. Which understanding
of Jesus Christ? is not an entirely silly question even within the
confines of the New Testament, let alone the history of the
Christian community, its thought and practice. Without denying
a basic convergence and coherence of the teaching of the New
Testament and of the historical Christian community, moral
theologians have to confront their own dilemmas and obscurities
in discerning the Jesus Christ of their faith and discipline. With
what concept of Jesus Christ is Titus asked to 'bid slaves to be
submissive to their masters . . . so that in everything they may
adorn the doctrine of God our saviour' (*Tit.* 2 : 9-10)? More
frighteningly, in the name of which Jesus Christ was the Inquisi-
tion introduced and heretics put to the stake? And for which
Jesus Christ did Ian Smith and the Rhodesian Front Government
believe that their oppressive regime and constitution would preserve Christianity? More painfully still which Jesus Christ was
at the stake in the religious wars of the sixteenth and seventeenth
centuries, in the continuing divisions of Christians today and in
the religious contribution to the hatred, oppression and violence
in Northern Ireland?

The rhetoric of the preceding paragraph should not obscure
the difficulty and the pain of the questions it poses for moral
theologians in their efforts to outline in critical and constructive
fashion a moral way of living for believers in Jesus Christ today.
The historical allusions have indicated how far particular interests
affect and sometimes distort the understanding of Jesus Christ
and the morality he embodies. But the fundamental lesson for
moral theology may be how the explicit or implicit (even unconscious) understanding of Jesus Christ, whether articulated in a
liberationist Christology or concealed in more traditional formulae, is determined by moral stance. Any naïve attempt to
develop a moral theology directly from Jesus Christ as presented

in biblical witness and Church doctrine will inevitably fall victim
to the hidden moral presuppositions of the moralist himself. The
circularity which affects the relationship between morality and
God also affects that between morality and Jesus Christ. It must
be consciously and critically confronted.

One way of conscious and critical confrontation to which
moral theologians have paid insufficient attention is the investigation of Jesus Christ and the development of Christology, from
a deliberately moral perspective. Despite recent excellent work
by biblical scholars on the moral teaching of Jesus and the New
Testament, and despite the rich flowering of Christology from
a variety of doctrinal points of view, theologians concerned with
morality, with the notable exception of liberation theologians,
have not undertaken in any formal and full way the task of
'moral Christology'.[15] Until they do their Christian theology of
morality will be as uncertain of its identity, as fragmentary in
its context and as confused in its structure as Shakespeare's play
without the Prince. It corresponds in fact much more closely to
the other side of that play provided by Tom Stoppard in *Rosen-
crantz and Guildenstern are Dead*.

Locating Jesus Christ. Whether the moral theologian's perspective is dominantly theological or dominantly anthropological or
seeks some dialectical relationship between the two, he will as
a Christian theologian seek to give some central, if formal, role
to Jesus Christ. Having considered the problem of identifying
which Jesus Christ, one has now to consider the problem of
identifying where one finds Jesus Christ. The problems are not
dissimilar. Which and where form at least related questions. To
answer the question 'where' by appealing to the Bible raises for
the moralists difficulties analogous to those raised by the question
'which'. And so it is with the historical doctrines of the Church.
The historical Christian community and its self-affirmation and
identification in the liturgy encounter similar difficulties for both
which and where. It may be worth considering a little more closely
the difficulties and possibilities of responding to the question
'where'.

Encountering the divine in and through the human is essential
to understanding Christianity and Jesus Christ. That the human
provides the locus of the divine seems to be a widely accepted

consequence of the event of Jesus Christ and the Christian doctrine of Incarnation. But which human? Jesus Christ certainly.
But where does one encounter him today and so locate the divine?
The question raises all the doctrinal, apologetic and epistemo-
logical issues Christianity is heir to. In hopelessly compressed
and totally inadequate fashion one may reply that Jesus Christ
is encountered in every human being, that the saving thrust of
the Incarnation is to call all men to be sons of the Father and
that the trans-historical character of the Resurrection whereby
the man Jesus is fully present to the Father as only-begotten Son
makes him present by the power and gift of the Father to every
man in his historical existence, transforming the core of his being.
'As long as you did it to one of these least ones, you did it to
me!' (*Matt.* 25 : 40). '. . . you in me and I in you' (*John* 14 : 20).
'I live now not I but Christ lives in me' (*Gal.* 2 : 20). For the
Christian moralist preoccupied with men's response to one another,
Jesus Christ is located in that other.

By the Gift and Power of the Spirit
    The trinitarian character of Christian living as found particu-
larly in St Paul awaits the same kind of systematic exploration by
moral theologians as the person and achievement of Jesus Christ.
More specifically, the Spirit has been even more neglected by
moralists than Jesus, despite the role biblically and traditionally
accorded to him as gift guiding into all Christian truth (*John*
16: 13), empowering Christian action and enabling the Christian
to identify himself finally as son by saying 'Abba, Father' (*Rom.*
8: 15). 'Moral pneumatology' parallel to 'moral Christology'
requires urgent attention and development. It is all the more
urgent in view of the possible collapse of community guidance
into merely juridical command, and of personal conscience into
arbitrary and self-interested decision. Only a fuller understanding
of the role of the Spirit in community and person can prevent
such collapse and lead to a more adequate theology of the Church's
teaching role in morality and of the responsibility and resources
facing the individual in his conscience judgment. The more elusive
but no less demanding problem of community conscience is even
more dependent theologically on an understanding of the gift and
power of the Spirit.
    The increased attention to the role of the Spirit which the

Charismatic Renewal has aroused in the Churches should encourage moral theologians also to reflect on this topic. For all the
evident richness which the renewal has brought to Catholics, the
moral theologian will feel a little disquiet at the speed and
certainty with which the voice of the Spirit is sometimes discerned
as well as at the ease with which the linked ideas of providential
and providence are often invoked. A slight acquaintance with
history and hermeneutics reveals the practical risks and theoretical
difficulties of any uncritical approach to discerning the Spirit or
interpreting providence. As both Spirit discernment and Providence bear directly on moral response by Christian individual
and community, a critical investigation of them is a primary
responsibility of the moral theologian.

Conclusion

The tortuous journey which this chapter undertook in quest of
moral theology remains inevitably fragmentary and erratic. The
quest cannot expect to be completed in substance or coherent in
method before its goal is reached. And like the crock of gold at
the end of the rainbow it is a receding goal; new problems and
new methods will tend to make previous achievements obsolescent. Continuity there can and should be. Discontinuity will also
play its part. Even now the diversity of civilisations, societies,
generations and individuals within the Catholic Church alone
creates a certain discontinuity obstructing any single monolithic
moral system. Some kind of differentiated moral approach is
clearly required between population policies in Calcutta and
Cahirciveen, political methods in South Africa and Northern
Ireland, sexual activity by sixteen-year-old single adolescents and
twenty-six-year-old married adults. Beyond that kind of 'objective' diversity but related to it is the pluralism which some moral
theologians recognise in regard to the 'subjective' diversity which
occurs today in the Catholic Church due to lack of consensus on
specific moral issues from contraceptives to violence.[16] Such
pluralism must not be an easy option, an excuse for self-indulgence by liberal theologians or believers. One should keep in mind
the words of J. B. Metz: 'Theological pluralism today too often
expresses no more than a mindless capitulation to the sorry status
of theology itself.'[17] Mindless capitulation cannot be entertained

by responsible theologians. Their responsibility is to seek to improve the 'sorry status of theology'. Theological pluralism has to be earned by intellectual sweat. Yet it may be a necessary concession to past and present failure, a healthy recognition of the limits of theology and theologians, and a call to repentance, conversion and development of the theological community in its quest for a moral theology.

Morality and Prayer[1]

IN the theological as distinct from the practical cooperation
between the Churches which has become such a feature of our
times, insufficient attention may have been paid to the characteristic of the Churches which most impresses the ordinary believer
and unbeliever, that they are worshipping or praying communities
which uphold certain moral standards. Of course there has been
extraordinary development in prayer shared between the Churches
and quite valuable growth in inter-Church moral activity, particularly on social issues. But has there been adequate theological
reflection on the relationship between prayer and morality as
distinguishing characteristics, particularly in the light of the rather
'radical' developments in both these which have taken place in
recent years? The liturgical changes in the Roman Catholic Church
in the wake of Vatican II[2] would have been almost inconceivable
fifteen years ago. And they are now being followed—for some,
overshadowed—by the renewal in personal and community prayer,
described as 'charismatic' or 'pentecostal'.[3] The changes in moral
understanding are no less far-reaching and have long since crossed
Church boundaries. For two Churches such as the Church of
Scotland and the Roman Catholic Church in Ireland, where traditionally church-attendance, personal prayer and a fairly rigid
moral code have enjoyed great strength, the changes are, despite
certain enriching and liberating effects, also the source of some
confusion and pain[4] and place the traditional bonds between
prayer and morality in urgent need of theological reconsideration.

Such reconsideration was inevitable. The age-old association
between religion and morality,[5] which subsumed the relationship

between prayer and morality, has had its own peculiar swings even with the Judaeo-Christian tradition. While presumed to be mutually illuminating and supporting, in fact one frequently enjoyed periods of dominance at the expense of the other. Those who honoured with their lips but not with their hearts. (*Is.* 29: 13) belonged to a long line of Hebrews and Christians for whom a certain distortion of religion suppressed or distorted morality. But moralism also had its turn in obscuring or reducing the central saving truth and power of the covenant of God and ultimately of Jesus Christ. The creative tension which ought to exist between the two and was proclaimed and lived by Jesus has frequently turned into a destructive exploitation of one or the other. It would be too much to expect that Christians and their Churches today were not exposed to these perennial temptations and did not sometimes yield to them. The *semper reformanda* of the Reformed tradition, which the Roman Catholic Church has proclaimed once again as hers also, will provide the stimulus here as elsewhere for the theological task which is a necessary part of the reform and which has become all the more urgent in the face of radical change.

Such a theological attempt in its bearing on the day-to-day living of Church members (in prayer and moral activity) could have the useful side-effect of overcoming the divisions between Christian theologians and Christian preachers/practitioners which have appeared—and sometimes in ugly form. The ultimate goal of the theologian's task is to attempt, out of his study of the Word and the Christian tradition, to assist ordinary Christians and Christian communities to understand and respond in prayer and life to the divine call offered to them in Jesus Christ. In grappling with the prayer-morality relationship in the new situations he will be attempting to provide assistance more directly than usual and finding himself more closely engaged in his reflections with daily Christian living.

It is hardly necessary to point out as a final introductory note that this is a theological and not a sociological exercise. No attempt will (can?) be made to correlate church attendance, personal and other prayer, statistically considered, with moral achievement, also statistically considered. Yet attention must be paid to experience, the obvious experience of changes in prayer and morality which require no statistical back-up and the personal experience, individual and shared, of new forms or needs in prayer and morality. It is with this kind of experience as stimulus that these theological reflections begin.

Pre-Vatican II Understanding of Prayer and Morality

Scholarly qualifications can be fatal long before they reach their first century, let alone their first millenium. Yet it is necessary in reassessing the relationship between prayer and morality to define fairly exactly one's starting point. I am concerned here with pre-Vatican II understanding within the Roman Catholic tradition. It is with that tradition that I am most familiar and to it my professional competence is really confined. However, I hope that what I have to say will find traces of convergence as well as divergence across the denominational divide. I have deliberately selected the period prior to Vatican II, and the particular relationship between prayer and morality that characterised that period is well exemplified by the manuals of moral theology[6] which during that time enjoyed such influence in the training of Roman Catholic clergy and their subsequent preaching. It does not mean 'traditional' which is much broader in scope and rightly should take us back to New Testament times. A prevalent (controversial) weakness is to identify one particular phase of tradition with all of tradition, the particular phase which happens to suit us.

However, before tackling the manual treatment of the association it is necessary to recall the popular understanding of prayer and morality which were dominant at least among Roman Catholics in that period and to a large extent still are.[7] Prayer was simply understood as speaking to God or communication with God (and this included listening to him). It did not, of course, confine itself to petition but included praise and adoration, thanksgiving and regret or sorrow, leading to repentance and reconciliation. For Roman Catholics, the public and central act of prayer was the Mass although it was an event (the word was not used and certainly not in any technical and theological sense) as were the other sacraments. There were other public prayers, paraliturgical as one might now call them, such as Benediction of the Blessed Sacrament, novenas and devotions of numerous kinds. And there were private prayers for the individual, the family or a particular group on a special occasion. For completeness one would have to advert to a variety of practices of private personal prayer, oral and silent, meditative, contemplative and mystical. But some elements of the more advanced forms were considered to reside in the more primitive types.[8] There was in addition the wider understanding of prayer as all that one does: *laborare est orare*. This was given concrete expression in the practice of the 'morning offering' whereby one 'consecrated' to God all one's activities for that day. It could also be expressed in terms of one's intentions to offer this or every work to God or by describing ones' work as always done for the love or glory of God in sound Pauline terms. (1 *Cor.* 10 : 13).

The morality[9] contemporary with the prayer-phase catalogued earlier was for the most part expressed in terms of a legal code of dos and don'ts, commands and prohibitions. God's will was the moral law and it was either directly revealed in the Judaeo-Christian tradition (e.g. ten commandments) or accessible by reflection on human nature, the natural moral law (or both). The expression of these primarily in legal form and their intertwining (e.g. the content of the ten commandments was for the most part also natural law morality) were further compounded by the admix-ture of a voluminous code of canon or Church law, so that the prohibition of eating meat on Friday (a purely Church law) could be taken as morally equivalent to the prohibition of adultery —as both could be thought equally to involve serious sin and merit eternal damnation. The resilience of priests and people, more important perhaps of the Spirit of Christ, rose above many but by no means all of these confusions and limita-tions.

This rather obvious and simple outline of pre-Vatican II approaches to prayer and morality seemed a necessary introduction to considering how the relationship between them was under-stood.

Presuming an awareness of the tension and temptation between the prayer and morality poles discussed earlier and presuming that the tension was not always creative or the temptation always resisted, one still wants to know how the manual theologians and the people envisaged the relationship and so could hope to cope with it.

Prayer[10] as a duty of the virtue of religion was regarded as of

moral obligation in various ways. This involved as usual a combination of divine (revealed and natural) and human ecclesiastical
law. So Catholics were obliged by law to attend Mass on Sunday.
They were also obliged to pray frequently throughout their lives
(this was sometimes interpreted as daily or in terms of morning
and evening prayers). And they were obliged to pray in particular
situations for light to know their moral duty and strength to do
it and to resist the temptation to evil.

One might not unfairly characterise the relationship as predominantly extrinsic in concept. There was a moral obligation to
pray and this was couched in rather legal and so extrinsic terms
—coming at the individual as it were from the outside, whether
from God or the Church. In relation to other moral obligations
prayer was of assistance in seeking light from God to understand
the obligation correctly and strength or grace from him to fulfil
it as correctly understood. Undoubtedly the light and strength
became internal to the person as granted by God, but the concept
and image of the connection between them and the prayer for
them was, I should say, also predominantly extrinsic. One asked
God for help and the help came or it did not, but any inner
connection between the asking and the help was not given much
attention, at either theological or popular level.

The prayer for forgiveness and the gifts of repentance and
forgiveness for moral failure suggested a more intimate connection but it was not expanded upon in other areas. The 'morning
offering' and 'good intentions' consecrating of all one's activities
to God were also intrinsic in concept as referring to God activities
somehow foreign to him and so to communication with him, i.e.
prayer.

There were appeals to experiences of inner illuminations and
strengthening by God which did issue for example in special
vocations, but these were not considered, for example, in the
typical moral treatment but as exceptions to be dealt with in theology
of vocation, with criteria for distinguishing true from false or,
in more advanced cases still, under the rubric of mystical theology.
Moral theology and popular moral thinking were not concerned
with such exceptional phenomena. The predominant links were
extrinsic in moral obligations to pray or in the use of prayer to
obtain light and strength to fulfil one's moral obligations, although
in the prayer to obtain forgiveness the connection was understood

in a more intrinsic way, but the potential for intrinsic connection in the 'morning offering' was scarcely adverted to.

Prayer and Morality in the post-Vatican II Era

The developments in understanding of prayer, particularly liturgical prayer, and of morality, which we attribute to this era had emerged in various ways to prepare for Vatican II itself. But they became predominant and official modes of teaching and practice after the Council.

The earlier simple and unscientific catalogue of types of prayer has been profoundly changed in content in the last decade. The community character of the Mass or Eucharist (a term in increasing use) has been newly emphasised for example by the use of the vernacular, the priest facing the people, the participation of laity in reading, bringing up gifts, bidding prayers, kiss of peace. These reforms have also been extended to the other sacraments. However, the other forms of public prayer in novenas and other devotions have undoubtedly declined, although they may be seen as increasingly replaced by prayer groups and developments such as the Charismatic Renewal movement, although without as yet the same clerical leadership or backing.

The most recent theological attempt to overcome the limitations of the manual approach to moral theology and its popular presentation began before World War II in Europe and reached its peak in the fifties and sixties.[11] A theology of Christian life, based on the human being called to share in Christ's sonship of the Father and brotherhood of all mankind, and derived more directly from the New Testament, began gradually to displace the legal system of the manuals although the undoubted achievement of these latter works provided a valuable challenge and corrective to some of the woollier forms of 'love-ethic' which began to emerge. .

This development of moral theology as a theology of the Christian life based on a Christian anthropology (ontology) is still far from complete.[12] Yet at the same time a quite different, if complementary rather than contradictory, approach is emerging, to which I shall have to return later.

The most striking consequence of these developments for our problem, the connection between prayer and morality, is the

manifestation of inner and intrinsic connection between the
liturgical activity of the Christian and his moral activity.[13] The
liturgical activity explicitly proclaims his incorporation into
Christ's response to the Father in self-surrender as Son, his
resultant adoptive sonship of the Father and brotherhood of all
men. And this is effected through the gift of the Spirit whereby
we are buried with Christ to rise with him to a new life (*Rom.* 6)
in which we are empowered to cry Abba, Father (*Rom.* 8). The
prayer which Jesus himself taught us to say begins Our Father
(*Luke* 11). The moral living which he summarised as love of
God and love of neighbour (*Mark* 12: 28-31) finds its basis in
this share in the gift and call to divine sonship of the Father
and to the universal brotherhood of mankind which this entails.
Each particular moral act and the moral life as a whole is to be
a realisation of that sonship and brotherhood which we explicitly
recognise, manifest and celebrate in liturgical and private prayer.
The Christian life, like the Christian liturgy, has a basically
trinitarian structure, directed towards the Father through sharing
in the sonship of Jesus Christ by the sending of the Spirit. Our
prayers for light and strength in moral situations are articulations
of our need for the spirit of sonship within us to find expression
in our moral understanding and in our moral response.

A good deal more might be said about the more precise content
of such a Christian way of life and how one is to discover it, if
one does not accept any simple theory of divine inspiration in
every moral situation. However, that is a task for another time
and place.

More relevant here is the theological basis with which such
a trinitarian approach to moral theology could provide the prayer-
renewal which is at present such a feature of the Roman Catholic
and other Churches. It must be admitted that the moral theologians
themselves in their work did not anticipate such a powerful
development or have the fully developed theological understanding adequate to the task. Despite a recognition of his essential
place in the scheme of things, the Spirit remained the poor relation of the Trinity in the renewal of moral theology as well as
in the renewal of the liturgy. The appeal to the Spirit in the new
prayer movements has put the theologians on their mettle and
one of the great practical advocates of shared prayer was one of
the great pioneers in the renewal of moral theology, Bernard

Häring. Other theologians writing in these islands too, such as Simon Tugwell[14] and Peter Hocken,[15] have attempted to do fuller justice to the role of the Spirit, while keeping him within the Trinity. The temptation to treat him in isolation is not one all prayer enthusiasts can resist.

Yet formidable work remains to be done in theological reflection on this prayer movement itself and its relation to daily living and morality. It would be impossible to deny the sense of liberation, which ought to be a feature of authentic prayer, which the movement has given to many people, as well as a sense of personal and communal integration at least as far as the group is concerned. (In this context the phenomenon of healing requires careful if positive evaluation.)[16] The dangers of excessive emotion undoubtedly exist, although the sheer lack of any emotional dimension in so much of even the reformed liturgy is not particularly praiseworthy either, given that the emotions are a God-given and integral part of man. More worrying from the ecclesiastical point of view are the dangers of elitism and sectarianism, although how far they exist is very difficult to judge. And for the moral theologian with his sensitiveness to the complexities of moral situations and to the mysteriousness of God's providential relationship with the world, there may appear to be for the less discerning a too easy temptation to appeal without question to what 'the Spirit told me'. Indeed there may be a deeper danger that the world in itself would be ignored in such an exclusively religious atmosphere.[17]

In my view these renewals in liturgy, shared prayer and moral theology remain basically positive, and include solid achievements which will undoubtedly persist. It is perhaps too soon to offer any final theological analysis of the Charismatic Renewal movement, or balanced judgment on it, yet it might attend to some of the limitations which have emerged in the liturgical and moral theological renewal. And these limitations may lead in turn to posing the question of association in reverse form, that between morality and prayer, rather than prayer and morality.

From Morality to Prayer: A Reconsideration of the Bond

The more obvious difficulty which renewal in prayer, liturgical, shared and private, faces is what is rather loosely known as the phenomenon of secularisation. Without wishing to enter the tangled debate on this thorny issue, I think that it can be safely said that the cultural context in which our minds are shaped and so our prayer(s) learned and expressed has far fewer explicitly religious elements in it than it had even some decades ago and even in countries with such obvious public and private religious expressions as Scotland and Ireland. For many people this secular cultural context has made God, the transcendent and religious dimension of life, unnecessary or irrelevant or at any rate much more remote and obscure. It has made the traditional prayer concepts, formulae and structures, however renewed, strangers to one's daily thinking and living. A lack of inner connection which threatens a lack of inner conviction can sometimes be discerned even among those with a firm desire to maintain and develop their prayer life.

This would in part explain a certain sense of disappointment with the liturgical renewal in the Roman Catholic Church which some experience. Undoubtedly the expectations of many were raised too suddenly and too high, while the implementation by others has been partial and grudging.

More profoundly perhaps the expectations were simply mistaken at times. There was a suggestion that a community-based liturgy with fuller participation by the laity would quickly inspire and sustain the reform of society as a whole, breaking down the barriers of race or sex or nation in such places as twentieth-century America. When this did not happen except in particular groups and for individuals, the liturgy lost in significance for many earlier enthusiasts. The value of the liturgy in wider social renewal should not be ignored, but it is not a substitute for social moral action and the connection between prayer and moral action needs to be soundly based.

At popular and more reflective level the problem of the relationship between morality and prayer, a facet, as I have said, of the relationship between morality and religion, has to face the reality that, while there has been a traditionally very close association between morality and religion/prayer, morality itself is older and wider than the Judaeo-Christian tradition and that today it is taken for granted as essential to human living by people who reject or neglect religion and prayer. Confirmed and perhaps accelerated by the secularisation process, however that is to be more precisely understood, morality both in its popular impact and as the subject of rigorous reflection, is increasingly regarded as an autonomous human phenomenon.[18] Where the autonomy is absolute and no relationship to any transhuman or transcosmic reality is accepted, one is faced with one of the many brands of humanist morality. Accepting morality in its immediate and reflective state as autonomous does not however commit one to such absoluteness, which is basically derived from a philosophy of life which is not necessarily implicit in the analysis of morality itself but attempts to answer questions raised by, but going beyond what that analysis provides. Such questions are not answerable in terms of moral analysis alone although they open the way to a discussion of philosophies of life, including Christianity, as providing—or not providing—some satisfying answers for enquirers.

Among the many possible approaches to moral analysis, I prefer for the task in hand to concentrate on the moral experience as it occurs in the concrete situation. This experience is at its purest in the form of unconditional obligation to do or avoid something however unpleasant or disadvantageous it may be to me. And the final source of this obligation is another person or group of persons. In its most developed form the morality is an aspect of interpersonal relations (individual or group) which expresses an unconditional obligation or call, at least to recognise and respect the person(s) as person(s) and to make a particular response of food or shelter or education or comfort, according to the particular situation. The unconditionality which affects recognition, respect and response as three not always distinguishable phases of the same reaction, is founded in the character of the personal source as constituting a world of its own, a creative centre of knowing and loving, deciding and acting, which I as subject may not seek simply to use/abuse, to violate, to possess, to diminish or to eliminate. He is in that sense ultimately other than I am.

Because I am equally person and other, the call to recognition and respect is mutual, although the particular concrete response, e.g. providing food, may affect me (the subject) more immediately than the other (source of the call). In the reciprocal interchange, recognising or distinguishing the other in his otherness develops identification of the self; respect for the other involves accepting and respecting the self; responding to the other involves seeking potentialities in the self or self-development.

The other person is however not simply source of call and so of burden, but comes to one as a creative, new and unique world, a gift or present in the literal sense of being given or presented to one and in the further sense of being (at least potentially) enriching for one. But this has to be qualified by our equally undoubted experience of the other as threat, potential or actual, at an individual or group level, provoking us to fear and self-protection. This ambiguity affects all our moral interchanges, although the direction of the overall moral call would seem to be to enabling the gift to triumph over the threat.

This moral or ethical analysis could be taken much further (and has been elsewhere)[19] as have meta-ethical questions which it raises, about the meaning of this human otherness with the unconditional obligations and inviolability which it involves; about the value or ability to go on attempting to enable the gift to triumph over the threat in a world which has experienced Auschwitz and Hiroshima and a thousand other lesser horrors; about the fulfilment available for subject or source even in the most favourable circumstances; and about the possible undermining of the whole moral enterprise by the absurdity of death. It is here, it seems to me, that Christianity corresponds and responds to the ethical analysis and meta-ethical questions: with its covenant structure relating God to man and man to man in a basically gift-call compounded by threat (sin) situation, with its understanding of human otherness as originating in the image of God the Father, the absolute other, and completed through its sharing in the divine sonship of Jesus Christ, and as finally assured of the triumph of gift over the most horrible threat, of meaning over absurdity in the suffering, death and resurrection of Jesus.

This mutual coherence, illumination and intrinsic connection which the Christian can observe is not offered here as a proof from moral analysis for the existence of God or the truth of Christianity. The humanist of whatever type would try to answer the meta-ethical questions, supposing he accepted the ethical analysis, from his own world-view. The scope of my argument is to provide Christian believers with a way of accepting the autonomy of the moral experience, but then seeking to understand its deeper connection with their faith in Jesus Christ—their awareness and acceptance of the God of Jesus Christ which have been given to them in the gift of the Spirit at baptism.

Morality and faith is of course only a step away from morality and prayer. And it is by considering morality in terms of this analysis of human relationships and understanding that our moral responses as between people involve, first at the genuinely moral and human level, that I believe our awareness of God, our prayer-life, can be enriched and expanded.

The recognition and respect of the other as other, which are essential phases of genuine moral response, are often simply implicit and taken for granted. Yet precisely for the task in hand they deserve more attention. Sensitivity to the unique world of the other in its actuality and potential, that is to the mystery of the other, with the respect and even awe which this induces in one's best moments, are in themselves enriching for me and my relationship, implying enhanced self-awareness and self-acceptance; moral awareness and the awe it inspires enrich the humanity of the world generally and can provide in a changing and more secular culture a new context for religious awareness and awe.[20] Prayer may be formal and empty, lack inner connection and conviction because of the poverty of our human relationships and their moral implications. Unless more attention is paid to recognition and respect for the penultimate other, the recognition and respect for the ultimate may lack any real roots. The true basis for an intrinsic relationship between morality and prayer is to be found here.

In the Christian perspective the human otherness which demands this unconditional recognition and respect derives from, if it remains (inadequately) distinct from, the final other we call God.[21] Image and sonship are the Judaeo-Christian ways of understanding of how the ultimate mystery is accessible to us in human form. So the moral response to the human other can and should by its own inherent dynamism expand into a response to the ultimate other; it can and should expand into prayer.

A fresh insight into this is provided by the Hebrew understanding of God as holy,[22] in a word which meant absolutely other, or as it was later (more obscurely) termed, transcendent. This holiness, with the awe it inspires, he shared with people. The renewal of holiness as awareness of and sensitivity to otherness will have to be alive for people with people if it is to be

alive for people with God. Renewal in prayer is not just dependent on or related in some extrinsic fashion to a good moral life
and relationship, it can be seen as an expansion of these
relationships.

The reciprocity of such relationships and the dialectic of
other-recognition/respect and self-identification/acceptance shed
a certain light on a problem rendered acute at least at the popular
level in our own time,[23] the contrast between the God-up-there or
out-there or beyond and the God-within, between the transcendent
and the immanent God. In recognition and respect for the human
other one can and should be opened up to the God-beyond, while
in the dialectic effect of further identification and acceptance of
the self (also a human other) one can and should be opened up
to the God-within, the immanent God. It is this God-within, the
immanent God, which is also accessible to us in our community
identification. By taking account of the historical character of
human relations and moral responses as they build up and move
into the future, one is summoned to an awareness of the God-
ahead, the eschatological God. And all this is dependent for its
historical offer to each one and for its understanding on the
original divine creation and incarnation. The absolute other,
whose creating and saving deeds in the history of Israel and Jesus
Christ gave human relations their divine significance, is also
accessible in these relations as the God of the past as well as
the present and the future, of man's origin and development as
well as his present sustaining and transforming power and his
future destiny.

In this necessarily compressed treatment of one aspect of moral
analysis and its impact on understanding prayer, the perennial
temptations to distortion and suppression are the more blatant.
Clearly, sensitivity to human others may not in fact be expanded
into awareness of the absolute and divine other. And for non-
believers this seems undeniably true. (I do not wish to get
engaged here with the quite different problem of how far this
sensitivity may have an inevitable 'implicit' or 'anonymous' relationship with the God of Jesus Christ,[24] because even if one
granted this, prayer in the strict and explicit sense does not arise
for such people.) For Christians the temptation could be to reduce
their Christianity and their prayer-life to a similar 'good neighbourliness' on family, local, national or world-scale. The penulti-

mate would have obscured the ultimate, perhaps to the point of becoming the ultimate itself and so creating an idolatrous humanism.

Such temptation can only be avoided by insisting on the true meaning of the penultimate as derived from, dependent on and directed towards the ultimate. And for this, of course, direct and explicit attention to the ultimate in liturgical and personal prayer, shared or individual, is essential. The close relationship between true and full other-recognition (including relationship to the absolute transcendent other) and true and full self-identification (including relationship to the absolute immanent other) means that the 'idolising' of the penultimate prevents true and full self-identification; and this in more traditional terms is called 'damnation'.

The other temptation, to which the earlier presentation in both pre- and post-Vatican II phases might seem more open, could easily arise here too; the distortion or suppression of the penultimate for the sake of the ultimate, the distortion or suppression of morality for the sake of religion or prayer. Where the human other is seen as finally derived from the ultimate other, the temptation to use him as a means to the ultimate other could become very real. Yet unless the human other is taken fully seriously as a world in herself/himself and for her/his own sake, his true reality is lost and the God we seek at his expense is not the God of Jesus Christ, of creation and salvation. And as one, in the move towards God, suppresses the other, so one suppresses the self and there is no basis for a proper relationship between God and the self either. Like all other human and cosmic realities, the call to renewal of prayer and of awareness of God by a renewal of human relationships and of morality, has its threat as well as its gift elements and can never be entirely unambiguous.

It is worth recalling at this stage the gift and threat aspects of human relationships and their moral dimensions. Concentrating on the gift for the moment, I feel that one of the primary moral activities is simply that of thanksgiving for the presence of others, a celebration of their presence as gift. With the source and guarantee of this human otherness in mind, it is fairly easy to establish an inner connection between this primary moral call and activity and the thanksgiving for and celebration of the gift of the ultimate other. Where the Eucharist forms the explicit centre of such thanksgiving and celebration, it is easily connected in mind if not in practice with thanksgiving and celebration parties for immediately human reasons. And proper understanding and genuine celebration of both can and should be mutually enriching. The mission which began with a (wedding) party concluded with a last (Eucharist) supper. The inner connection is based on the genuine humanity of the man who was God but was practically exemplified in the life of one who came eating and drinking, only to be accused of being a drunkard and a glutton (*Luke* 7: 34).

The gift is always qualified and sometimes obscured and apparently overwhelmed by the threat. At both individual and group level, from battered babies and wives to football hooliganism to Northern Ireland or the Middle East, one can hardly escape noticing the prevalence and reality of the threat. The cry and the prayer are for peace and reconciliation, for the triumph of the gift over the threat. To many people these cries and prayers seem hollow and evidently fruitless. Perhaps once again the penultimate has been ignored for the sake of the ultimate, the moral situation misunderstood or ignored or inadequately responded to, while refuge is taken in prayer. At least a moral awareness of threat as obscuring gift and of the call to enable the gift to triumph over the threat would shift the prayer from the lips to the heart (*Is.* 29: 13). Efforts at reconciliation begin by taking the others fully seriously with their own unique world, their limitations, fears and hatreds, as well as their actual and potential achievements. Such moral response may be rebuffed or inadequate or meet with what is for the present at least an intractable situation. Yet it has to go on, for the call is insistent and persistent that we should seek to enable the gift to triumph over the threat. And the battering husband or mother, the hooded gunman or hostile soldier, the football hooligan or threatening rapist, are also gifts whose enriching potential one cannot see (perhaps they cannot see) and yet must seek to discover and encourage to emerge.

'Love your enemies' (*Matt.* 5: 44) is how Jesus summarised the appropriate moral response to threat, the effort to transform it into gift. In pursuing this line, great risks may be involved and at the high point of moral response, one may have to lay down one's life even for one's enemies. The significance of this only becomes clear in the life and death of Jesus, but in the persistent attempts to reach the other as gift rather than threat, one is reaching for his mystery as image of God and Son of the Father. So, one is reaching for that divine mystery. The explicit prayer which one then voices for peace and reconciliation is the translation into words of what the search for God involves, as one seeks the true gift of humanity in one's enemy. Reconciliation is no cheap grace as Jesus showed, and it is frequently bought only at the price of human suffering as one or both individuals or groups persist in their efforts to overcome the threat element by the gift element, and so liberate true humanity and encounter its final mystery.

Such struggles today are conducted on the grand scale between exploiting or warring groups.[25] The efforts at reconciliation will be efforts to restore true recognition of and respect for the other group as gift rather than threat and then to find the appropriate solution which will embody that recognition and respect. The final argument against violence is that by eliminating one side to the dispute, it refuses ultimate recognition and respect and prevents mutual gift from replacing mutual threat. The immediate excuse for violence is that the powerful and entrenched (the basically threatening) refuse to recognise and respect the exploited and oppressed (the basically threatened) or to provide structures enabling such recognition and respect to grow into mutual enrichment and the removal of threat and exploitation. The commitment to overcome exploitation and oppression, with a sense of justice for all and readiness to undertake the same training programme, the same risks as the men of violence (institutional or physical) will enrich our sense of human others and provide flesh and blood (incarnation) for the words of appeal for peace to God or to others, which flow so readily from the mouths of the comfortable. And in the faith which fuels the loving commitment, the committed discern and experience the mystery of God even as Jesus did, above all in the oppressed and the marginal people, while remaining aware of it in the oppressor, his needs and even his particular impoverishment. Engagement in the pursuit of social justice at local, national and international level is about recognising, respecting and responding to the inviolable otherness of all human beings; at the level of Christian understanding it is also an encounter with the absolute other in whose image and sonship all men share.[26]

It is, I believe, possible to consider other areas of moral activity, such as sexuality or verbal communication and to discover the same kind of inner connection between the appropriate moral response to the other and the response to the ultimate other or God. From a different angle it is equally possible to take most of the traditional categories of prayer: adoration, thanksgiving, petition, contrition, in their vocal and silent forms or even more developed and mystical forms, and see how they have their parallels at the level of moral interchange between people and could be greatly enlivened and enriched by starting from the understanding of moral response and expanding into prayer. Along the same lines, the theological virtues which might well be called the 'prayer' virtues in their traditional meaning of having God as their immediate object (unlike the moral virtues which relate directly to men) could be more richly understood by considering their human parallels, faith and hope in men as well as love of them, not simply as parallels, but as human realities relating human others but open to expansion to the ultimate other and to the transformation which that involves. However, if the point has not been sufficiently made by now that through moral experience and a deeper understanding of it, one is opened up to prayer-experience and a fuller commitment to it, further elaboration will scarcely help.

Conclusion

Theologians are sometimes known to yield in arrogance to the temptations of exclusiveness or totalitarianism in their analysis and solution of difficulties. It is not a temptation which I experience particularly strongly here. I am too well aware of the strength of the prayer-life and moral-life of the people in that era which I have criticised as (inevitably) having a somewhat extrinsic understanding of the relation between prayer and morality, at least at the theological level. Again, I am very well aware of the achievements of liturgical reform in my own Church and of the potential for good which the new prayer movement is already displaying, despite my reservations born of the inability of some very good people to connect inwardly with the predominantly religious thought and words used here. Threat elements are inseparable from gift elements in these movements, and could lead to liturgical and prayer communities estranged from, if not indifferent to the world in its 'secularised' state. My object has been simply to complement these developments by endeavouring to show that a reconsideration of moral relationships and responses can provide the dynamism for a prayer-development which avoids some of the limitations or threat-elements of the others discussed, while inevitably involving its own. And it is an approach which could increase communication between the 'study-bound' theologian and the Christian on the street, while it would seem also to have the advantage of cutting across denominational boundaries.

3

Morality and Spirituality[1]

The Renewal of Moral Theology and its Relation to Ascetical and Mystical Theology

IN the renewal of moral theology in which Father Häring's *The Law of Christ* proved such a seminal work, the artificial distinction between moral and ascetical theology and mystical theology was in principle overcome. The double standard of Christian living, symbolised by the precepts and counsels and to be realised by laity and religious, the less perfect and the perfect, gradually lost its significance. In Christ all men are called to be perfect as the Father is perfect (*Matt.* 5: 48). The grace of adoptive sonship of the Father and brotherhood of Christ achieved through the gift of the Spirit (*Rom.* 8) provided the basis for all Christian life and the lives of all Christians. The continuity between liturgy and life, between public prayer and private prayer, between response to God in religious and ascetical exercises and the response to the neighbour in moral virtue rested on the sonship and brotherhood which were called into play in these diverse situations. Mystical prayer itself became an intensification of a son's awareness of his Father, his brother Jesus Christ or the gift of his own sonship, the Spirit. In this dynamic trinitarian base of religious and moral life, the Charismatic Renewal movement and other prayer movements are firmly grounded. Spirituality as the more personal experience of religious and prayer life has the same ultimate objective basis as morality. Contemplation and action coincide in their deepest meaning and justification.

While all this is true in principle, it must be admitted that in neither moral nor spiritual writing and teaching has it been sufficiently elaborated. Spiritual literature still tends to lack integration into the overall structure of the Christian life and to cater for the elite. Moral theology pays lip-service to its continuity with ascetical and mystical theology but in its literature and teaching continues to concern itself with the more traditional moral areas, albeit in a new setting and with a new awareness of the positive open-ended character of the moral call. This is partly due to the inertia of history and tradition.

The renewal of moral theology is only partly accomplished. Fundamental moral theology has received much attention but many areas in special moral theology are more influenced by advances in the empirical sciences than they are by the basic change in moral theology itself which *The Law of Christ* so strongly signalled. Indeed one might make the very same criticism of Häring's pioneer work. His fundamental approach embodies his original insight but that is not carried through very strongly in volumes II and III which deal with what is known as Special Moral Theology. However, the range of subject matter covered in these two volumes and in other works dealing with special moral theology reveals how difficult it is to cover matter in the recent tradition of ascetical and mystical theology within the confines of a moral theology course or text-book. These topics have tended therefore to get crowded out of the moral theology course which should properly take care of them and have failed by and large to find a satisfactory home elsewhere.

Spiritual theology or the theology of spirituality can provide the time and the space but is exposed to the risk of reviving the older artificial distinctions between spiritual life and Christian life in general, between spiritual theology and moral theology as a theology of the Christian life. It is likely to make its greatest appeal to religious and end by giving us two grades of Christian in the Church once again, the perfect and the less perfect or imperfect. And this at a time when the whole trend of theology and not just moral theology is insisting on the basic equality of the vocation and mission of all members of the people of God despite their diverse functions (*Lumen Gentium*).

There remains, therefore, an important task of developing and integrating theological reflection previously associated with ascetical and mystical theology and now sometimes treated as spiritual theology into the moral theology which in our own time has rediscovered its basic sources in Scripture and doctrinal theology. The groundwork has been to a large extent done by people like Häring. It is not surprising, given his theological base, that he has become more preoccupied with prayer and prayer movements in recent years. This is in many ways a logical follow-through from his original moral theological work and strictly speaking belongs to it. It is the inner connection between the morality of the Christian and his prayer-life that distinguishes for me Christian morality from morality in general. The Christian moral response not only has as its ultimate power-base sonship in and brotherhood of Christ, it opens the moral subject up to the transcendent in a way parallel to prayer. Indeed if one were to follow the lead of some more recent attempts to develop a theology of morality rather than a moral theology, by taking as one's starting-point the moral experience itself, this openness to the transcendent would be even more striking and more distinctive.

From a Theology of Morality to a Theology of Spirituality

It is not the purpose of this essay to try to supplement the *Law of Christ* approach to morality by developing it to include matters traditionally treated in ascetical and mystical theology or currently in spiritual theology, however necessary that task may be. In recent years I have become more keenly aware of the need to complement the *Law of Christ* approach by starting the analysis of morality not from revelation and the Person of Christ in particular, but from human moral experience. This moral experience is discernible in itself and can be analysed and structured in a way that confirms the fact that it is older and wider than the Judaeo-Christian tradition. The moral analyst who is also a Christian believer must confront his analysis with his Christian faith and see how far they illustrate, cohere with and confirm each other or are even intrinsically linked. This leads to what is more properly termed a theology of morality than a moral theology and forms the subject matter of my book *Gift and Call: Towards a Christian Theology of Morality.*

This is far from a purely academic exercise, a kind of intellectual experiment in the laboratory of one's study to see how far one can go in devising yet another approach to morality for the Christian. At the pastoral level many Christians find it difficult to connect immediately with a morality couched in strongly religious and Christian terms. That is not, in our secularised world, how moral problems express themselves. They feel the need to take moral problems in their own human terms as they occur in their experience and that does not usually involve an awareness of the basic trinitarian structure of Christian living or even such concepts as sonship and brotherhood, however true they be and however valuable it is to alert people to them reflectively. But neither is this primarily an apologetic exercise, aimed at making the moral conclusions whereby Christians live more credible to non-Christians, although this could be a useful side-effect. This approach has its own justification in the manner in which so many people, including Christians, actually experience their moral lives and require an analysis and understanding whereby they can order them in a way that immediately connects with their own thought processes. The relative autonomy of morality, its distinction from and ultimate connection (for the believer) with religious truth provide valuable insights into many areas of moral living. In more traditional terms it can be seen as a fresh development of natural law without the artificial limitations which that concept sometimes suffered by being set apart, as it were, from the overall human experience of failure (theologically: sin) and gift (theologically: grace).[2]

In earlier essays I attempted to relate this approach to morality as a human phenomenon to the person, achievement and teaching of Jesus Christ, to the task of discerning God's action in the world and to the reality of prayer.[3] I wish to follow through these attempts here by relating morality as a human experience to some of the traditional concepts in ascetical and mystical theology. As in the case of prayer, I find that by following through certain aspects of human experience to the limit, it is possible to find connections for people to whom ideas of asceticism or humility for example are either unreal or distorted. In this fashion it may be possible to give real human roots to some of the great Christian ideals and renew in the light of human experience the spirituality which is already being renewed in the more objective light of revelation.

This is a hazardous undertaking because in invoking experience, one is ultimately forced to depend on one's own. One has no direct access to anybody else's. Of course, through various social communications in books, lectures and conversation and because one is to a large extent a child of one's age, one can hope, if not properly assume, that one's experience is shared in some degree by others. The proof of that will lie with the readers, in how far they find echoes of their own experience in what is presented here.

More difficult still is the task of focusing honestly and fully on one's own experience. The shifting sands of that experience frequently elude verbal expression—still more, intellectual analysis. The influence of various subconscious and unconscious forces and the perennial temptation to dress up in public what one discovers in private create difficulties that cannot simply be shrugged off. How much they interfere with the analysis presented here, it is simply not possible to establish *a priori.*

A final limitation on this particular enterprise must be conceded. It is obviously not possible to cover the whole range of human attitudes and activities that might provide the roots for all aspects of the 'spiritual life'. The few attitudes and activities selected and the related spiritual realities do not exhaust the number of possible human roots for these realities. At work here again is the personal equation of the analyst, a professional theologian with a strong pastoral interest, working in a particular institution, country and culture at a particular time. It should be remembered, however, that while particularity imposes necessary limitations, it is also essential to a living theology. The day of the simply universal theology and theologian is over.

The Human Roots of Ascetical and Mystical Theology

Asceticism, both semantically and in traditional usage, refers to a certain training required for a more intense Christian life, whether in the world or—more usually—in the cloister. It involved certain renunciations of which the paradigmatic ones were those of the cloister, in the vows of chastity, poverty and obedience. The more general concept applied to all Christians and the ascetical practices of fasting, almsgiving and prayer derived from the Sermon on the Mount frequently inclined towards the model provided by John the Baptist, who lived in the desert and came neither eating nor drinking, rather than to that of the more sociable Jesus, who came 'eating and drinking', associated freely with sinners, had friends and went to weddings and parties and yet could make the crucial demand that if anybody would come after him, he must take up his cross and follow him. For Jesus, meeting his fellow-men never made him less a man as the 'flight from the world' ascetic might have it, taking as his charter *The Imitation of Christ* rather than the New Testament.

In recent years the Church itself has seemed to abandon or at least considerably reduce the emphasis on the traditional ascetic practices. The 'black fast' of Lent disappeared many decades ago and now we have only two official fast days in the year. The pre-communion fast has become little more than a gesture. The more positive evaluation of the world as indicated in the documents of Vatican II, particularly *Gaudium et Spes,* has undermined to a large extent the *fuga mundi* mentality. The changing role of the laity with the recognition of the diversity of vocation in equality of Christian dignity has affected the special status hitherto accorded religious life and its presumed ascetical superiority. Marriage has been rediscovered as Christian vocation and sacrament in a manner that creates real difficulties for the defenders of virginity as the more perfect state. Democratic patterns of relationship have considerably altered the practice of obedience and there is a definite crisis in the reflection on and practice of poverty in large, opulent institutions with a financial security for the individual religious unknown to a large percentage of mankind.

In this ecclesial and cultural situation the appeal to ascetical practices, as they were known, seems either irrelevant or hypocritical. Some acceptable alternatives have emerged, such as fasting in order to share with the hungry of the world. But many good Christians are genuinely puzzled about the meaning of asceticism as part of a Christian life-style today and rather put off by the apparently negative emphasis of the more traditional practices.

Here it may be possible to formulate a general principle in relation to the practice of the Christian life in the world and then to make (very) selective application of it to the more particular aspects covered in ascetical and mystical theology or theology of spirituality as we now have it. The roots of Christian living lie in human attitudes and activities which we can directly experience. When these attitudes and activities are pursued to their limit, a certain mysterious element, at least in the form of a question mark, is experienced. In Christian faith this mysterious element can be identified and interpreted as the presence of God, the Father of Jesus Christ.

My earlier analysis of this for the moral life as a whole, in *Gift and Call,* concentrated on the basic moral relationship between human others and how the contact with the mystery of the human other could open one up to contact with the Ultimate Other, the final transcendent reality we call God. Along these lines I should like to attempt an analysis of readily experienced human phenomenon as a way of leading Christians, alienated perhaps from the previous concepts and practices, to find a connection between their day-to-day experience and tasks and some of the growth points in Christian spirituality.

Asceticism

It is a commonplace of educational theory today that people are best trained in a particular skill by being set definite tasks or projects. The five-finger exercise approach cannot be simply dismissed as suitable only for children but for the more developed and the adult the task or project establishes a goal, stimulates the interest and focuses the attention. Focusing the attention over the period necessary to accomplish the task is one of its most demanding aspects as every student and teacher knows. Attention at work in the fragmented and distracted lives which most of us lead is not easily maintained. The habit of it ensures better work, more skill in performing it and greater satisfaction and enjoyment for the worker.

In the Christian understanding of work today as a sharing in the creative and redemptive work of God himself, one can see how attention of this kind has a theological and spiritual significance. It makes the worker a co-creator and co-redeemer as through his skill he overcomes the chaos of fallen nature and releases the creative forces of the cosmos.

Not all work can be so readily interpreted in this way. Not all Christian workers can be brought to share this vision. Yet from the farm to the factory floor, from the business office to the university library, the ultimate justification of work rests on this co-creative and co-redemptive dimension. Work that is incapable of any such interpretation is either inhuman in itself or performed in inhuman conditions—a not uncommon state of affairs.

The persistent attention demanded is a positive attitude, yet it will not be without its negativity and pain and difficulty. In overcoming these, the attentive worker shares in the redemptive work of Jesus Christ. His personality, skills and achievements are marked with the cross of Christ. However, in the ultimate satisfaction in the fruits of his labour, he shares too in the Resurrection, anticipating the eschatological transformation into which he and his work will be integrated.

Any discussion of the spirituality of students and other workers must recognise the ascetical—i.e. spiritual training—quality of attention at work and understand the Christian significance of this human experience. The presence of God in his cosmos is revealed to the faithful and attentive.

More important and more demanding than attention to work is attention to people. Some of this occurs spontaneously or almost, as with the mother who gets up in the night to attend to the crying baby. As we grow older and the circle of our family, friends and acquaintances grows larger so does the area of responsibility and response. In the global village of today, everybody is literally my neighbour and makes a corresponding call upon my attention. The range and variety of our attention necessarily depends upon the range and variety of our relationships with other people. The closer the relationship the more attention is demanded. On the other hand the more urgent the need for attention, irrespective of the previous relationship, the greater the obligation to attend.

Attention may be a relatively impersonal and professional affair, as when we say somebody who was in an accident received the attention of a doctor who chanced to be passing by. Even then there will be some personal recognition by the doctor of the personal presence of the injured other and some sympathetic concentration on his particular needs. The attentive skill which the doctor has acquired in his previous medical experience will predominate but in a personal context, which would not be evident in the case of sympathetic treatment of an injured dog.

A cartoon which I saw some time ago seemed to me to reveal much of the pain and disorder of modern life. A white-coated psychiatrist with professionally horn-rimmed glasses is looking disdainfully at an uncertain and sheepish patient. The patient explains, 'I have this feeling that everybody ignores me.' 'Next please!' replies the psychiatrist. A more poignant illustration occurs at the end of Arthur Miller's play *Death of a Salesman* when (if I correctly recall it) the 'hero' salesman Willie Loman calls out despairingly, 'For Christ's sake, will somebody pay attention?' almost a contemporary secular rendering of 'My God, my God, why hast thou forsaken me?'

Attention demands first of all recognition of the other as the different and unique world which he constitutes. It is not an almsgiving brush-off or a cocktail party contact, filling the time until somebody more important comes that way. The recognition of attention requires and displays genuine interest in this different human world, this gift of the other, whose achievement, failure and potential have a profound human significance. The interest in that significance is properly for the other's sake—not, for one's own, as a useful contact or somebody one can use to make further useful contacts. The 'contact' man is not interested; he is merely using people for his own advancement.

The genuine interest manifests itself in sensitivity to the complexity of the other's world, to the light and shadow in his life, rejoicing in the achievement and sympathetic to the failure. Out of that sensitivity is born a responsiveness to the real needs of the other which always include the need to be taken seriously for himself, the need for attention.

With limited time, energy and other resources, the degree of attention which one can give to another will never be adequate. One has to accept this as a condition of human living. Yet in many cases one should accept very sadly. The maturely attentive person has to make choices and establish priorities so that his resources are organised in the way most helpful to the others: those to whom he must be continuously attentive at home or at work and then the wider range of people, eventually embracing the whole world, to whom he must turn his attention from time to time.

The quality of the attention is more important than the extent. Where that attention develops over the years an interest, sensitivity and responsiveness in more immediate relationships, the thrust and skills of it, the basic orientation, will come readily into play in new situations with new people. The Good Samaritan, as distinct from the Levite and others who passed by the injured man on the road to Jericho, had by then that spontaneous gift of attention which was not content to 'attend' to the stranger on the roadside but took him with him to have him looked after at the inn.

That kind of attention with friends, acquaintances or people one casually encounters does not grow easily and spontaneously. It is usually the fruit of much effort and concentration. Even the mother rising in the night to nurse the baby has to discipline herself in her sleep and work if she is to be an attentive and sensitive mother. On the broader horizon without the natural bonds of motherhood or family, the struggle can be more intense and the pain more acute if one is to be really attentive to the other. And yet in this noisy, fragmented civilisation the whole world seems to echo the cry of Willie Loman for attention.

It is an attention that frequently involves dying to our own selfish interests and rising again to share the interests of our fellow-man. In doing so we transcend our own petty world to encounter, even enter, the world of the other. In this encounter the ultimate mystery of the other touches us and opens us up to the mystery of the Ultimate Other, whose image and son or (daughter this human other is. In attending to one of these least ones we attend to Jesus Christ himself (*Matt.* 25) but frequently at a cost, the cost of taking up our cross and following him.

The way of attention to others is a human demanding way. With its repercussions throughout our whole life-stance and orientation, it is a basic training and ascetical way. In its final encounter and in the pain of its path it is a Christian ascetical way. The human roots of Christian asceticism may be found at least in part in the difficult yet exciting and finally fulfilling way of attention to others.

Humility

Fragility of Humanity

There are many aspects of human and moral experience that could provide a starting-point to the understanding of humility as a central Christian virtue. Yet it may be one of the hardest of the virtues to understand and practise in our ambitious and competitive civilisation. The image-seekers, or the advertisers who manipulate public opinion to sell their product, human or artefact, must find great difficulty in accepting and implementing any notion of humility. It simply wouldn't be good for business, whether that business is politics, entertainment, or even scholarship, let alone the more conventional exchanges of commerce.

Yet even beneath this hard and glittering surface, the vulnerable and fragile reality of humanity continues to assert itself. Some of the tragedies of show-business, such as that of Marilyn Monroe, reveal this very painfully. The fragility of our humanity, threatened in so many ways by mental and physical hurt and faced with the final threat of disintegrating death, may be cloaked or kept at bay by the social and psychic as well as the chemical drugs of our time. Yet if that fragility is not totally evaded (and how can it be?) it offers a felt experience of our weakness and contingency from which one may begin to explore anew the reality of humility.

Interdependence of Mankind

A somewhat different starting-point is the increasing sense of interdependence which is beginning to affect individuals and societies around the world. The threat and potential of nuclear war may not be as readily felt as it was in the fifties and sixties, although the prospect of exporting nuclear fuel and technology to an increasing number of countries for basically commercial reasons is giving new cause for alarm to politicians such as President Carter. And the threat of accidental or deliberate nuclear explosion is ever present, drawing mankind together in self-protection. The hazards of terrorism, now an international phenomenon, serve to promote further this sense of interdependence. The oil crisis, the various fishing disputes, the problem of conservation and pollution, demand solidarity in solution and heighten once again the sense of interdependence. The problems of racial and sex discrimination together with the need for international standards and structures for dealing with dissenters, prisoners and minorities of all kinds underline this interdependence. Above all the widening gap between the affluent and poor countries should alert us to the potential dangers of inequality but primarily it should summon us to solidarity with poor countries in sharing goods, technology and personnel to help them resolve their enormous difficulties. Those clearly deprived and enslaved by our economic and political systems serve to illuminate our own impoverishment and slavery to the priority of goods and trivial satisfactions over truly human living and relationships. Their liberation is partly a condition of ours, blind though we may yet be to much of the slavery into which we escape so comfortably.

To acknowledge our interdependence at family level, at local and national level, at international level, is one protection against that family, local or national pride which can be so destructive. A sense of that interdependence, an eager acceptance of it, provides a real insight into our actual condition. Out of that insight may come a wider and deeper awareness of the fragility and dependence of all creation, including mankind. It is the way of humility, which becomes Christian humility with the recognition that the secret of that dependence and the ultimate guarantee against the final consequence of that fragility is the Father of Jesus Christ. The interdependence like the attention focuses on equally vulnerable men and needs some ultimate hope for its survival. That hope is supplied in the acceptance by God of the fragility and interdependence of men in the life and above all the death of his Son Jesus Christ and in the divine triumph over the final fragility of death through the resurrection.

A lively sense of our interdependence is essentially the way of the humble. The further interpretation of that in the light of faith in the Creator-Saviour God of Jesus Christ reveals the Christian significance of such humility.

Man the Learner

A fresh insight into the virtue of humility is made possible by taking a particular aspect of our interdependence, as learning beings. In the very early days of our dependence, as infants and children, on others, we have to learn from them how to walk and to talk and all the other myriad details of ordinary living that we take so much for granted as adults. In this connection we might well ask ourselves, 'What have we, that we have not received?'

The learning process does not cease with childhood or with the end of formal schooling. The fully human being is a permanent learner. In this way his life is enriched and developed. He remains open to other worlds and does not stagnate in a closed world of his own. The willingness and application in continued learning increases his sense of dependence and of incompletion. It prevents him from becoming like one of the stiff-necked teachers of the law who were unable to open themselves to the radical character of Jesus' message.

For the true learner, no message so long as it is true is too radical. The provisional world-view which he has formed on the basis of his previous learning may be shattered again and again. What matters is the fuller encounter with the truth. Along this learning line he is continually made aware of his own limitations and inadequacies and sometimes in a disturbingly painful manner. His pursuit of the truth at whatever cost contains no satisfactory inner-worldly explanation. Transcendence is at work—the pull of the ultimate mystery. The search for understanding is an attempt to grapple with this mystery and to realise how inadequate one is in the face of it and how dependent one is on one's fellow-learners to continue the search. For the true learner there is no other human being from whom he cannot learn and yet there is no human being who can be more than a pointer—in his knowledge and particularly in his being—to the final encounter with truth. The humiliation involved at times in the search, like the humiliation involved in coming to terms with some great novel or work of scholarship, issues in the humility of the genuine learner. To lead a truly learning life is to lead a humble life because one is inevitably humiliated by one's ignorance and limitations. To lead a learning life it is not necessary to work in a university or school or to have any particular academic talents. The profusion of human talents indicates a profusion of ways of learning. Some of the great learners, wise and humble men and women, have never had much formal schooling.

For all the pain of the learning process, there is a joy and an exultation at times that prevents humility from centring on the self or assuming any self-denigratory expression. The learner shares the pain and the joy of death and resurrection. His new life issuing from the death of his former world leads to further learning, awareness of limitations, pain and again new life. His humility is secured in the process; his identity and self-acceptance guaranteed against the destructive threat of self-rejection and self-denigration by his recognition of the direction of the process, the universal summons of it to all men and the joys of discovery and fulfilment which at least occasionally come his way.

To learn of Jesus who was meek and humble of heart is to realise that in him God trod the learning path of mankind from baby-talk and baby-walk to the heights of the Transfiguration, from the depths of abandonment in the Garden and on the Cross to the fullness of knowledge of the Resurrection. Jesus not only points the way and provides the model: he is the very goal of the learning process whether we focus it on the world created through the Logos or on men created in the image of that Logos and called to share its very divinity.

Tolerance

It is not usual to find the topic 'tolerance' figuring in a discussion of spirituality, or of morality for that matter. I choose it here as a topic that may be particularly appealing to this generation, as it is certainly very necessary. Although the word itself sounds weak (it is difficult to find a suitable alternative), the issue is one of great and positive human importance, and can be seen to have a deeply Christian significance.

The appeal and the necessity of the word have both social and personal dimensions. In Northern Ireland as in the Middle East, community intolerance between the diverse groups is the source of much suffering. On a wider canvas class and racial discrimination contradict the very brotherhood of man announced in Jesus Christ. Under various totalitarian and even apparently democratic regimes, intolerance of the dissenter can lead to the most horrible torture and death.

At a domestic and local level tolerance is no less necessary and frequently lacking. The development of the nuclear family without any substitute for the safeguards provided by the extended family of the past, raised exaggerated hopes of fulfilment for the isolated married couple or family with sometimes appalling consequences in cruelty, beatings and finally total marital breakdown. The pressure of life in the enclosed territory of some of our city slums and suburbs so lowers the threshold of frustration and intolerance that 'muggings' and vandalism become regular outlets.

Given these personal and social problems even in predominantly Christian and Catholic areas, it would be a very individualist discussion of Christian life and morality that ignored them; and a very elitist and 'spiritualist' view of Christian spirituality that did not consider the place of tolerance in Christians and others actually living together. However, there is a much more positive and creative side to the tolerance in question here than that involved in merely keeping the peace.

The question of tolerance is sometimes posed in terms of the difficulties of combining truth and freedom. This may help with some of the social problems listed above. But it is essentially negative in its direction (how much must truth yield to freedom or vice versa) and crude in its application. A far more refined and positive virtue (it is not too much to call it so) is in question here.

Tolerance is basically the capacity to recognise, accept and respect the existence of a different world from one's own. The recognition, acceptance and respect are at issue in every interchange between men from the most intimate in the home to the most international. Unwillingness or inability to recognise the other as different, to accept him and respect him in that difference, constitutes the problem of intolerance with all its bloody and other consequences.

The recognition which leads to acceptance and respect is not as easy as may at first appear, otherwise the intolerance we know would not exist on such a vast scale. The difference itself may be experienced as threat provoking fear rather than complementary gift inviting acceptance and respect. So much intolerance arises through fear of the different which is recognised as such but excluded from acceptance and respect without further investigation. This exclusion may be based on previous experience of similar different others or even of the same other and the fear which provokes it closes down the subject to any fresh consideration of the other. With fear in possession, intolerance has an easy sway. Many a blow struck in the home, like many a shot fired in communal strife, manifests a defensive reaction born of fear. Indeed, many a defensive reaction by churchmen, attempting to exclude or repress the different, arises from the same fear of the different and largely unknown. With our continuing ecclesial difficulties the virtue of tolerance has a large role to play in enabling people of different interests and tendencies but all genuinely committed to the Church and the truth of Christ, to live together in peace and then combine creatively.

Recognition and acceptance of the other as different form the minimum basis for living together in peace. The more creative aspect of tolerance demands that respect which goes beyond any uneasy peace, any cold war co-existence or any merely indifferent live and let live. Respect involves a genuine appreciation and encouragement of the difference as basis of a potentially enriching relationship. It allows for a creative interchange which can only grow out of genuine difference accepted and respected. All the creative growth in the world depends on the interaction of the different. At the conscious and free, human and moral level, this interaction demands mutual recognition, acceptance and respect. Through such interchanges families develop, the Church is enriched, social and cultural development takes place.

'Creative' is a key word here because it means following the intention and example of the Creator. The profusion of his creative activity finds its best witness in the harmonious acceptance and blending of the different. The fear and rejection which intolerance expresses is the shadow side of that creation, part of the ambiguity introduced into it by man's sin. Overcoming the fear and rejection then is not only creative but redemptive. The tearing away of the veil in the temple (*Matt.* 27 : 51par.), the breaking of the barriers between nations, classes and sexes (*Gal.* 3 : 28) and the struggle of the whole of creation (*Rom.* 8 : 19ff) towards the reconciliation accomplished by God in Jesus Christ (2 *Cor.* 5 : 18 ff.) unmask the Christian meaning of the gradual establishment of tolerance as a personal and social reality.

Intolerance has been interpreted as the unwillingness to recognise and accept differences between men. Because he is different he cannot share my world. My world has room only for beings the same as or similar to me. The theological implications of this attitude are truly awesome. Since only people in my image may inhabit my world, only the God whom they reflect may inhabit it. The image of God is confined to people in my image. He is reconstituted in my image and becomes a veritable idol. By intolerantly excluding the different, one is impoverishing access to the diverse images of the mystery of God and ultimately reducing that mystery to the sole image one can accept. Feuerbach is truly one's religious mentor and not the New Testament or Augustine or Aquinas or the Councils of the Church. The very catholicity of the Church, based on the universality of the God of Jesus Christ, calls for tolerance as a positive and creative quality in the lives of Christians.

Celibacy, Poverty and Obedience

It is feasible and necessary to find a human starting point for many of the other more conventional characteristics of the 'spiritual life'. I have already attempted to do this for celibacy (*Gift and Call*) which I take to mean not primarily a restriction but a new freedom to love. To love is to love in human fashion which always involves the total human being including his or her sexuality. So celibacy becomes a freedom to love sexually in a new way, reflecting once again in its affirmation and renunciation (of marital love) the way of the Creator and Redeemer.

Poverty has been the subject of much reappraisal in theory and in practice. As a necessary aspect of the lives of all Christians it renounces service of the money-God in the search for ever-increasing wealth. Positively it indicates a willingness to share one's goods, skills and very person with the deprived and needy.

A special vocation which should act in some sense as avant-garde witness for mankind as a whole involves community of goods for a particular group but with that openness to wider sharing to which every Christian is called. To pretend that the teaching, nursing and other professionally oriented orders can be witnesses to actual poverty in the midst of their necessary institutions and equipment is foolish. Community of goods would correspond more accurately to the reality and provide a very valuable witness. Finally, there is the vocation of those called to share temporarily or permanently the actual living conditions of the most neglected and deprived in the community. Perhaps it would be better to reserve the word 'poverty' for people in this situation. To remove the further ambiguity in Christian attitude to poverty which at once exalts it and condemns it, all Christians should join with the most deprived in solidarity and protest against their condition (Gutiérrez). The visible symbol of this solidarity and most potent instrument of protest would inevitably depend on those who actually join in living out the marginalised existence of these people.

Obedience as a Christian virtue is undergoing a similar questioning. Its role in the religious life in particular is the source of much confusion. Perhaps the most useful human starting-point is that of availability to others. This kind of freedom to drop everything to attend to the needs of others we find very admirable in Christian and non-Christian. Without exploring here all the ramifications of such availability and its relationship to the traditional vow and virtue of Christian obedience, it is possible to see how the obedience of Jesus was expressed in terms of this availability to human others and the ultimate other, his Father. A particularly unpopular and misunderstood virtue could well be rehabilitated by examining more fully this availability in human life and in the life and death of Jesus Christ.

The elements of the 'spiritual life' discussed here, some at length and others very cursorily, are clearly not exhaustive of that life. Neither, indeed, are the particular human starting-points adopted here, the only possible ones for any of these elements. The purpose of the essay was to try to root in ordinary human living some of the outstanding characteristics of Christian spirituality in the hope of enabling some people of our generation and our civilisation to connect with them in an intelligible and vital way. The task of recasting our whole thinking on spirituality along these lines is a formidable but necessary one, not to replace but to complement the more conventional analysis springing from the central truths of Christianity rather than from immediate human experience.

4

The Moralist and Christian Freedom[1]

THIS paper starts from certain questions which have arisen for the lecturer in relating his understanding of morality with its presupposition of freedom to the teaching on Christian freedom so evident in the Pauline writings, firmly founded in the rest of the New Testament and influential from time to time in the life and teaching of the Church, if not in the works of conventional theology or Christian ethics. To be fair, the tradition of Christian ethics, in so far as that is a 'reformed' Churches phenomenon, has been much more conscious of such teaching and questions than the tradition of moral theology, in so far as that is a Catholic phenomenon. The latter tradition tended to ignore the problem entirely, or to leave it to the biblical scholars as an exegetical problem or to the dogmatic theologians as a problem of doctrine.

As an integral and influential part of a theology of morality or Christian living it did not figure in the Catholic manuals of moral theology, even new style such as Häring's *Law of Christ*. Its role in the Reformation tradition was undoubtedly more evident but how much more illuminating or influential it was in either the 'Puritan' ethic or Anglican moral theology may be open to question. At any rate the very structure of that approach, with the Bible or revelation as its basic starting-point and final criterion, does not offer any immediate aid in the tasks confronting so many moralists today (and this moralist in particular) who have a quite different approach to analysing morality and its relationship to Christianity.

This is not a paper about the relationship between Christianity and morality in general. That is much too wide and to some extent too well canvassed a topic to examine here. And it is not in particular a paper on the question to which the whole relationship between morality and Christian faith is too frequently and, in my judgment, misleadingly reduced: how far is there a specifically Christian morality or ethic? The paper is obviously set within the wider context of the relation between faith and ethics. It will inevitably involve a certain general stance on that question which should be briefly clarified at the beginning.

I take the view, not unreasonably or eccentrically I hope, that morality is primarily a human phenomenon. It is older and wider than the Judaeo-Christian tradition. And while there are close historical links which are intellectually significant to the believer, these links are no longer relevant or meaningful to many people today. Further, much of the morality which we might think of as at least Christian in origin, has an intelligible and defensible meaning and value outside the Christian and faith discourse. This applies I believe even to such central tenets of Christian morality as the primacy of love and the necessity of repentance. Some of the other values one is simply recovering for the wider human community from what the Jewish and Christian communities previously borrowed and integrated into their particular religious covenant relationship with Yahweh and the Father.

Without wishing to labour the point I am assuming here that morality is primarily a human phenomenon and that it is a matter for the Christian moralist, the Christian who is engaged in analysing morality, to examine the connection which such a morality may or may not have with his Christian faith, although here I will confine myself to that aspect of the Christian faith, or perhaps preferably that perspective on the Christian faith as a whole which we may call Christian liberty or the liberty of the children of God.

In a mood of optimism I might assume that Christian faith and Christian liberty are sufficiently well-defined and understood in the theological and Christian community to provide at least one clear and fixed partner in the relationship or interaction I wish to examine. Such optimism is not easily justified and the difficulties in finding an agreed understanding of Christian liberty will undoubtedly return to haunt us.

The other partner is more obviously fluid and difficult. What human phenomenon of morality is one talking about? How does one choose among the welter of conflicting theories and practices? Undoubtedly much of the discussion about human morality and

Christian faith or human and Christian morality suffers from the vague and even vacuous notion of human morality assumed.

One of two strategies may be employed, often unconsciously. One way adopts an empirical strategy and selects a particular non-religious moral position whether of an evolutionary humanist or Marxist or whatever kind. But this is seldom the road taken by Christians except in so far as they wish to promote or refute evolutionary humanism or Marxism in the name of Christianity. It is more usual to understand the human as defined within the theological tradition: that which is distinct from the divine presence and activity as available through Revelation, Incarnation, Redemption, Jesus, the Spirit, the Church, word, sacrament and grace. It is basically a theological definition of the human and provided the basis for the development and integration of the Natural Law tradition within Christian moral theology.

Its limitations, practical or theoretical, for our purposes are multiple. At the practical level it is not a definition of the human with which anybody else works and in speaking of the wider phenomenon of morality as understood and shared by other human beings it would not make much sense to them. Also, there are not in this theology any pure human natures free from grace and sin wandering round which might act as guinea-pigs for such observations or indeed any observers free from the darkness of sin and illumination of the Spirit. Such an exercise of non-existent *ratio mere humana* on a non-existent *natura pure humana* which some natural law morality assumed could hardly suffice for the practical science of morals.

One should of course recognise the need for abstraction which faces all scientists, even the most practical, and still more sympathise with the difficulties of finding an alternative strategy. Mine contains its own difficulties which the reader no doubt will be quick to seize on. The worst of being a moralist is that one eventually has to choose, even if one can do no better than the lesser evil.

In order to maintain a certain order and clarity in the dialogue between my understanding of morality and my understanding of Christian freedom I will take moral analysis in stages and relate it at each stage to Christian freedom. This will have the advantage of offering an incomplete picture of both at any particular stage and so while avoiding some confusion, lead to some partiality and distortion. Here I must confine myself to certain aspects of both themes but I trust they will be significant aspects for the reader as well as for me.

My particular approach to morality as a human phenomenon is to examine the morality I know, experience, try to live by; conscious that I did not invent it but was, to begin with anyway, born into a historical society in which I was informed and trained as a 'moral' being. That historical society is of course western society with the further refinements of a particular era, country, Church, family, etc. I acquired moral categories of thought and patterns of action and reaction before I was able to reflect on them critically, and so before I could appropriate, reject or modify them in a personal way and act out of them as out of myself, and not as simply the focal point of various determining forces, outside or inside.

As I became through time and relationship and activity a person in my own right, I could begin to understand and live by the basic discernment of a right and a wrong in human behaviour and of a freedom to do that right or wrong, however conditioned it might be by past experience or current pressures.

Let me look at the moral experience in the more precise situation of writing this chapter. I am conscious of course of a certain freedom to abandon the whole enterprise whatever my promise to my publisher. However I am also conscious of an obligation, duty, call, to explain as well as I can what I understand by this topic, and I know that if I did try to evade that obligation, it would return to judge me by my failure to fulfil it, to behave in morally right fashion, to do the good demanded of me.

What strikes home on reflection is that while I experience this obligation, my readers are the source of it. Moral obligations are primarily interpersonal. The ought or call aspect is not only compatible with the freedom aspect but presupposes it. I am not convinced by the moral analysts who essay to account for moral responsibility while maintaining a determinist position. But that is to stray too far from my theme.

Let me explore the interpersonal a little further.

The source of my obligation and the focus of my response lie in others. This is critical to my understanding and (fitful) living of morality. Others provoke, call me out of myself. The first stage of that call is that I should recognise and respect them, the final stage is that I should respond to them in terms of the particular call—in this case by writing this paper. Of course there are reciprocal calls and obligations: it is up to the serious reader to recognise and respect me as a person by endeavouring to read and understand what I have written. But the reciprocity goes deeper. In my very recognition of the existence of my readers, I more fully recognise myself, become more fully aware of my own character. I am apprehensive of my readers' reactions and yet I am stimulated by them.

And of course my acceptance and respect for my readers puts me at ease with myself, enables me to accept myself. My resources, actualised in writing on morality and liberty in response to my readers, increase or develop my own understanding. The cocktail party query about 'how do I know what I think about the Rhodesian settlement until I say it' may be more properly true than we realise—and may have some application in the written sphere too.

The thrust of my discussion here is complex but essential to my understanding of morality. It is in recognition of, respect for and response to others as persons with particular needs that we behave morally, exercise our freedom, and in the process gain in understanding, acceptance and development of ourselves. This occurs simultaneously but the focus is on the others through which the enrichment of the self occurs. The enrichment combines as here, in an apparently paradoxical way, deeper differentiation or actualisation of the resources of the self with higher integration of these resources. In the course of his morally good history the person becomes more developed in his resources or talents so that he has more to offer in response and is more integrated in himself and in his orientation to others. He is able to offer his increased resources more readily, fully and effectively. That process is what I would call moral maturity, liberation or adulthood. In that process the fragile freedom to choose the good which was his initial starting-point has become deeper and fuller freedom of engagement with and commitment to others which makes him a virtuous man rather than a man who simply performs a virtuous act, a man of character in the fruitful sense in which the American moralist Stanley Hauerwas analyses morality. He is not only the man who does not pass by on the other side. He does not have to agonise about appointments missed or trouble or expense incurred, as he finds a man beaten by robbers on the road to Jericho. The reference to that most powerful piece of New Testament teaching provides the obvious point of Christian connection with my earlier analyses of moral call and response, freedom and liberation.

Christian Freedom and Personal Morality

While the explicit doctrine of Christian freedom is elaborated by Paul in his letters to the Romans, Corinthians and Galatians, and there is a significant passage in John 8, the background to it all is undoubtedly the freedom displayed by Jesus himself in the Synoptic accounts of his own life, attitudes, teaching, and finally of his death and resurrection. We do not need to get deeply entangled in the difficulties of tracking the exact words and deeds of the Jesus of history to derive from these faith documents the freedom which Jesus manifested in relation to the Law, the sabbath, the Temple, religious and social conventions, the authorities of this world, its demonic forces and death itself.

The words and deeds of Jesus as recorded in the Synoptics cohere very well with the explicit teaching in John and the detailed elaboration in Paul on freedom from sin, the law, falsehood and death, accomplished through new life as sons of the Father in Christ by the gift of the Spirit. In this sense freedom in Christ in its meaning, origin and implications is a particular perspective on the whole saving work of the Father in Jesus the Christ, extended to his followers by the coming of the Spirit.

Such a doctrine poses some immediate problems for morality as I have presented it so far and indeed for any presentation of human morality. The first and most obvious of these appears to be the abolition of morality or at least the undermining of its significance by the abolition of the law. It will not suffice to say that it was the cultic and purificatory laws with their accretions from the traditions of men which were abolished, leaving the moral core untouched. It was the very law itself. Paul was quite insistent on this even though he resisted the conclusions of libertinism drawn by some of his followers among the Galatians. Such temptation has continued in Christian history with the frequent aggressive response among the main-line Churches of resorting to a legalistic and self-saving concept of the (moral) law which was certainly rejected by Paul.

In a different fashion Christian liberty has, in combination with the ideas of grace, election and predestination, tended to eliminate human freedom and thereby the whole value of moral striving. The peculiar irony whereby this tendency issued in a work-ethic which in turn influenced the kind of *laissez-faire* capitalism which horrifies many Christians today (not all of course!) reinforces the sense of bafflement which many moralists feel in trying to connect moral endeavour and Christian liberty.

Christian liberty is a divine gift whereby we are transformed from our death-laden, sinful condition to sharing the life and status of sons. Our behaviour is to be expressive of that sonship. As the sense of the imminence of the Parousia receded, that behaviour was seen to have a finer dimension, to be something that had to be expressed and developed over time. That expression had to be characteristic of the new life. The guiding characteristic was, above all, love but the more detailed structure of the loving behaviour was explicitly if not completely provided in the New Testament directives (which included many of the directives of the Law and the Prophets as well as some original teaching and some further borrowing from contemporary Stoic morality). The guidelines did not disappear. Libertinism was not an option for the Christian and he was still held accountable and free in his behaviour. Yet the principle of salvation was the conferring of this freedom of the Spirit which set men free from sin to respond freely in love and set them free from the law as a means of achieving justification.

Can we accept or even reconcile such a concept of liberating gift with the human phenomenon of morality as I have described it? It is wise to remember the limitations of our language, concepts and eventual understanding in trying to relate the absolute mystery of God and the relative mystery of man. It is however cowardly evasion to pin up the sign 'mystery' on the doors of our studies or of our minds and repair to drinks and dinner. An apophatic theology should be the final phase of our theological enterprise, not the first. Only then will we recognise what we have to be apophatic about. It is much.

In the moral enterprise the person is, at least to begin with, simply recipient of moral ideas, attitudes, actions and habits. We see him as gradually becoming his own moral person although out of the resources which he has received and which as we saw he may reject, modify or personally appropriate. But at least in moral awareness as in all awareness, in moral activity as in all activity, he begins as a learner, a recipient of the given or gift. It is as a creative recipient that he becomes his own moral person and expresses his gifts creatively in a way which is his own rather than simply derivative and may transcend the understanding and activity which he has learned. The morally outstanding clearly do. However there is no denying the original gift.

Shifting focus from the moral agent or subject to the personal object who provokes or calls him out of himself to recognition, respect and response, I suggest that creativity in moral response is in fact a response to the gift of the other as a different and potentially enriching world. It is the cherishing of this gift of the other, the recognition and respect and response to his need as other which reveals how paradoxically the other is liberating for the self in the self's moral response. Moral activity is not therefore self-liberating or self-creating except in so far as it is focused on the other in forgetfulness and surrender of the self. If I were to write only for myself (a not unheard of practice) or more subtly try to use you, the reader, in some way, to make an impression or a reputation, I would obviously not be responding to you as you are, recognising or respecting you. But still more I would be defeating my own purposes, enslaving myself in my own needs for prestige or whatever and refusing to allow myself to be liberated by the people for whom I am writing. (No matter how badly this chapter may read to you, you may console yourself later by the thought that you were helping to liberate me.)

The more serious further point takes the gift of the others and the self and the mutual liberation which moral interchange involves to the point of integration, adulthood or maturity which, as we saw earlier, enables us to respond out of more developed and more available resources in a fuller, more personal and what we might now describe (summarising recognition, respect and response) as a more loving way. Good moral behaviour is not self-centred or self-justifying but other-centred and other-concerned.

If this understanding of morality is valid then the parallels with Christian liberty hardly need underlining. Is there more than a parallel? Am I merely saying that at least one way of structuring the moral life provides channels for the liberating Spirit? And was there a dishonest rigging of the structures to allow this? Or have I in fact rendered the Spirit superfluous by discovering in or attributing to the human patterns of morality the gift-like liberating power which the New Testament and Christian tradition reserves to the Spirit? In face of this dilemma I must move on to the next phase of my moral analysis.

In introducing my analysis of morality I rejected the more general theological approach of a reasonable examination of human nature, abstracting reason and nature from the Christian realities of faith, sin and grace. I wanted to take man in his human condition and moral behaviour as I found him or at least as I found myself. But I could only do it in stages and this meant abstraction and so some inevitable distortion.

The distortion which concerns me at this moment is that due to idealising of the interpersonal exchange in terms of mutual gift with reciprocal calls to recognition, respect and response and consequent mutual enrichment and liberation. This is an abstraction because the others are for us, as we are for them, always ambiguous, mixtures of good and evil, potentially enriching and potentially destructive, gift and threat. Which of these elements predominates, which of them is allowed to predominate, will influence how far our interaction is one of love and acceptance, enrichment and liberation, and how far it is one of fear and rejection, destruction and enslavement.

Where the gift predominates love drives out the fear, and mutual enrichment and liberation take place. This is clearly the direction of good moral response but it is not the direction always followed by one or both parties. Indeed fear and rejection play a very large and evident role in our personal and social lives with their consequent enslavement and destruction. One can see this in the most intimate of relationships within the family, between colleagues, in the university or profession or trade union, in the religious order or Church at large.

If the *Imitation of Christ* could to our incredulous ears maintain that one never meets another man without coming away less a man, it was concentrating on the fearful and destructive role we may play in one another's lives and entirely neglecting the other side of the ambiguity, the loving and enriching role which we play. In life as we know it the ambiguity is not resolved and indeed in a particular human history may issue in final tragedy. It is the liberation from this ambiguity that we seek through self-protection and self-justification in doing what we ought to do and protecting ourselves against the reality of others as too threatening for us. It was that ambiguity which Jesus confronted in his own life. We sometimes read the gospels too easily on a cops and robbers, goodies and baddies model. Both Jesus' disciples and his critics were a mixed lot. They both took destructive roles in the final climactic confrontation in which the divine gift of Jesus had assumed such threatening proportions for his enemies that they sought to liberate themselves by having him killed.

The final attempt at liberation determined their own enslavement and provided the gateway for Jesus' final triumph over the threats of sin and death. In the risen life of Jesus, man's threat to and fear of his fellow men is definitively overcome. True freedom, freedom in the truth, is achieved for mankind. The sending of the Spirit is the extension of that freedom to our lives, ensuring the final resolution of the ambiguity of gift and threat, providing the resources of power and energy and understanding to express that liberation in our lives even in face of the rejection from which we may wish to fly back to the safety and slavery of Egypt.

At this stage I feel that the parallelism between moral living and Christian freedom is developing into an inner connection. However, before one can judge whether I am simply collapsing one onto the other, it is necessary to look at further stages or aspects of moral analysis.

I have already made clear that the moral understanding and moral behaviour of the individual agent is dependent on and derived from social categories and patterns of morality. Nobody becomes a moral subject on his own. It is always in society. And nobody behaves as moral subject purely on his own; it is always in relation to other people. The most individual of moral actions have been influenced by society and have an impact on society.

Yet there is more to the social dimension of morality than this. It might be said with certain safeguards that social morality, the moral behaviour of groups of people towards other groups of people is the primary moral challenge of our time and should be given appropriate priority in moral analysis. It is not possible to develop this point fully here but it has been my recent major concern. At any rate as the great moral challenges from violence and war, poverty and starvation through racial, sex and class discrimination and exploitation affect large and identifiable groups of people and can only be tackled by large and organised groups of people, it is clear that the concentration on the individual as moral agent or object of moral response must yield to the group as moral agent and object of moral response. The conceptual difficulties in such moral analysis are great but not insuperable and the practical urgency is immense.

My concern here is to relate such incipient social moral analysis as there is to the notion of Christian liberty. In some respects this task has been anticipated by the Liberation Theologians of Latin America and elsewhere. I may be permitted to add my pennyworth. My reaction to the Liberation Theologians is in general favourable to their Christian concern for the marginalised millions, their insistence on praxis, analysis of social needs and structures as anticipations of theological understanding, and their more general interpretation of God's liberating activity in the world, and the call to Christians and other Churches to commit themselves to this. However this is not a considered critique of liberation theology. It is relevant in so far as it bears on some of the issues of concern here. These include the relation between morality as social and Christian freedom. Liberation Theologians lack a social ethic which would provide a mediating role between the faith insights based on Exodus or God's liberating role in Jesus Christ and their concrete if provisional recognition and realisation in society.

However, before and apart from liberation theology, ethical analysis had seen something of the need and manner of developing a just society at the local, national and international level. This can be understood in various ways which must take account of the two poles of person and community, or individual and society where society is understood as a pattern of relationships or series of such patterns binding individuals together in a recognisable context for a recognisable purpose. The interplay of individual and society is critical to such a social ethic. Its criterion might be described as the promotion of deeper differentiation of the individual and sub-groups within a higher unity of the society. This could be applied very easily to the family, for example, and to other societies such as the Churches with sometimes startling results.

Both the unity and the differentiation demand institutions and structures which shall be both protective and promotive. The protective ones may be developed into recognised human rights and the promotive ones will ensure equality in sharing the various resources of society as well as participation in its decision-making processes.

My more immediate concern is with the differentiation and the respect for the person or sub-group with the (comm)unity, its structures and institutions. Sharing the ambiguity of all things human these structures, institutions and the people operating them will be at best a mixture of protection/promotion and exploitation/destruction. Their effect will be, as far as the good of the society and its members is concerned, partial, fragile and provisional. At worst it will be predominantly destructive/ exploitative. In any event, whether in its predominantly if provisionally good or its predominantly evil character, society and its structures will demand transformation with a view to the fuller differentiation and liberation of its members. That is the basic direction of all social ethics. Does it cohere with our doctrine of Christian liberty?

A prima facie reading of the New Testament and certainly much of the Christian tradition on the matter might suggest that Christian liberty concerns the individual primarily and even exclusively. That that will not quite meet the case is evident from the overall understanding of Old and New Testament as concerned with the saving of man-in-community rather than as an individual. The saving is of course the liberating. More precisely Christian liberty applies to the new mankind with its new Adam as head in Christ. It derives from men's status as sons and co-heirs, with a relational or community status. It is confirmed by the spirit of unity and community at baptism, the rite of initiation into the new Israel, the new people of God.

At the level of ecclesial community the coherence between social morality and Christian liberty is undeniable. But can social ethics be limited in this way? If ethics as such belongs to the wider human community, this would seem to apply *a posteriori* to social ethics. There are profound theological problems here about the relation between God's saving activity in Jesus Christ, the Church and the wider community of mankind. Let us be content for the moment to say that as the Spirit of Christ is the bearer of Christian liberty, the range of the Spirit's presence and activity determines the range of Christian liberty. But let us not forget to pray that in that recognisable locus of the Spirit's activity which we call the Church the gift of his liberty may not be stifled by the oppression, exploitation, discrimination and division Christians are so ready to condemn in other societies.

The final stage of my moral analysis has been near the surface of discussion since the beginning. I refer to the time-laden, historical character of mankind which pervades his moral life just as it does the rest of his life. In morality the temporal and historical condition of person and society is discerned in so far as the past sets the conditions in both limitations and resources, for present and future action. Yet both the individual and society can and do transcend the past.

The future remains open as the zone of free decision and moral behaviour, of transformation for individual and society. In that sense morality is more concerned with creating the future than remaining faithful to the past. It cannot ignore the past without remaining its prisoner. But in understanding and harnessing it, it can transcend it. The new, the discontinuous and the revolutionary can and do happen in individual and social history. Such an understanding of time and history with its implied attitudes to past and future permit person and society to become, in the present, subjects rather than objects of history, arbiters of their own destiny rather than creatures of fate.

But time past and time future share the ambiguity of gift and threat, of destruction and creativity characteristic of all human reality. The past in its ambiguity may be discerned and accepted in a predominantly gift and liberating way. The future may be entered as a further creative stage. But not without threat and fear, vulnerability and hurt. Finally disintegration and death await the individual man but societies and civilisation too. The future which beckons also casts its shadow. For many this shadow is too much. For some it presents a serious question about their efforts, their hopes, their fulfilment and their liberation.

The doctrine of Christian liberty does not immediately banish the fears or eliminate the historic destruction. It does however sustain the hope of final liberation and fulfilment through the power and after the fashion of Jesus Christ.

Christian liberty then, because it is already and still to be, at once an actual and eschatological reality, survives the fragility of time, the provisionalness of human achievements, the destructiveness of all human failures, even of human death itself. It survives as an indicative and an imperative: indicative of the meaning, resources and destiny that finds expression in our moral lives; imperative of the need to give it that expression in the tasks of personal and social morality which face us.

5

Social Ethics and Christian Freedom[1]

THE general context of the relationship between social ethics and Christian freedom is the relationship between ethics and Christian faith, which has become once again a lively topic of debate among theologians and moralists. I do not propose to review that debate here. Instead, I hope, by shifting the focal points of the debate from ethics to social ethics and from faith to Christian freedom, to take a fresh look at a rather murky area in which the question of relationship between ethics and Christian faith has been too easily transposed into the question of how far there is a specifically Christian ethic. And that question is in turn too easily subdivided into questions of content and motivation with unhelpful and unclear 'yes' and 'no' answers.

There are, however, other and perhaps deeper reasons for examining the relationship of social ethics and Christian freedom. The question of ethics and Christian freedom has haunted Christian thinkers since the days of Saint Paul and has provided some of the most intense debates and disruptions within the Christian Church from Paul and Augustine to the Reformers and their critics and into our own time with Barth and Bultmann and a host of other important figures. The debate has for some people reached a new stage, and one intimately connected with social ethics, in the phenomenon of Liberation Theology which has emerged within the last decade, particularly in Latin American countries. Meantime, the moralist at least cannot finally ignore the persistent question raised about morality and freedom *tout court*, whether by philosophers, psychologists or sociologists. On this occasion I wish to concentrate attention more particularly on the relationship between specific topics indicated by the title and advert to the wider contexts and historical debates in at most a passing way.

Social Ethics

In the Christian as well as the philosophical tradition of ethics, social ethics is a relatively recent arrival. Ethical reflection in the Christian west has been notoriously concerned with individuals and one-to-one relationships. Of course, morality has been understood as a social phenomenon, a matter in and of society and sometimes in a reductionist way that disposed of any intelligible notion of freedom. But the focus has been for the most part and the longest period on the individual and his actions. Despite the efforts and achievements of the last century by moralists and theologians, theoreticians and practitioners of a wide variety, ethical reflection is still dominated by the individual agent as starting-point and paradigm.

The limitations of such thinking are becoming increasingly obvious. The social origins of the individual's own moral categories and the social influences on and of his moral behaviour are nowadays taken for granted and form the basis of much research, reflection and reform. Even in apparently individualist moral challenges arising in one-to-one relationships such as truth-telling or promise-keeping the social dimension is operative. More significantly the most serious moral problems of the day, in range of influence and difficulty of resolving, are social problems in the fullest sense; problems that derive from the needs of groups, large groups, whole societies, even of continents and which can in turn be responded to only by groups with the necessary resources and organisation. Faced with such problems the moralist's traditional model of the individual agent appears alarmingly inadequate. If a group moral response is called for, does this not suggest a moral responsibility of the group with all the attendant difficulties of group moral awareness or conscience, group structures for decision-making or choice and effective response? Questions of this kind seem to me to reveal the poverty of our current moral analysis and pose particularly acute difficulties for Christians and others who have become much more sensitive to global problems of peace and war, affluence and poverty, of overfed millions and starving millions, of oppression and freedom based on distinction of race, class, sex or geography. The socially structured character of these problems

and the way western Christians are for the most part involved
on the exploiting side are indisputable. The limitations of Christians' analysis and response make their situation more painfully
acute. The understanding and living expression of an adequate
social ethic and its relationship to Christian freedom may help
to relieve some of that pain.

The social character of all ethics has already been indicated.
It is not possible to learn to distinguish right and wrong and
behave accordingly except in the context of some society. Ethics
then has both a personal and social dimension. It would be better
treated as both personal and social at all times. More rigorously
stated, morality and reflection upon it revolve around the two
poles of person-in-community and community-of-persons or
society. Community or society may be regarded as a particular
or global pattern of relationships whereby persons are constituted
within a particular context while they in turn constitute the community in that context. The family, for example, is a pattern
of relationship whereby John and Mary become parents while
Thomas and Anne become children.

The basic source of this personal-social character of ethics is
the personal-social condition of mankind. A human person is/
becomes a person only in community. A community or society
(we will use these terms interchangeably for the moment) is
constituted of persons. Person-in-community and community-of-
persons provide the focal points for human behaviour and development and so for moral behaviour. The respect for, value for and
parallel moral response to the person is understood and accomplished in community whether by individual or social agents. The
person in turn responds morally to others directly or through
community structures in a manner which enriches the community.
The destruction of or damage to person by his reduction to an
instrument of the community, and the destruction of the community by reducing it to the mere instrument of a person or
persons, mark the direction of immoral activity at the social level.
The direction of morally good activity is that which both promotes
the good of the individual person and the good of the community
as a whole. It may be described as combining fuller development
or deeper differentiation of the person, of particular groups of
persons with fuller development or higher unity of the society
or community. Deeper differentiation leading to higher unity is

one summary of the general direction of social ethics within societies as diverse as the family, the state and the international community.

Such a generic description needs to be examined in detail in relation to particular communities and to the more detailed pattern of relationships which form the more precise social contexts in which human beings exist, develop and behave. So, for example, the political relationships of the state (and between states) will serve this differentiation and unity by preserving internal order and external peace but under the law and by recognising basic human rights and operating through structures in which the person as citizen participates. That the state is not exhaustive of the total pattern of relationships of the people who as citizens constitute it and that, accordingly, citizenship is not exhaustive of personhood but that society and person transcend state and citizen, forms a critical aspect of social ethics. Otherwise, fundamental human rights would be meaningless; reform or transformation of the state inconceivable. However, such a distinction should not be invoked to maintain exploitation and privileges which are opposed to deeper differentiation and development for all the members of society. And higher unity would, for example, transcend the class, racist and sexist divisions we know and enable the victims of these divisions to be more fully differentiated or developed and so liberated.

Characteristics of Social Ethics

The basis of social ethics we have seen to lie in the dipolar condition of mankind as personal and communal. Its moral direction, while focusing on both these poles, is discernible as deeper differentiation of the personal leading to higher unity or community. Some further characteristics of persons-in-community relevant to our discussion will prepare the way for an examination of the interaction between social ethics and Christian freedom.

The relationship between person and community is at once founded in biological nature and transcends it. To take the example of the family, once again : parenthood and childhood are normally established by biological unity and relationship. The biological unit of the child comes into being through the biological unity of father and mother. Yet, that biological unit and that biological unity become in time human person and human parents through a caring and loving relationship which has an increasingly deliberate and free character. This interplay of nature with engagement, choice and freedom characterises not just the domestic but also larger groupings such as the tribe or the nation. The unity of the biological substrate is clearly a necessary condition, but the transforming character of human freedom is essential to human society. In more sophisticated societies the free human creation of bonds and structures may appear dominant. Without attention to the biological they will prove eventually either unstable or unfair. The manifold discriminations we know frequently involve a conscious or unconscious rejection of the basic biological unity of mankind. And social aggression and instability are frequently related to frustration of or inadequate provision for the biological.

This transformation of biological unit and unity into human person and community expresses in another way the task of social ethics. And it reveals the time-laden, historical condition of the social, the ethical and the human. It is only in time that the individual unit becomes a person and the wider group a community. The becoming is time-laden with the heritage of the past but it is in its orientation towards the future that the human being or community discovers its true moral task. Ethical call or obligation occurs in the present. The resources of response are prima facie determined by the past. But the future orientation is decisive. It is for the future that the decision must be made. And in that decision and making of the future, the past may and sometimes should be transcended. Of such decisions is history made. History-making, becoming the subject of the historical process, the determinant of one's own destiny, is a critical and distinctive aspect of human ethical activity, personal and social. The subjectivisation of history as against its objectivisation, whereby person and community are subordinated to past decisions and current structures, describes the thrust of social morality as it ranges from Northern Ireland to Latin America.

The prospects as well as the lessons of history cannot be regarded in terms of unrelieved progress. Regress has characterised human endeavour and achievement at least as much as progress. The ambiguous character of historical development with its mixture of good and evil underlines a number of critical points for the social ethician and subsequently for his dialogue with Christianity. The ambiguity itself reveals the inherent difficulty of discerning and promoting the ethically good. Our best discernment is obscured by past mistakes and misunderstandings and by the heritage of weakness and malice endemic in our mental and social structures. The limitations of discernment are re-echoed and reinforced in our mixed attempts to respond to moral and social needs, involving, as response must, some shedding of our self-preoccupation, self-protection and self-interest.

Even when we overcome these negative forces to respond in predominantly positive fashion, the achievement is both fragile and provisional: fragile, in that it may be disrupted or destroyed by a re-emergence of the negative and destructive forces; provisional, in that it is at best a stage on the way. Final and definitive achievement of morality in society, of complete differentiation in fullness of unity, does not seem to belong in time or history at all, much less in the ambiguous history we know.

The ambiguity may, in practice, lead beyond ambiguity. Social ethical endeavour can end in complete frustration or destruction. The most developed societies we know have fragmented and decayed no less than their individual members. And the inevitable disintegration in death of every person in community throws its own question-mark over the enterprise of social as well as personal ethics. The choice for the moral agent and the moral analyst has always seemed to me to lie between heroic absurdity and some final definitive transmoral significance. One may avoid such a dilemma, I feel, either by refusing to take morality seriously enough, or by avoiding the ultimate questions it raises but cannot answer. Neither course commends itself as morally and intellectually responsible.

The Christian Connection

It is obviously at the level of this dilemma that the Christian connection arises. I do not believe that one can argue apodictically from such a dilemma to the truth of Christianity or of any religious or world view. One may opt to settle for heroic absurdity as the best available solution or at any rate no worse than others on offer. On the other hand, one's choice of a transmoral world view as answer may be non-religious or religious without being Christian. For the Christian who has on other grounds chosen his world view, the connection may have its own irresolvable difficulties. This Christian, at any rate, does not see how he can evade confronting ethics and in particular social ethics with his Christian faith, although he is by no means certain that any easy harmony will be achieved. This he finds particularly true when he comes to consider as part of his Christian faith Christian freedom. For the synoptic writers it is embodied above all in the person and activities of Jesus Christ and for John and Paul in the status which believers in Jesus Christ enjoy.

Christian Freedom: Individual or Social

As I have already suggested, the connecting points between Christianity and ethics have been seen as predominantly individual. Indeed, some commentators would see this emphasis on the individual and his responsibility as one of the distinguishing features between the Old and New Testament. And such individuality would certainly seem to fit better with the more obvious understanding of Christian freedom derived from the synoptic accounts of Jesus or more formally presented in the theologies of John and Paul. If ethics can, as I believe, no longer be treated in any separate individualist fashion, but must be seen as personal-social, the relationship suggested by the title of this chapter seems even more problematic. Yet, despite the dominant moral tendency to approach the New Testament in an individualist way, the thrust of Jesus' own preaching of the Kingdom with the freedom which it implied and of the discussion by John and particularly Paul of the context, mediation and meaning of Christian freedom has a clearly social dimension.

The Kingdom to which men are summoned, which Jesus demonstrated or inaugurated in his work of exorcism, for example, and illustrated in his parables, involves certainly the quality of personal decision. Yet, it is a kingdom, a table-fellowship, a community of friends, of sons who are free in regard to the temple tax, and a group distinguished by the deepest social bond of all, love. For John, only the true sons of Abraham enjoy this freedom. And the status of sonship and so of brotherhood conferred by the reception of the gift of the Spirit is the basis of freedom for Paul, a freed community in which the old divisions of sex or race or class are no longer relevant. Entry into this freedom in community is by rebirth. A theological substrate replaces or complements the biological in the formation of the new Israel, the new mankind under the headship of the New Adam.

The Pauline view of this community with its unified existence in Christ established by the gift of the Spirit makes ample provision for the personal gifts and development of all. The diversity of gifts ensures the enrichment of the community. Responsibility in their use is demanded for the building or edifying of the community in that unity established in Christ.

However, such an apparently neat coherence between the New Testament understanding of freedom in Christ and the social dimension of morality presents at least one immediate problem. What of those outside the Christian community? It has been part of my thesis that morality and ethical reflection thereon are wider and older than Christianity. But can Christian freedom then be co-extensive with the world of social ethics? Does it have to be to maintain the connection I have espoused? The two possible responses that Christian freedom is available through the gift of the Spirit to all men, or that that freedom is limited to the explicit Christian community both pose problems that go far beyond the terms of this debate. For myself I would say that Christian freedom is clearly co-extensive with the writ of the Spirit. The Spirit may be properly manifested in but is not confined to the recognisable Christian community. Neither is Christian freedom.

Christian Freedom and Human Freedom

More pressing problems for the moralist arise when he considers how Christian freedom might be/should be understood in a way which undermines the basis of his own work, that is, human freedom.

The first of these ways was confronted by Paul himself and clearly entered into the calculations of Jesus as recorded in the Synoptics. If freedom is, as is so often made clear, a freedom from the law, is not the Christian free from moral obligation as normally understood? Is he not open at least to the temptation and the charge of libertinism? Libertinism was clearly not acceptable to Paul or to Jesus, but how did they still maintain freedom from the law? The distinction between purification, ritual and moral laws, adopted by some traditional commentators to resolve the difficulty will not do. It was from the Law as such that Paul declared Christians to be free and Jesus himself was clearly understood as a challenge to the Law which in him was fulfilled but transcended.

A similar objection may be made to the explanation that in Jesus men were given the power to fulfil the Law which still retained at least in its moral core its validity as Law. It is here, however, that one is beginning to approach the glimmerings of an answer to a problem that has troubled Christians over the centuries and sharply divided them at such times as the Reformation. The solution may lie, not in more exact and exacting exegesis of the New Testament texts, important as that will always be, but in a renewed understanding of morality or the charter of human behaviour as not primarily legal and individualist.

Morality as legal, as a series of obligations or a system of laws, divine by nature or by direct command—and as such the diverse Christian traditions understood it—is essentially burden. The freedom whereby Christians are set free is clearly from that burden (*Gal.* 5: 1). Yet, morality analysed in human terms or historically understood in Judaeo-Christian terms is in its basis salvific gift. In human terms the basis of moral obligation or call is human others who as different worlds and irreducible centres of awareness, love and creativity, present themselves as potentially enriching or gift. It is in the recognition of, respect for and response to this gift of the other(s) that the I or we behave morally. Simultaneously we become more self-aware, self-accepting and self-developed, in other words increasingly mature or liberated. This applies in personal and social relationships.

Such a view of morality provides the human basis for the freedom whereby Christ has set us free. Creation is reaffirmed and deepened by incarnation. The freedom of the Christian requires expression in line with the liberating activity of morality but now expressing the deeper reality of divine sonship.

Yet, human relationship, personal or social, which forms the basis of moral call, response and liberation, is never pure gift. Ambiguity is its continuing characteristic. Men are a mixture of threat embodying fear, of potential destruction as well as of gift promising enrichment and liberation. The mutual fear is inevitably enslaving, issuing in defensive or offensive retaliation and destruction. In regulating this fear, in attempting to control its worst effects, the various traditions of morality have played and continue to play an important protective role. That protective role lends them an especially legal character and historically and socially they have provided the necessary structure of law, conceived in religious or civic terms. But, while these traditions, including the late Jewish tradition, might protect men from the worst of their fears, they could not release or liberate them. That could only be achieved by the triumph of the gift over the threat. This means the restoration of the truly gift character of men to one another by driving out fear, by abolishing the barriers of division, by taking and overcoming the destructive character of mankind at its worst in its deliberate killing of fellowmen. In his death and resurrection Jesus Christ displayed the love which is fully gift. Morality becomes fully a morality of gift and liberation as the burden of the Law, with its protective/self-justifying character derived from fear, is replaced by the liberating status of common sonship of the Father and universal brotherhood of Christ. Freedom from the Law is freedom from the failure and fear of Adam, from the mark of Cain, from the isolation of Babel. It is freedom from sin, mankind's mutual destructiveness, and from death, the definitive historical expression of destructiveness and destruction.

The source of that freedom is God. Its medium is man; uniquely, the man Jesus Christ; derivatively and ordinarily one's fellowmen. The freedom of the Christian happens in and through one's fellowmen. They constitute the gift or grace of salvation or liberation. Society is the locus of God's liberating activity. Social ethics is its expression.

My neighbour is all mankind may now be written 'my liberator' is all mankind. Love of God and love of neighbour may now be translated into liberation by God and liberation by neighbour. The manner of that liberation, the basis of it, the most delicate expressions of it, are to be traced in and through the social relationships of mankind as they emerge in attitude, action and structure. The charter of attitude, action and structure whereby men in Christ set one another free is the discovery and achievement of social ethics.

6

Secularity, Christianity and Society

THERE is a certain confusion about the relation between such terms as 'Christian', 'Secular' and 'Society'. This chapter is an attempt to make more explicit the sources and implications of such confusion.

'Secular', 'secularisation' and 'secularism' are themselves used in very many different ways with varying nuances and overtones. It is probably impossible to define and confine any of these words in an absolutely consistent way which will at the same time receive complete approval. The term 'society' is even more elusive and in combination with secular or Christian frequently constitutes a sort of hypnotic blur that refuses closer definition and yet is used in an obsessive way.

'Secular', derived from the Latin 'saeculum' = (this) age, might be more properly related to 'eternal', 'transhistorical' or 'transcendent'. In usage it has been contrasted with 'religious' within as well as without an explicitly Christian context (e.g. religious and secular clergy), and with 'sacred'. The extension of the usage/domain of the secular in replacement of the religious/sacred in theoretical understanding and practical achievement constitutes a central strand of the process of secularisation. How far this strand is neutral, positive or negative in relation to Christianity in society requires much more detailed discussion. However, it might be useful to consider here another usage of the term 'secularisation' as simply decline in religious belief and worship, for us in Christian faith and worship, which would seem totally negative as far as Christianity in society is concerned. The major difficulty about this judgment is that of providing criteria of genuine Christian faith and worship for comparison between different societies and between different periods within the one society. Church attendance, registration of Church affiliation on census forms or acceptance of basic liturgical ministry of the Churches at birth, marriage and death provide some indications which remain however at a relatively superficial level. The long-standing embarrassment of purely nominal Christians and the concern frequently expressed about marrying in church 'non-practising' Christians or baptising their children confirm the unease which many people have with such criteria of the strength of Christianity in society at any particular time. The shedding of such nominal members, if characterised as secularisation, might appear to some Christians as growth rather than decline, positive rather than negative. Further refinements and variations in the meaning of secular will I hope emerge later in the paper.

Contexts

A major source of difficulty in attempting to discuss secularity, society and Christianity is finding ways of describing society which will allow for progressive clarification and refinement. The same source of vagueness and confusion operates in much of this discussion about Church and world. What is attempted here is far from being entirely adequate but it may offer some basis for progress.

Men live in a bewildering variety of overlapping, interrelated and inadequately distinct contexts with accompanying and equally confused patterns of relationship. The totality of these contexts and patterns of relationship may be taken here as 'society'. The contexts are defined (at least partially) by men focusing/being focused on particular and discerned aspects or needs or objectives in the total human situation. For example John is an Anglican, an Englishman, a husband and father, an engineer, secretary of the local golf club, interested in classical music and member of the British Labour Party. It is the same John who exists and behaves as all of them. He is not partly English, partly husband, etc. Each of these describes him (in his totality?) in a particular context with a particular set of relationships because he is focused by or on a particular element of the total situation. New elements and so new contexts of the total situation do emerge. With accession to the EEC he becomes a European 'citizen' with new rights, prospects and obligations. With the death of his wife he becomes a widower. With the development of science and technology he becomes a *chemical* engineer. With the opening of a new university in his area he becomes a lecturer in engineering rather than a practising engineer. With the decrease in people seeking full-time ministry in the Church he is ordained and acts as a part-time minister. With the advent of the general election he becomes the local Labour candidate and is elected Member of Parliament which means that he no longer has time to be secretary of the local golf club although he remains a member. A trivial example of the interaction of contexts.

John's fellow Englishmen and his fellowmen in general live in an equally complex and changing set of more or less formalised contexts with their own particular pattern of relationship and their interrelationship with one another. Some of these contexts are clearly more important than others, e.g. being a father as against being a member of the golf club. A very exact hierarchy is not however easy to establish, being an Anglican as against being a father. And even where it is, criteria for behaviour in terms of time and energy explicitly devoted to activity in one context rather than another are difficult to establish. Engineering may take considerably more time and energy than fathering without necessarily being regarded as more important.

In an effort to introduce some order into this bewildering variety of contexts I assume in John and his fellowmen the basic spiritual-material endowment which issues in his knowing and choosing capacities and has the obvious sexual, social and historical dimensions making him male or female, born out of and into a relational structured situation and acting and developing in time or history. With these assumptions (and I recognise how much explanation they may require now and in the later discussions of contexts) I suggest that the contexts in which men act may be arranged in families. These families of contexts which display closer similarities and interplay are not exhaustive; at best they are provisional and inadequately distinct. They may however, enable us to conduct the discussion in a more ordered way.

Group Contexts

The first family of contexts focuses on the organisation and development of men in groups. Much of this organisation and development nowadays may be accounted for in the three contexts of politics, economics and culture. The political context is at its widest the international order (or disorder) to which all men belong and on which they depend for peace, order, some affirmation and protection of basic rights as well as the opportunity and the structures to develop communication and cooperation. Its more developed expression is the more limited context of the state with its responsibility for order within and peace without and its increasing awareness of its obligation not only to compose the diverse interest groups but to use its overall resources and powers (legislative, executive and judicial) to affirm and uphold human rights and to create a more equitable distribution of goods, services and opportunities. It is not easy adequately to sum up the state's objectives. The common good or welfare, temporal good or welfare can all be at once too vague or empty and too comprehensive and so repressive of other contexts. There remains however a certain minimum of peace, order, protection of basic rights, etc., which the state must uphold and which forms the basis of the political context. Further activities depend to a certain extent on the needs and aspirations of the people themselves with due recognition for the validity of quite different (families of) contexts which nowadays may be expressed in terms of human rights which demand protection in the political context, e.g. the right to religious freedom.

The distinction and interaction between the political and economic contexts at national and international level have become extremely complicated. The oil-crisis, the recurring monetary crisis, the problems posed by the multi-national corporations and the widening gap between the rich and poor nations are continually exercising governments at international meetings while individual governments through taxation programmes, national investment programmes, and the provision of all manner of welfare are tied in so much of their activity by economic considerations. How far the economic context does and should remain independent of the political context with its own inherent dynamism and how far it can and should be controlled by the political, nationally or internationally, are questions of critical importance but enormous complexity.

The cultural context is bracketed here with the political and economic because they have so often developed in close relationship and had a great deal of mutual influence. Culture taken in the broader sense as a way of life develops historically through the people's sharing common resources in face of common tasks with obvious political and economic implications. The more self-conscious cultural identity which developed over the past couple of centuries with the rise of nationalism frequently led to the establishment of (nation) states (Treaty of Versailles). States in turn through their political power over education and communications have promoted a particular cultural identity. Economic developments such as industrialisation led in turn to new ways of life and new cultural identities among the industrialised masses which have in turn begun to call a good many of the economic and political tunes in our countries through trade unions, for example.

The object of this rather obscure discussion of what may appear obvious realities is to let these contexts emerge individually in their own right and in their interrelation with one another. They enjoy a certain coherent meaning and an independence irrespective for example of the religious adherence of the people involved. This would seem to me one of the clearer ways of understanding 'secularisation' or 'the secular'.

Vocational Contexts

The second family of contexts concerns men in their personal achievement, development and relationships, what I call the vocational, educational and familial contexts. Clearly these three contexts interact closely with the previous set. The vocational may for a particular person be basically defined by the political if he is a professional politician or civil servant for example. And vocational cannot today be divorced from economic. The interaction of education and family with culture, economics and politics requires no particular elaboration either, yet these contexts can retain a meaning and value for themselves. How far they should in the face of political or economic reductionism/imperialism and how far they have a special interdependence in maintaining their independence vis-à-vis the first set are important questions which I can only indicate here.

The vocational context varies enormously and in the affluent part of society it is easy to forget that so many people have no job; so many who have jobs simply have them thrust upon them without any real choice on their part; so many find no personal satisfaction or development in the jobs they do, which simply provide them with money to exchange for other goods. For other people (a small minority?) there is a choice and there may be considerable satisfaction and fulfilment. The satisfaction and fulfilment or lack of them have their primary basis at any rate in the work itself in its relation to the particular capacities of the worker (e.g. craft work) and in its relation to the discernible needs of other people or the wider society (e.g. looking after the aged). The recognition of such intrinsic worth in their work might appear desirable for all and the only effective protection against the extrinsicism and alienation which an exclusively 'money' attitude to work produces.

The educational context might be confined for ease of discussion to the more formalised development which people are offered in institutions devised by society to prepare them to live and make a living in society, schools at various levels and at various stages in a person's life (refresher courses, continuing education and retraining nowadays). However, the interaction and overlap with family, culture, and all the other interests, are very extensive. In so far as such formalised education is a sharing of an initiation into the heritage of one's society and in so far as it involves the acquisition of personal maturity and professional skills for life in that society it may have a coherent value and meaning of its own that is recognisable though never separable from the other contexts in which the learner lives. This is probably the most disputable and certainly one of the most difficult contexts in which to distinguish the basic elements. The difficulties are not only those of 'religious' *v.* 'non-religious' education but also the relations of family, school, society and now some radical questioning of our schooling coming from people like Illich and Freire.

The context of the family might seem, on the other hand, the least disputable and clearest. However, the very wide range of family patterns which have emerged in anthropological studies, the developments which have taken place even in our own memory, the diversity of pattern even in this country show undoubted and important elements of continuity but also important elements of discontinuity. What may be important is that at least some recent developments seem to have taken place irrespective of religious affiliation of the people involved, e.g. nuclear and extended family, decline/increase in number of births, age and variety of schooling, relations with peer group, working mothers, age of children going to work, choice of work, age of marriage and manner of choice of partner, care of ageing parents, etc. The continuities as well as the discontinuities observable can have a meaning and coherence which immediately at any rate need not evoke any religious resonance.

Moral and Religious Contexts

The third family of contexts are the moral and the religious contexts. It has been taken for granted by Christians that they are intimately related and that they have important roles in relation to all the other contexts listed. It is the more exact definition of these roles that is at the heart of the present discussion.

Despite the traditional close association it is necessary here to discuss the moral and religious contexts separately and better to begin with the moral. However, this is not the place for an exhaustive presentation of the basis and structure of morality although questions about these can scarcely be avoided in any full discussion of its role in relation to activity in various other contexts. Certain assumptions must then be made about morality which will however be made clear, could be justified and are, I believe, shared by Christians generally.

Morality is concerned with human behaviour in so far as it is free, subject to the free decision of the individual or group. The first assumption then is one of freedom of decision and action for the individual and group, not an unlimited or unconditioned freedom, but a freedom situated in concrete people with concrete possibilities open to them. It is further assumed that in some areas of human activity at least a basic distinction between right and wrong ways of exercising that freedom exists, a distinction so basic and compelling that the agent *ought* (is obliged) to behave in the right way and not to behave in the wrong way. To behave in the morally right way is to do and be good; to behave in the morally wrong way is to do and be evil. While there is a very extensive and diverse history of the understanding and practice of moral behaviour it is further assumed here that on this planet morality is a peculiarly human phenomenon, resting in the human capacities to know and decide freely and on a certain understanding of the value and distinctiveness of human beings. Respect for that human value in individals and in groups has been expressed in many ways: by respecting particular values in the interchange between beings, e.g. human life itself, truthfulness in communication, justice, chastity; by formulating and respecting particular moral laws to express and protect these values, e.g. thou shalt not kill; by attempting nowadays to embody an increasing number of these values in declarations of human rights; by giving to the most basic expression of these rights in society the protection of the political power in the law and its sanctions.

Men can know and decide freely about a right and wrong which are not simply arbitrary or their own private inventions. Morality is a subjective and objective reality. Relations between morality and the other (families of) contexts turn on the subjective knowledge and freedom with which the individuals and groups act in these contexts and the 'objective' right and wrong founded (for the writer) in some understanding of the intrinsic worth of the human being. The special character, inherent dynamism and recognisable autonomy of the political context for example is at once judged and challenged by the manner in which it respects and expresses and promotes the intrinsic human worth of all men. Some obvious consequences nowadays of such relationship between morality and politics would be the equality of all men as citizens before the law with a developing understanding and formulation of their basic rights which may range from protection of human life to guarantee of a minimum wage. It is not possible or appropriate to attempt to derive a political system from moral values but the system may and should be judged morally as destructive or oppressive of men in their basic worth and it may and should be challenged to go beyond the present level of political organisation to a fuller and freer stage of development. The moral challenges of racial discrimination, class inequality, underdeveloped countries, corrupt or destructive institutions (e.g. prisons), and 'marginal' people such as itinerants and prisoners confront us all in the political context where the organisation and resources to meet them can be found.

In the economic context similar moral judgment and challenge with the implied concrete criteria can be recognised and applied both in the simple individual-to-individual situation and in the more complex group-to-individual and group-to-group situation. Because of the very close intertwining of politics and economics the moral judgment on economic forces destructive or exploitative of man's intrinsic worth and the moral challenge to economic forces from deprived individuals or groups will normally require political action of restraint and promotion.

The cultural context presents similar if more subtle difficulties and demands similar lines of approach. The morally good or evil at folk level as well as high culture level can be discerned implicitly or indirectly in its expression and promotion or destruction of the humanity of man. The more conventional difficulties such as art and pornography have been widely canvassed in recent times. A more neglected area is that of the destruction of certain cultures or ways of life by colonisation, industrialisation, even Christianisation and the moral assessment and challenge involved. And there is an area also relevant to Ireland in the moral responsibility for minority cultures and the moral decision involved in issues of cultural identity at local, national and international level. The human achievement involved in such cultures, the destructive consequences of their neglect or suppression for the people identified with them as well as the impoverishment thereby of wider human society should make one take very seriously this moral judgment and challenge.

The moral complications and applications in the second family of contexts have always received considerable attention. What may have been neglected is the autonomy and diversity actual and possible in these more personal contexts. In the educational context for example the autonomy and diversity seem to have been frequently diminished by State and even Churches in ways that demand a fresh moral evaluation and challenge. However the intrinsic human worth together with the derivative values of justice, truth and chastity for example have been subject to such development and refinement in the moral tradition within and without Christianity that it is unnecessary to discuss them further here.

Some general conclusions at least implied in what has already been said might be formulated at this stage. The moral context does not suppress the meaning, validity and consequent autonomy of the other contexts. The moral context in particular judges and challenges the imperial extension of one context at the expense of diminishing or suppressing any of the others, e.g. the political at the expense of the familial and vice versa. The moral context has its own meaning, validity and consequent autonomy both in relation to the contexts already treated and, as I hope will be clear, in relation to the religious context which I must now discuss.

The religious context I treat here simply in Christian terms. Because the relation between the religious and other contexts varies so much with the major religions, any preliminary survey would be entirely superficial even if I had the competence to deal with them. My Christian treatment will inevitably reflect on my own Catholic tradition although I would hope that it will not be completely unacceptable or unrelated to Christians of other traditions.

I have had great difficulty in finding a satisfactory starting-point in trying to relate the religious/Christian context with the others. It may serve our purposes well enough to begin with the kind of questions Christianity attempts to answer for man about his deepest meaning, significance, value, his ultimate origin and final destiny. These questions it answers in its central doctrines of Creation, Covenant, Incarnation, Redemption and Consummation as related and realised in the Old and New Testament, in the people of Israel and fully and properly in the person of Jesus Christ, a realisation still to be completed for historical human beings and the cosmos. The relationships of these Christian doctrines to the contexts discussed above would seem to be:

one of affirmation of them in their basic value and validity, as belonging to God's creation;

one of judgment on their relative, dependent and ambiguous character;

one of challenge to them to develop their positive potential more fully and overcome the negative elements in the ambiguity;

one of empowerment to do this through the ultimate saving power of God in Jesus Christ;

one of guarantee of final significance and fulfilment in the Resurrection and Parousia. However, Christianity will also and very directly affect other contexts through the medium of the moral context with which it is intimately connected.

It would be possible to discuss the contexts individually and in detail to see how far the relationships outlined here properly apply. This would demand an assessment from the Christian point of view of the meaning and validity and autonomy of each of these contexts from the political to the moral as well as an assessment of the moral in relation to the others and indeed from this point of view of the meaning and validity of the actual differentiation of contexts itself. It would then be possible and necessary to relate the Church as the divinely fashioned visible embodiment of Jesus' saving message and power to the different contexts. In particular in the Irish situation with such a differentiation of contexts and such an acceptance of basic Christian stance of affirmation, judgment, challenge, empowerment and final guarantee in the light of Jesus Christ, the Churches should be able to make progress towards a common understanding of and approach to such difficult contexts as the political, cultural, educational and moral. But this is a full programme of work for years ahead. I have conceived my task as introductory, particularly in trying to sort out the complexities of that hold-all word 'society' before it is qualified as Christian or secular.

Two unargued but implicit conclusions suggest themselves to me at this stage. 'Secularisation' would be treated as a process of differentiation and therefore as potentially of great positive value. It is when the differentiation is distorted or restricted and one relatively autonomous context such as the political or economic (more insidiously) constitutes itself the absolute, subordinating if not eliminating all others that the objectionable 'secularism' occurs and it is a form of idolatry, the worship of a false absolute or God. Secondly Christianity/Churches may yield to similar temptation to become a political or social power or at least an ideology which will in turn diminish or eliminate other contexts and thereby diminish itself. Maintaining the correct relationship, always one of tension, demands great understanding and commitment under the guidance and power of the Spirit.

7

The Worth of the Human Person [1]

PART of the irony of the human condition is that we become more aware of the human values of health or freedom or love when they are threatened or denied. This is all the more true of the more elusive worth of the human person in general. By a further savage twist of the irony, an Auschwitz, by revealing the degradation of its victims and of its masters, can shock us into horror at the evil of which man the master is capable, a new consciousness of the worth and dignity of man the victim and the usual firm resolve of 'never again'.

Experience of the denial of the true worth of the human person —or at least of serious risk to it—is necessary to awaken most of us to its reality. Such negative experiences may not be safely consigned to other times and places. However much we may try to insulate ourselves from the current assaults on human worth through killing and torture, through exploitation and discrimination on the basis of race, sex, economics and religion, the protective barriers will never be quite high and secure enough. Some of the more sensational occurrences do get through, however carefully selected and edited. No insulation can finally protect us from the hurt and neglect of daily living in which we experience, trivially at times, some denial of our worth as human beings, some threat to our human dignity. The indignity of pain and suffering and the apparently final dissolution of human worth in dying await every man and compel at least the reflective to seek some positive understanding of the worth of the human person.

Practical Safeguards

Reaction to such large-scale destruction of the human person as Auschwitz received juridical expression in the phrase 'crimes against humanity'. People with very divergent basic philosophies of humanity seemed to be able to combine at a practical and negative level in excluding certain attacks on humans as immoral, whatever the state and its law, the superior and his command might say. At the practical but positive level this issued just thirty years ago in the Declaration of Human Rights and its continuing consequences from Strasbourg to Helsinki. The shock of Auschwitz had a powerful positive impact as well as the negative one.

There is a great deal to build on in the declarations, conventions and court activity of the last thirty years. How vulnerable that achievement is and how much remains to be done can be discerned by reading the latest bulletins from Belfast or Umtali, from Moscow or Buenos Aires; still more by reflecting on the bulletins we will never receive. The fragility of the present achievement is clearly demonstrable in practice. The declarations remain too often just that—declarations. Even where they are made concrete in institutions of laws and courts they may be evaded or manipulated or simply suspended. The concept of the National Security State provides all the necessary power and some of the respectability for denial of basic human rights. The struggle for the practical recognition and protection of human rights as expressions of the irreducible worth of the human person must be pursued if one's affirmation of that human worth is to mean anything.

Theoretical Justification

The theoretical difficulties of adequately justifying human worth are no less daunting than the practical ones of adequately expressing and protecting it. Formulations such as 'crimes against humanity', and 'degrading and inhuman treatment' and 'human rights' survive uneasily between divergent and even contradictory practice and divergent and perhaps contradictory theoretical justification. What I have to say about the basic meaning and justification of human worth is not necessarily as acceptable as the conventional formulations or the condemnations of certain current practices. And it must be said briefly and crudely.

The continuity of the human being with the wider physical world in which he exists I take for granted. It is the discontinuity that seems significant for our immediate task. That discontinuity may be described and analysed in different ways. I regard as essential to it the individual human's awareness of himself and of the world about him which enables him to take a position in relation to himself and to that world, to make choices about them. This conscious ability to possess himself (to some extent) and the freedom to dispose of himself (in some degree) provide one way of understanding the human being as centre of knowing and feeling and deciding, of understanding and relating to the world, not simply reducible to or replaceable by the knowledge, feeling and freedom of anybody else. She or he is a unique, irreducible and finally inviolable reality. At least that is the claim which each one's existence makes on the rest of mankind. It is that uniqueness, irreducibility and inviolability which found human rights and claims, just as they provide the source of human development and creative contribution in society and history.

Person, Community, Society, State

It is in society that each man comes into existence, achieves his development and contributes in turn to the social forces by which he is formed. Individualism ignores the mutual dependence of person and community, isolating the individual to the point of total discontinuity with his fellows and reducing society or community to purely intrinsic relationships. Collectivism ignores the final irreducibility of the person and transforms society into the determination of the ant heap. The maintenance of continuity and discontinuity, of dependence and independence between persons in community is essential to the recognition, development and protection of the worth of the human person.

Much of the difficulty in understanding and implementing this programme derives from the elusiveness of the general concept of society or community; and from its relationship to the concept of the more precise and very powerful social reality of the state. Without providing a total political philosophy, I take society in general to refer to the total complex of structures and relationships in which a person exists and develops through family, through language, through economic structures. State I take to be the legally institutionalised and organised aspect of these structures whereby the members of society cooperate and are protected under the law. Without the legal institutions of the state, society would disintegrate and personal worth be impoverished and destroyed. However, just as the person must be distinguished from and yet maintain its continuity with the wider society, so must the state be distinguished from while maintaining its continuity with society. The distinction between state and society and their mutual dependence are essential to the recognition and protection of personal worth. The temptation of the liberal politician is to exaggerate the distinction and in the name of freedom abandon the weak to the forces of the strong. The temptation of the socialist is to exaggerate the dependence and in the name of protecting the weak from the strong substitute the constrictions and conformism of the bureaucracy. Totalitarianisms of the right and the left ignore the relationship and tension altogether, and identify society with state, state with party or ruling clique or individual dictator. Critics of the government become traitors to the state and have no place in society. Keeping the right balance in the relationship between state and society and distinguishing still further between the various institutions of state and the people who operate them in service of society are essential to maintaining the worth of the human person.

Christian Foundation of Personal Worth

In the history of western society and state the Christian distinctiveness of the Church and its mission made a critical contribution to the distinction between state and society. In a social situation in which the Church proclaims and maintains its freedom to carry out its mission, society can no longer be identified simply with state. The original persecution in the Roman Empire or current persecution and restriction East and West confirm this. Of course the Church has had its temptations also. From being the Church of the catacombs in Rome or the Church of protest, for example in Rhodesia and Latin America today, it can easily drift into a close relationship with the power structures of the state and so obscure the basic distinction of state and society to the great impoverishment of the person.

The Church's responsibility is the more acute and its betrayal

all the greater if one recognises the need for some ultimate foundation of personal worth. The irreducibility and uniqueness of the
person with their potential for creativity and claim for protection
do not yield any finally satisfactory explanation in purely cosmic
and evolutionary terms. In Christian tradition personal worth
finds its ultimate significance in the doctrines of man's creation
in the image of the absolute and ultimate reality known as God,
and of his final destiny in reaching fulfilment with that God of
Jesus Christ. The Church's commitment to recognising the worth
of every man stems from her basic beliefs. Her role in upholding
these basic beliefs can be critical in maintaining a basic intellectual
justification of personal worth and providing at least one area
in which the person is not crushed by collectivism or abandoned
to the exploiting forces of the strong.

Temptations of the Church

The Church has its own internal temptations and dangers. The
most serious is its failure to recognise its limited, historical and
indeed sinful character by identifying itself with the kingdom or
rule of God. The distinction between Church and kingdom has
some affinity with the distinction between state and society. At
least the practical denial of the distinction (and nobody would
deny it in theory) could lead to a kind of ecclesiastical totalitarianism. If Church as people of God is identified with Church
as institution and so with the people who rule the institution,
the identification of Church with God's rule or kingdom means
the identification of human institutional Church and divine gift
of kingdom, of human and divine rule. Critics of institutional
rule could then be treated as opponents of divine rule and traitors
to God's kingdom, and the worth of particular persons diminished
or denied. The Church has constantly struggled to overcome this
temptation but, given the equally important Christian doctrine
of human sinfulness, not always successfully. The history of the
Churches gives ample evidence of varying success and failure in
meeting that temptation.

The reality of another Church failure which Christians today
feel challenged to overcome, the divisions between the Churches,
could by a curious paradox provide a safeguard against the
identification of Church and kingdom. When all the Churches

in their better moments acknowledge their own responsibility for the divisions and recognise in their fellow-Churches the saving truth and power of Jesus Christ, each should be less inclined to identify itself or the collection of divided Churches with God's kingdom or rule on earth. The pain of division may have the humbling effect of maintaining a realistic sense of their distinction and even distance from the full historical realisation of the kingdom. For this, of course, each Church requires a genuine humility and openness in regard to other Churches, a deep sense of their God-given worth. We still seem rather far from that in Ireland.

Kingdom and Society

In expressing and promoting God's kingdom as it must, the Church must also be open to the wider society and the expressions of God's creative and saving activity there. The recognition, development and protection of human worth is central to that. Part of the Church's responsibility is to cooperate in that recognition, development and protection by affirming and accepting what is truly human, questioning what is questionable and rejecting the dehumanising. The correct theoretical understanding and proper practical expression of the relationship between Church and state must serve the worth of the human person. The Church undertakes this in its preaching and promotion of the kingdom of God, by which it is also judged. That kingdom is realised not only in the Church but in society as a whole to which the state attends in its laws and institutions, services and servants. In this analysis the Church and state meet not directly but through the relationship of kingdom and society which respectively they serve, on which they are dependent and by which they are judged. In assessing, therefore, the role of the Church in matters of law and morality for example, kingdom and society must play a mediating role. And precisely because of Church divisions, no individual Church may ignore the other Churches in its relationship to the kingdom and in their common search for values which reflect the emergence of the kingdom in society.

It is, then, in the search for, promotion of and protection of human values that the Churches exercise their wider role in society and find themselves in contact, conformity or conflict with the state. At the very least they must not confuse their own community with society either by subordination to it or by domination of it, at the same time upholding society's distinction from the state.

All this theoretical reflection has to be expressed and tested in practice. The fundamental law by which the state is instituted, the Constitution, should not allow any confusion of Church, society and state. It should be restricted to fundamental law in recognition, promotion and protection of human worth. Particular laws and other state institutions should be assessed in the same way. The thrust of this distinguishing of state, society, kingdom and Church is that terms like pluralist and secular may be unnecessary and inappropriate. The state in the proper sense is a secular reality belonging to this seculum or age, and an institutional framework for all members of society, religious and non-religious. Pluralist, in the sense of mixed religious allegiance, cultural heritage and social condition, is a factual description of society whose value will vary and which will ultimately be assessed by Christians in reference to the kingdom or in non-theological terms by its respect for human worth. The kingdom is historically pluralist in the rich variety of the modes and gifts of God's creative reign. It forms the mediating ground between Church and society as well as the ultimate test of the Churches in their fidelity to their mission of proclaiming and realising the God who so recognised human worth that he took it to himself in Jesus Christ.

8

Technology and Value Preferences[1]

TECHNOLOGY is such a polyvalent and pervasive concept that it is impossible to provide an adequate description. For the purposes of this discussion I regard technology as the progressive and purposeful mastery by man of the cosmic forces and resources available.[2] This view would take account of the very long history of man's struggle to ensure his own survival by intelligent utilisation of the world about him, and range from the invention of the wheel to spaceships, from the 'agricultural revolution' some 5,000 years B.C. to the 'green revolution' of our own times.[3] For all the antiquity of its ancestry technology emerged in the nineteenth century as a progressively accelerating reality and with correspondingly accelerating social impact.[4] Indeed social impact has to be reckoned as an essential part of today's purposeful development of technology, sometimes as the predominant motive-force as in the 'green revolution' already mentioned, and always at least as social cost in terms of disruption of people's lives, pollution of the environment or depletion of scarce resources.

Within this rather general concept of technology, certain distinct but interrelated facets emerge. Traditionally the tool-making character of technology,[5] whereby man extends his own powers of hand and eye and ear, has been taken as symbolic of technology as a whole. From the reaping hook to the laser beam, the tool in the narrow sense of physical instrument has manifested man's intellectual ingenuity in extending his bodily powers and so utilising his environment more effectively. Man as tool-maker has established his distinctiveness from the rest of the animal world and with the revolutionary progress of the last century and a half contributed to so changing the world in which he lives that he himself has been changed in ways as yet difficult to assess.

A rather different facet of technological achievement has been man's ability to understand and harness the cosmic forces and resources which surround him. The 'agricultural' revolution released man from day-to-day struggle for survival because it enabled him to plan ahead and provide for the future by regular sowing and harvesting.[6] He was no longer dependent on the whimsical abundance of nature. He was no longer simply fighting nature to extract a living from it, but by cooperating with it was, to a certain extent, controlling it. That control was to grow with the centuries but only in the last two was it to grow to such a degree that a fundamental change seems to have taken place and man became lord of nature in the very arrogant sense of that term. However, where control was bought at the price of cooperation, the truly 'natural' arrogance of technological man, the price is proving too great as the present environmental concern testifies.[7]

Natural and Man-made Environment

Human mastery of cosmic forces in this fashion is sometimes described as the replacement of natural environment by man-made environment and the image conjured up is that of a futuristic city like Brasilia or the shanty settlements of some of its fellow cities in Brazil, depending on the tint of one's spectacles. Yet at least since regular agricultural practices were introduced, man has lived in a decisively man-made environment, an environment purpose-built by man. Obviously the man-making was limited in scope and clearly related to the natural forces of the soil and vegetation and climate available in the particular place. Today many more men are almost entirely removed in their work and home life from any contact with the 'natural' rhythm of season or climate or the natural produce of earth and beast. Central heating, air-conditioning, refrigeration, prepackaged and precooked foods, enormous urban settlements, mass transport, synthetics of all kinds to eat, to wear, to shelter in, cut man off from the man-modified but still largely 'natural' environment which his ancestors shared with the beasts and birds and trees. That environment he observes at a distance as a source of food or water or he visits in package holidays. There is no doubt then that the immediate 'physical' environment in which so many people today live, work and play is man-made to an enormous extent.

This physical environment, precisely because it is to such an extent man-made, enters closely into and merges with the 'social' environment of man, the intricate networks of relationships in which each person and every group exist and develop or decline. The urbanisation phenomenon, a complex expression of contemporary technology, provides the framework for so much personal and group relationship. Transport developments from the steam engine through the motor car to supersonic planes clearly influence with whom and how we relate. The parallel changes in communication from the penny post to the communications satellite are of similar far-reaching social influence. As a social being who comes into existence at all as a result of a relationship however fleeting and casual between others and for whom mere existence becomes human living through the further relationships which are given to him or he acquires, the human person is profoundly affected by the technological transformation of so much of the basis for relationship in terms of housing settlements, transport and communication.

Given the complex interplay of all facets of human living, it is no surprise to find that such technological transformation has become critically evident in patterns of work and recreation. Some commentators on the development of technology would describe it, and with considerable justification, as primarily a transformation of work.[8] Certainly the industrialisation which developed in the West and is now sought and copied throughout the world, provided the most obvious examples of technological achievement in terms of use of cosmic resources to produce new goods, of harnessing of cosmic forces from steam to nuclear power to power production, of creating a new structure of society about the industrial process itself and of developing a new life-style throughout society through the goods and services provided and the needs for them stimulated. And naturally these very changes in the work-patterns exerted their influence on the leisure-pattern which became in turn the basis for production of new goods and services and for the stimulation of the appropriate needs.

The social impact of technology should not be conceived as simply extrinsic to the persons involved, any more than the modifications of the physical environment should be conceived as simply the neutral landscape within which society develops. The physical and cosmic belong to the intimate nature of man and his society; social structures and relationships belong to the intimate nature of individual persons and smaller groups. It is impossible then to separate these aspects of man and discuss or modify them in isolation from one another. The physical and social changes consequent on technology affect the mental structure and attitudes of the individual. His attitudes to 'nature' and 'neighbour', given the increasing remoteness of the one and the increasing proximity of the other, reflect mental structures peculiar to our 'technological civilisation'.[9] The potential enrichment and potential danger, the gift and the threat which the remoteness and proximity contain, stimulate appropriate mental adjustment. The mental impact of technological achievements and the ambiguity of these achievements will occupy us later.

Technological Ethic

In the build-up of discovery and invention through the nineteenth century, a mentality developed which saw technological progress as both enriching and inevitable. By the end of the century that vision, imaginatively and forcefully expressed in the novels of Jules Verne as it was to be later by H. G. Wells, had moved from confidence in the continued ingenuity of man to provide technical advance on a very wide front to a sense of the need to plan such technical advance in an organised way, to see it less as a simply technical achievement and more as a way of changing society or establishing a new kind of society. From a civilisation greatly influenced by individual technical achievements and excited and optimistic about the prospect of more, there was emerging a technological civilisation in which all aspects of life would be subjected to the technological method and that method itself was established in a systematic and organised way. Individual achievements from the radio and telephone to the motor car and aeroplane continued to make spectacular impact, but they both reinforced and fitted into a view of life for which technology as the application of science to solving life-problems became the symbol of success.

Implicit, but becoming more explicit, in all this was the transformation of all human tasks, problems and difficulties into technological task and problems. There was no problem that could not and would not be ultimately solved by technology. And despite steadily increasing scepticism confirmed by the notorious 'logistic' failure in Vietnam, a very strong residual faith in science and technology still persists in the developed countries and has no doubt yet to reach its climax in the developing countries.

Whatever doubts there may be about what technology can do, there is considerable assurance that whatever technology can do it will do, and whatever it can do it should do. In that sense its progress is still considered inevitable and good. No effective moral brake on particular technological developments has as yet been accepted, even for such destructive technology as nuclear weapons. The 'technological ethic' which identifies can and may or should, has consequences far outside the technological sphere and epitomises for many the 'technological civilisation', preoccupied with means rather than ends, where the instrument reigns supreme.

Ambiguity of Technological Achievement

Technological 'progress' has in recent times more clearly revealed its 'shadow side'. The ambiguity which is discernible in so many, if not all, human enterprises more and more compels the description progress-regress when speaking of the achievements of technology.

Such ambiguity was obviously at work in man's development of a destructive as well as a constructive technology. Swords are as old as ploughshares and no doubt attracted as much human attention and energy in their development and use. Nuclear warheads even preceded nuclear power stations and modern warfare has proved an enormous stimulus and working laboratory for so much technological 'progress'. The ambiguity at the heart of man has been faithfully mirrored in his technological achievements with their deliberately developed destructive potential as well as their constructive potential. The positive and gift aspect of technology has been balanced and sometimes overbalanced by the negative and threat aspect which men in consequence of their own and other people's selfishness have also fostered.

Such ambiguity at the heart of men might, in the various optimistic assessments of religious and humanist 'hopefuls', yield to education and/or conversion. The ambiguities at the heart of nature, or more precisely the ambiguities intimately, perhaps inextricably, bound up with technological development of natural resources irrespective of human intentions, offer in their natural condition a more formidable problem to the simply hopeful progressive, religious or humanist.

Energy and Resources

The limitations of planet earth and of its natural resources are now being increasingly recognised.[10] The oil crisis sparked off an awareness of these limits which affect many more natural resources than oil or other energy resources. Some authorities regard the energy difficulties as less critical than those evident in other natural resources such as mineral resources or basic metals.[11] (This is partly because energy consumption can be a bit more easily controlled, but much more because new forms of energy to replace the conventional oil, gas, etc. of today are conceivable and even now feasible.) 'Present reserves of all but a few metals will be exhausted within fifty years, if consumption rates continue to grow as they are'.[12] And new inventions and substitutes will provide for only a limited stay of execution and even if the acceleration could be stopped and present rates of consumption retained, only iron and chromium would last up to the middle of the twenty-second century.[13] The use of limited and non-renewable resources by particular societies (an estimated 80% by the West at present) or particular generations means less and less for other societies and future generations. The technological appetite for such resources which is still increasing exponentially has underlined the ambiguity which lies at the heart of man's technical mastery of the world and its resources. The energy crisis may well turn into a crisis of too much energy for too little raw materials rather than a shortage of energy. And of course the production of energy has its own shadow side in terms of pollution by industrial waste such as nuclear waste and consequent disturbance of the earth's ecosystem, the possibility of far-reaching effects on the climatic conditions by, for example, affecting the polar ice-cap, extending the tropical desert zone into the temperate zone and of course generally increasing the level of entropy, of non-useful energy in the planet with the ultimate prospect of a heat death.

Such prognostications are not as far fetched as they at first appear. At any rate more prosaic and more tangible evidence of the pollutant consequences of technology are readily available from Lake Erie to any modern fume-affected city. The disruption of the ecosystem, as it is called, by industrial waste from factories and power plants as well as by the accumulation of products which cannot be recycled, non-biodegradable in the awful jargon of the moment, is affecting the prospects for life and development of hundreds of mammal and bird species and thousands of plant species. In the logic of events and the unity of the ecosystem and biosphere, human life prospects will be seriously affected.

Ecological Effects

The ambiguity of technological progress is underlined with more than a touch of irony in the agricultural developments of recent decades, undertaken with such noble intentions and high hopes in face of the desperate needs of the undernourished or starving two-thirds of mankind. The reclamation of much marginal land, the increased use of pesticides and fertilisers, the development of monocrop farming and the introduction of new high-yield varieties of wheat and rice (the 'green revolution') have enormously increased food production but with consequences that considerably qualify, if they do not ultimately defeat, the noble intentions and the high hopes. Reclamation of land might seem the least ambiguous of achievements, yet the role of slobland and woodland and even hedgerows in preservation of the necessary balance and stability of the ecosystem by serving and preserving certain vulnerable species is being increasingly recognised. The monocrop farming which spread from the farms of the midwestern states of the U.S. around the world brings similar disadvantages, imbalance and instability. The use of pesticides and fertilisers was quickly recognised as a mixed blessing and some of the most widespread such as DDT are being gradually replaced in the West. The chemical run-off to lakes and rivers, for example, is destructive of marine life, while there is continuing upset in the checks and balances which 'nature' itself provides by eliminating certain predatory species or enabling a hitherto harmless species to reach pest proportions. With the development of certain immunities, these chemicals have to be applied in increasing doses thus enlarging the vicious circle.

Social Impact : Housing

So far I have been emphasising the 'cosmic' ambiguity of technological development by drawing attention to its negative impact on the cosmos and its resources. Its social impact for all its positive achievement has also its negative side. In terms of human shelter and habitation astonishing achievements can be recorded, yet they must be set against the limitations of the industrial towns of the nineteenth century and still more against the mushroom urban development of the twentieth century, not only in its shanty towns or endemic slums, or even the sheer effect of so many people living so close together with all the social evils attendant, but also in the shadow side of its positive achievements whether in terms of high-rise flats or sewage systems.

Transport

The technological developments in transport and communications have perhaps done more to change and in so many ways improve the social pattern of human living than any other. Yet the negative consequences are no doubt far-reaching and intimately related to the positive achievements even if we do not accept in all its stark conclusions Ivan Illich's analysis of transport development,[14] the negative features of that development through pollution of the atmosphere, disturbance of homes by noise, depletion of scarce resources both of energy and raw materials for construction and power, increasing use of scarce arable and building land for roads and runways and their subsidiaries, ever-growing risk to life and limb in accidents and, more ironically and frustratingly, to the deceleration of real mobility with the increasing acceleration of technical means. The more cars the slower travel becomes in our cities and towns; the more ring roads and their like are developed to overcome this, the more remote from one's home and destination they must be; the more and faster the planes the bigger become the runways and airports, the more remote from homes and city centres they must be. It may not be true to conclude that no real progress has been achieved in ease and speed of transport since the bicycle, but the built-in limitations of transport development, apart from the destructive side-effects, can no longer be ignored.

Communications

Communications technology may from the ecological point of view be regarded as 'clean', and its social impact has been enormously beneficial in developing a consciousness of the common destiny of mankind, in promoting a common understanding of their different peoples, their achievements and, on the basis of that understanding, promoting some organised common effort in tackling them, from famine in Bangladesh to earthquakes in Nicaragua. Their educational and recreational potential scarcely needs to be mentioned. But the potential remains a potential also for destruction, a threat as well as a gift. The danger of Big Brother watching you and bugging you, of distorted propagandist uses of the media, the exploitation of people for commercial reasons through advertising and the dangers of continuous exposure to scenes of violence, for example, provide the usual starting-point in discussing threat from the media. A more insidious danger of the communications revolution may be the growing inability to cope with the amount of 'communication' transmitted by the media or the amount of information collected and stored in computers. Such inability could eventually nullify communication or so trivialise it as to make it seriously misleading, while the growing information mountain without corresponding growth in judicious selection could paralyse human judgments in a variety of fields. The multiplication of channels of communications or of banks of information does not automatically lead to more personal community and more informed personal judgments. And they may at a certain stage of development inhibit such personal progress.

Work

While it may be too restricting to describe technology exclusively in terms of its transformation of work, the work-place as symbolised by the factory or industrial plant experienced earliest and deepest development. The shadow-side of the social and personal impact of industrial development has received its share of attention from students and critics of society. The break-up of traditional communities and the formation of anonymous and alienated ones, together with the associated disfigurement of the landscape, dominates many people's view of the industrial revolution. And the same mistakes bid fair to be repeated in the developing countries of Africa, Asia and Latin America, all while the West is having to face a fresh set of ambiguities with the onset of automation and cybernation.[15] And how far the industrial complex, old and new, is essentially exploitative of particular groups and how far that exploitation is maintained and endorsed by the weight of the technology itself is a critical issue for many thoughtful observers and participants.[16]

Medicine

The technologies of housing, transport, communication and work undoubtedly shape the fabric of society for good and ill, and so of the person in society. It is a mistake to think of them as purely extrinsic to the individual person, when his very conscious-ness is so intimately influenced by them. Matching the empirical i.e. sensational mood of the times, medication, one of the outstanding examples of technological developments, appears to enter more immediately into the shape of the individual. And it would appear to be a relatively unflawed achievement as the elimination of so many fatal epidemics and less serious health hazards, the increase in life-expectancy and the general improve-ment in health can testify. The ambiguity remains. The thalidomide affair provided a spectacular example of the dangers which modern drugs, so effective in so many ways, may still involve. And again without accepting the final extreme of the conclusions of Illich[17] (why one doesn't may be more difficult to show than is sometimes realised) many people involved in health and illness are concerned about the easy availability and prescription of so many drugs whose effects especially long-term are only vaguely understood. Like the agricultural drugs of pesticides and fertilisers, they replace natural processes or disturb them in ways that may be ultimately and seriously injurious. And this is not a matter for the particular individual or current generation only as the thalidomide case showed.

Apart from any inbuilt limitations, medical technology poses problems of choice in use of limited resources for complex technological machinery such as kidney machines of benefit to the few or much simpler apparatus of benefit to the many, with all the attendant difficulties of providing highly-trained medical and technical staff to back up the machinery as against the 'barefoot' doctor kind who could provide for a much wider clientele.

Medical technology, in common with all other types, depends on limited resources of money, raw materials and personnel and has similar hard choices to make, choices which will exclude some people to include others.

Population

Where the medical progress has shown its most effective positive results in dramatically reducing natal and peri-natal mortality and so increasing life expectancy to an enormous extent, another rebound effect has shown itself—the exponential rise in population which, in efforts to feed, educate and employ, must make growing demands on these diminishing natural resources of energy, minerals and land and on the accompanying technology with its accompanying negative consequences. Population growth at the present rate and with the present demand on structures offers, in the opinion of many authorities, the greatest single threat to the survival of mankind on this planet,[18] at best it enormously and continuously aggravates the negative consequence of every single aspect of technological growth.

Deeper Ambiguity

Some treatment of the ambiguity inherent in or associated with technological development seemed necessary to provide a framework for discussing moral choice. The attention of the negative side should not obscure the positive. Without equal awareness of the positive side in terms of the actual achievement for so many men and of the possibilities and options which it offers to all men, the real agony of the ambiguity will be missed. And the ambiguity discussed here has so far confined itself to the gift and threat elements arising out of particular technological advances. Yet such ambiguity in human life, personal and social, at work and play, did not originate with recent technology. And it is a matter of debate how far technology today endorses and increases, even creates, deeper human ambiguities. 'Alienation' of the worker, particularly in relation to his own work, is certainly older than recent technology, but the spread of industrialisation with assembly line production leading to automation may have increased it enormously and created new forms of it.[19] Yet the gradual elimination of unskilled labour by machines and the reduction in the West of the need for long hours of work to achieve high production, has its obvious positive potential. 'Alienation' in social and political terms, where so many have so little say in determining their own destiny, is not another innovation either. Yet the range of it within a particular society or state and in the international order is related to the range of power over production of wealth and social control which modern technology can achieve. The domination and exploitation of which the advanced countries are accused in relation to the less advanced industrially is not new, but in its form of 'economic neo-colonialism' depends on the technology of the plough-share rather than the sword and so may be all the more subtle, pervasive and difficult to overcome. The 'ambiguous' results of aid to the developing world which has widened rather than closed the gap between rich and poor underlines this difficulty. At the personal level the flood of consumer goods which modern technology has made possible has seriously affected people's desires, expectations and even needs in a way that it would be naive to describe as simply good or constructive or valuable for them. It is against this general background that some general ethical conclusions must be drawn about man's attitudes to and his development and use of technology.

Moral Responsibility

Faced with any ambiguous reality constituting gift and threat, with potential for good and evil, the moral subject seeks to discriminate between the gift and threat elements and to enable the gift to triumph over the threat.[20] Who the moral subject is and how the distinction between gift and threat is to be made are questions basic to the discussion.

Moral Subject and Moral Object[21]

The moral subject is first of all and obviously the individual human being. Our whole moral theory and practice simply assume this and, if they cannot build on this foundation (however it is ultimately justified), they lose their strictly moral character and become psychological or sociological studies and practices. And the individual human being is regarded as moral because of his ability to choose, his liberty to choose what he knows to be good or evil. Human liberty with the awareness it presumes, is the essential characteristic of man as moral subject and some distinction between good and evil in the choices facing him (and not just in his own mind or fancy) provides the correlative object for his moral activity. But the individual person is not an isolated being and does not enjoy or exercise his liberty in a vacuum, while the correlative *object* is an aspect of a web of actuality and possibility to which he responds conscious of the further strands of that web. In the enjoyment and exercise of his liberty, the moral subject is dependent on the wider *society* in which he first receives his existence and from which he learns his moral distinctions and practices, on *time* or *history* through which he develops this ability to discern and choose and act on choice, on the *cosmos* and its forces and resources which provide him with the necessary conditions for human living and so choosing. His very liberty as moral subject is socially, historically and cosmically dependent and conditioned. It is by acknowledging this dependence and understanding and utilising the resources which society, history and the cosmos provide that he can most effectively exercise his liberty.

The correlative object of moral choice which confronts him in any situation contains social, historical and cosmic strands because this is the world in which he lives. To choose an effective response he must in turn endeavour to understand and respect these strands.

The search for moral assessment of technological development must take into account the social, historical and cosmic dimensions of the subject and the object of moral choice. Where any of these is ignored or misunderstood, moral failure will occur. However, some more particular guidance is required in helping the moral subject to discern correctly the moral object of his choice.

Liberty and Equality[22]

Two very general moral features arise from the acceptance of the individual human being as the primary moral subject. (The role of the human group as moral subject which will be touched on later is more properly considered as secondary.) The first of these is the critical one of liberty. The ability to choose as central to the moral character of the human agent involves for the sake of moral living a correlative right to choose, the fulfilment of the social, historical and cosmic conditions which promote and protect that right while the right itself is understood not just as the right to individual actions by an individual, but more widely, socially and historically, as a right to decide one's way of life and one's destiny within the unavoidable limitations of social, historical and cosmic living, in particular recognising the limitations inherent in recognising similar rights in other moral subjects. Here emerges the second general feature of moral significance, that of 'equality' or the recognition as equally entitled to the right to choose and decide one's way of life and destiny of all human beings (with due regard for the same conditions and limitations).

Two basic and interrelated questions then for the moral assessment of technological developments are: how far do they recognise, respect, protect, promote human liberty? How far do they allow for equal consideration for all concerned in the exercise of that liberty? To revert for a moment to the more general ambiguities discussed above, it is clear that domination and exploitation at the local and international level inhibit the liberty of some and violate equality of consideration and treatment.[23] In so far as technology is used in this way, its use must be regarded as immoral. The enormous increase of options in so many areas, and the possibilities for participation in deciding between these options, which modern technology offers, constitute the gift element in this context, which can and should be brought to triumph over the threat of domination and exploitation. From that point of view, 'liberation' in political and economic structures to equal partnership is more basic than the apparently more urgent 'fairness' in distribution which we must now discuss.

Fairness

Closely related to the equality dimension, but including more the cosmic sphere, is this concept of 'fairness' in distribution of goods, services and opportunities for personal and social development. Basic to this concept are the considerations that liberty is cosmically conditioned. Without the basic cosmic conditions of adequate food, clothing, housing, etc., human liberty cannot properly or in some cases even minimally exist. Equality of respect for their human existence and liberty belongs to all men. The goods and resources of the earth in particular are at the service of mankind and may not be primarily regarded as the possession of particular individuals or groups. The social determination of mankind and the interdependence of individuals and groups which, through modern technology, has extended in some ways to form at least an embryonic universal society, involves concern by the privileged for the welfare of the deprived. Where technology is used to promote this fairness of distribution its gift aspect is again triumphing over its negative threat aspect. And while no technological developments can ensure this triumph overnight, it is clear that a good deal more could be achieved if the moral commitment existed.

This moral commitment must affect the individual, but to be effective it must affect him in community, as a member of a group. The decision that is needed to ensure fair distribution and to prevent domination and exploitation on a grand scale, must be a group decision, by states and groups of states. The individual is helpless; in voluntary and statutory groupings he can exercise his liberty of choice in favour of fairness, equality and liberty. The group itself at all the various national and international levels becomes the bearer of moral decision but not without self-contradiction, in indifference to or in spite of its various sub-groupings and individual members. The exercise of leadership in promoting such decision-making with the fullest participation by the community is one of the great moral challenges of our time. The technological means are at hand to meet the challenge, ignore or frustrate it.

Development Technology and Historical Conditions

The 'fairness' of distribution which starving peoples so urgently and obviously require, demands moral commitment and political will to turn the technological means available to us in directions in which they have only intermittently been employed hitherto. The transport technology, which has been rampant in pursuit of speed and comfort in the West or which has moved out into space travel or more threateningly concentrated on war mobility, could and should be more effectively directed to movement of essential goods such as food and clothing to the needy hundreds of millions around the world. That, of course, is emergency activity, no less necessary for the foreseeable future for all that. The aid to development on the spot is clearly more profitable in the long term. Yet the attempts to achieve this must not be at the expense of liberty and equality, so that more people become more dependent and achieve less and less control over their own lives. Some of the aid and its technology has been heavily inclined in that direction. And if this technological aid is in turn to respect the people aided and promote their control of their own lives, it must take account of their social and historical setting. Western industry has developed a technology which involves very heavy capital expenditure and yields very small employment return, where so often what is needed in developing countries is industry with high employment potential and low capital cost per job: labour intensive rather than capital intensive. To achieve this a different 'intermediate' technology is required.[24] From a different historico-social viewpoint, technological aid should take account of the traditional patterns of relationships in society with their checks and balances, their provision for needs and the needy, young and old, deprived and lonely and not simply disrupt these patterns without providing any alternatives. Given the lesson of earlier industrial development, the mistakes of the West should not be thoughtlessly repeated elsewhere, as they already appear to be in so many places with the introduction of modern technology. Efforts to ensure fairness of distribution and development should be the occasion for improving social and cosmic conditions, not for introducing new ones which diminish basic human liberty and equality.[25]

Technology and Future Generations

The historical line which has to be recognised and respected in treating of mankind does not just refer to the past. Future generations are also the responsibility of the present, and the social and cosmic conditions of their humanity must be considered because it will be affected by the present use of technology, whether one recognises that or not. The present health benefits enjoyed by much of mankind derive from the health care of past generations and will in turn affect the health of the future. The thalidomide tragedy may provide the headlines about how the future generations may be affected, but the whole biological and psychological future of the race is increasingly affected for good and evil by technological developments in drugs and agriculture, in transport and housing. Again the moral responsibility is one of discernment between the potential for good and evil, mindful of the cosmic, social and historical conditions in which human fulfilment may be achieved in freedom for all.

In the strictly medical field this will involve choices about investment of scarce resources and personnel in heavy technology of benefit to the few with consequent neglect of the needs of the many. Some of the difficulties of many such decisions would be removed if a more reasonable control were exercised over developments in the drug industry, for example, at present left to the 'market'. A spokesman for the WHO said recently[26] in Geneva that, whereas three to four hundred drugs would be perfectly adequate for the health needs of the West, some thirty or forty thousand were circulating. And undoubtedly some of the characteristic serious diseases of the West, such as heart condition and obesity, would be helped or prevented far more effectively by a different, healthier life-style than by any technological treatment or development. A life-style which would, in fact, increase man's control of his own destiny would release many medical resources for those in real need. Where medical technology is involved with maintaining what is really only a living death or else has recourse to euthanasia, a more realistic appreciation of death as well as life might form part of the life-style. It is in some such frame of mind that such emerging problems as genetic engineering will have to find an adequate moral analysis, with due account taken of the cosmic, social and historical conditions in which human beings enjoy and exercise their humanity as free and equal beings.

Depletion of Resources and Pollution

Man's future orientation as well as his present responsibility no longer permit him to ignore the impact of his present technology on the limited resources of the earth or the ecological disturbance caused by that technology. Husbanding scarce resources, developing alternatives, recycling, abandonment of polluting technology and the substitution of non-polluting are all obvious, indeed banal, exhortations. There remain the basic questions: how shall this be done, by what criteria are the decisions made and who shall make them? The 'no further growth'[27] approach takes very seriously the strain on resources and on the ecosystem, but it fails to take sufficient account of the strain such a policy would place on the Western world in terms of economic and social upheaval or to face the fact that this 'growth' in some technological and economic sense cannot be readily abandoned for the developing countries with any sense of fairness or without drastic consequences for present and future populations.

The other extreme of 'technology will see us through' is no less unsatisfactory, although its merit is to force us to take a new look at the control and use of technology in the public interest of all rather than in the private interest of particular groups. The capacity to store and retrieve information, to use highly-complex models to predict the possible consequences of particular strategies, could be of enormous use in devising effective means to deal with such problems.[28]

Perhaps the main conclusions to be drawn from the two extreme solutions is to recognise that technology is so built into our social structure and needs that it cannot be stopped short at a particular stage, let alone abandoned. The problems are not strictly technological but social with political and moral implications. If they can be solved it will be with the aid of technology as the servant of mankind not in submission to it as master.

Such dominance over technology and over the goods it produces is not conceivable except in group terms, at international level as well as national level, and indeed ultimately in global terms. And yet if new patterns of dominance and exploitation are not to emerge then group, even global decisions, must involve effective participation by sub-groups and individuals. The various proposals for a global strategy with decentralised control may appear utopian, yet they contain basic truths which we ignore at the peril of mankind.[29]

The criteria for these decisions turn mainly on the value of humanity as expressed in different forms such as liberty, equality, fairness, and at various levels, individual and social (including historical), as well as cosmic, such as biological. In all this the cosmos, more particularly the natural environment, ecosystem or biosphere (diverse but related terms) might be regarded merely as the setting for human endeavour and source of its raw materials without any worth of its own. There is much to be said for the view that Western thinking was dominated by this idea of 'man's dominion over nature' and so indulged in the 'rape of nature' which has led to such environmental and ecological difficulties. To what precise degree this is true (and how far it can be attributed to the Judaeo-Christian Tradition)[30] need not detain us here. It was certainly true to some degree but a more balanced view is now required so that man's respect for 'nature' is combined with his respect for man. For man is at once continuous and discontinuous with nature. To ignore the continuity is to create much of the ecological tension and destruction we now observe. To ignore the discontinuity and seek to submerge man in his natural environment as just one more conjunction of molecules[31] would eliminate him as a moral agent and make nonsense of his attempts to respect natural forces and resources, to accept a certain stewardship for them and to cooperate with them. It is inspired by this respect, stewardship and cooperation that he will finally ensure that the threat of his technology is overcome by the gift which will set him in harmony with nature also as mutual gift.

9

Violence and Political Change[1]

Reservations

I HAVE many reservations about the propriety of my writing on this subject. As a moral theologian I am not directly and actively engaged in promoting or preventing political change, much less in violence. And one cannot help feeling that all that moral theologians might have to offer (it may not be very much) must have been said so often, so clearly and, to judge by results, so ineffectively before, that another one of them will not bear reading. Faced with a subject that moral theologians among so many others do not seem to be able to discuss effectively, silence is the obvious counsel. Yet for the Irish moral theologian 'Violence and Political Change' constitutes the greatest and most persistent challenge of this generation. It confronts him in his own personal feelings and attitudes, as it does in the activities, and to use de Chardin's word, passivities of his countrymen. It may elude his professional analysis as a theologian and defy his influence as a moral leader. It continues to haunt him as an Irishman and a Christian in whose name the most barbaric exchanges take place.

It would of course be mistaken to see this as a peculiarly Irish problem or to see the Irish problem as an exclusively Irish responsibility. The problem of 'Violence and Political Change' is world-wide and civilisation-old. Responsibility for the Irish version rests inescapably on both sides of the Irish Sea. My task here is to analyse some typical and contemporary characteristics of the universal problem, and to apply this analysis to the Irish situation in the hope of illuminating, however modestly, the responsibility we share; I am not concerned here to repeat the ritual condemnations, necessary though they may be.

Modesty becomes any attempt by a theologian as a relative

'outsider' to probe in Christian faith the tangled world of political violence and change. The methodological difficulties posed by 'outsider' analysis of such complex issues have always been more acute than theologians, with much consequential vacuity and irrelevance, were wont to acknowledge. Given the recent work by the 'Liberation Theologians' of Latin America with their insistence on theological reflection and analysis founded on engagement in the enterprise of liberation, it is no longer so easy for the rest of us to evade these difficulties. Theology as faith-analysis has always proclaimed itself as 'inside' study (*fides quaerens intel- lectum*). Yet theologians have too often considered engagement with faith an adequate basis for 'theologising' about areas of life to which they were total strangers. 'Insider' insight at some level into sexuality or business or politics or even violence would seem no less necessary to effective theology in these areas than personal Christian faith. The limitations of this writer and perhaps of his readers derive primarily from lack of such insider experience, insight and reflection.

Of course it would be foolish to exclude in doctrinaire fashion all reflection on such problems by people without full-time or extensive personal involvement. Some of the most percipient analysts of situations can only exercise their talent by having the leisure and detachment of the outsider. Their percipience is also related to their 'insider feel', some sharing or continuity in experience due to actual circumstances and creative empathy. It is on the basis of such 'insider feel' arising out of circumstances and, I hope, my empathy as a concerned citizen with an Irish back- ground that I make bold to use my scholarly detachment to examine in faith the relationship between violence and political change.

Definitions

Hard on the heels of difficulties in method come those in defini- tion—of violence, politics and political change. Without presuming to resolve the difficulties surveyed in the vast literature, I will opt for certain working definitions and hope that I may be able to refine as well as justify them in the course of this chapter.

It is of course important to distinguish force from violence. Yet I feel the whole discussion may be preempted by the too nice insistence on this distinction and the definition of violence as the 'unlawful or excessive use of force'—a procedure adopted in that otherwise excellent report produced by the Joint Working Party of the Irish Council of Churches and the Roman Catholic Church in Ireland (pp. 8-12).

I prefer a descriptive to a normative approach at this stage and to define violence primarily in terms of deliberate physical destruction of people (through death or injury) or of property. Violence in this sense is readily extended to at least certain kinds of psychological destruction of people—for example, in psychological torture or brain-washing. It may, in my view, be also legitimately extended to the social or structural destruction of people ('institutional violence') although this will merit more cautious consideration later.

Politics and political change provide equal opportunity for variety in definition and misunderstanding in discussion. I opt here for certain functional descriptions, which yet imply a particular ideological stance and no doubt contain their own variety of meaning and possibility of misunderstanding. I take politics and political change to be about providing peace, justice, freedom, and at least the opportunity for fulfilment to all the people embraced within the particular political structure. It is no longer easy to determine the limits of the political structure. In Britain for example it faces internal devolution to Scotland and Wales and is already engaged in the wider political structure of the EEC as well as the broader structures such as NATO and the UN. Yet the run of its effective writ may be fairly closely defined at the different levels of international and national responsibilities and capacities. It is also difficult to describe more exactly what is meant by peace, justice, freedom and fulfilment. I can only resort again to crude functional description in terms of fairness of distribution of goods, services and opportunities; of equal protection of basic rights and liberties (including primarily the right to life); and of effective participation in decision-making about one's destiny. How more precisely this is to be expressed in terms of structures and laws need not concern us here except in so far as expression is seriously defective and there are diverse proposals as to how it should be radically and urgently changed. I say 'seriously' defective because all political structures are somewhat defective through incompetence, neglect or malice or just the sheer inertia of history. And I say 'radically and urgently changed' because some change is going on all the time and it is radicality and urgency which raise the prospect of violence. But that is to anticipate a little.

Ends and Means

The relationship between political change (or political preservation without change) and violence belongs to the general category of relationships between ends and means. In itself, the end is the more important and ought to have first place in the discussion in accordance with solid scholastic practice (*Finis etsi sit postremus in essecutione, est tamen primus in intentione*, Aq. I-II, 1 ad 1). However in most discussions concerning relationship, what is usually primary is the other fellow's violence (as 'terrorist' revolutionary or defender of the status quo) and my political goals. So the IRA or the PLA and their sympathisers will harp on British or Israel's practice of torture and other military 'violence', carefully underplaying their own as merely the necessary reaction to attain peace with justice and other desirable political ends. An equally unthinking upholder of the status quo, and there are many, will be blind to the destructive activities of army or police and postpone all effective tackling of the political issues involved. So the discussion centres on the secondary issue of violence and in an inevitably fruitless way, because one sees only the other fellow's violence and is blind to one's own.

Violence is related to political change or preservation as means to end and so is in a subordinate role. To understand the problem intellectually and solve it practically, this has to be constantly borne in mind. However, although subordinate to ends, means bear their own importance, an importance that at the level of violence becomes a matter of life and death. It is this importance which tempts the 'preservationists' to concentrate on the violence in the restoration of 'law and order' and at the risk of ignoring the political ends. But it also leads many supporters of change to question the validity of the ends and means analysis as applied to violence or at least to qualify it radically. Where deliberate killing of people is undertaken for change or preservation, in this view the end is already undermined. Politics and political ends exist for people. Where people are suborned to the point of elimination in pursuit of some alleged 'political' goal, a destructive distortion has occurred. The means-end relationship is no longer adequate, because an intermediate end, a particular political structure, has been given priority over a much more ultimate end, the human person. Logically this might apply to preservation as well as to change and some people would insist on this through the abolition of capital punishment and other legal practices and through the development of alternative forms of national defence to that of military strength.

Without wishing to dismiss either this latter school as naive and unrealistic or the defenders of 'legitimate killing' as illogical in their opposition to 'violence as a means of political change', I should like to turn from the end-means debate to wider anthropological and theological considerations which may shed some light on these difficulties.

Social Destructiveness and the Inertia of History

Violence as a means of political change is invoked on basically two grounds: Firstly, the social and political situation requiring change is so totally destructive of a majority or minority of the people that it may already be labelled violent; secondly, the prospects for any other method of change succeeding are so remote in time that there is certainly no other hope of success for this or the next generation. Social destructiveness and the inertia of history combine to frustrate all non-violent attempts to achieve some equitable measure of genuine peace and justice, freedom and possibility of fulfilment for the deprived. In such situations, widespread today as in the past, young men's thoughts lightly turn or are turned to violence.

In his social nature man exposes all the ambiguity, that mixture of good and evil (of grace and sin as theologians might say) which is characteristic of every dimension of humanity. Three elements of this truth have to be kept continually in mind. Man is social by nature. There is no way he can come into existence, survive or thrive apart from some minimal social context. This social context is not only essential to him but good for him; it is potentially enriching for him. It is no less potentially destructive. All three elements—the necessity of society for each man, its potential for good and its potential for evil—have occurred and recurred in all societies we know. It is not too much to presume they will continue into the indefinite future. Secular utopias or kingdoms of God on earth are not, in human wisdom, for the foreseeable future. In faith, they are recognised as not belonging within history at all. This is not the preliminary to a counsel of despair of social and political change or an excuse for opting out. The extent of this ambiguity, the manner of this mixture of social good and evil depends immediately on human effort. Admittedly graced human effort in the Christian perspective but still authentically human. Without the courageous and persistent efforts of men who discern and espouse the good, the evil in the mixture will dominate. They may not be able to eradicate but they can arrest and even reverse the destructive trend in social structures. They must bend their efforts towards this, at times more in hope than in faith, but the best of them recognise they have no other choice. And Christians among them recognise that evil has been definitely conquered in Jesus Christ even if the historical realisation of that conquest will always be slow, painful and partial.

This recognition of the obligation to fight social evil invokes mankind's assumption of its responsibility in history, in time, as ambiguous a dimension of mankind as the social. It is only in time that progress can be made, that social structures can be changed. The most successful revolution and its implementation in subverting evil social and political structures takes time. Time, as we say more truly than we know, is of the essence, of the essence of man. There is no escaping time or the temporal/historical dimension of man. And time is on his side. It is in and through time that he develops and grows, that his structures change, develop, improve. Time constitutes his most critical resource for his development. Yet time is also against him. In our time, or not in our time becomes critical for him as time slips by and progress cannot be reported. For the people at the bottom of the heap with only one life to lead 'Not in our lifetime' becomes a cry of despair or destruction. On the lips of an Ian Smith (now suitably modified by time) or of someone else at the top of the heap, the slogan becomes the solace of the privileged. In terms of social or political change time may be gift or threat. When it appears only as threat, as potentially destructive, the frustrated seek to overcome time. Haste, urgency replace gradualism—the haste which Thomas Merton called violence in time. And the inertia of history, already alluded to, provokes many to try such violence.

The dilemma for the radical reformer and revolutionary as well as for the gradualist is acute. Only through time can change be achieved. Yet too gradual and time-laden a change will achieve nothing in time for so many of this generation. The attempt to compress time by violence eliminates quite a number of people, privileged and disprivileged, from historical existence altogether. The violent revolutionary sacrifices at least one group in the present for the sake of future generations. The gradualist or the preservationist tends to sacrifice another. Either way, time is some people's enemy and more people's opportunity. Its ambiguity remains unresolved except in the eschatological perspective of the Christian where the Resurrection message proclaims the final triumph of man's historical struggle—his fight within time and his fight against time. The socially concerned, with or without Christian perspective, feel obliged to enter the historical struggle to arrest, reverse and if possible overcome the destructive social and historical forces including privilege and inertia. It is only such concern and such engagement which finally give them the right and the insight to pronounce on the question of means, and in particular on the question of violence. That much at least the Latin Americans might teach us.

Violence v. Non-Violence

Scholarly detachment can provide valuable or at any rate interesting perspectives. Can it provide answers? Can it at least help equip the concerned and engaged to decide between violent and non-violent means in search of political improvement? Let me dally for another scholarly moment on the word 'search'. The radical as well as the gradualist reformer have to be humble enough to admit that theirs is a search. Whatever the thoroughness of the analysis, the refinement of the vision, or the shrewd calculation of the means, the goal to be achieved will be revealed only in time. It cannot be accurately forecast. All the reforms and revolutions we have known bear witness to that. If the end is still a matter of 'search' and not of accurate forecasting, greater difficulty still surrounds the choice of means. Of course much is already decided about the end, in considerable negative detail about what must be removed as destructive, and in broad general perspectives, what the constructive replacement must be. Similarly it is possible to recognise the unsuitability of certain means either to remove the destructive or introduce the constructive. And suitable means can and must be found. Hesitancy and caution are initially in order but a choice must finally be made.

Focusing discussion here on the suitability, moral suitability that is, of violent means, we assume the seriously defective social structures amounting to what is now described as 'institutional violence'; the concern and engagement of those who have to choose; and a genuine desire to choose the morally appropriate means to achieve the political changes demanded by the situation. On the basis of a moral calculator that might be described purely in terms of choosing the lesser evil, it would seem impossible to rule out definitively for all times and places the choice of violent means. One might adapt the traditional criteria for a just war— of a just cause, last resort etc. One might calculate more simply but carefully that a brief if intense escalation of the actual violence in the situation through violent revolution will, by replacing the destructive structures with constructive ones, considerably reduce the overall violence in the situation and the continuing destruction of people. However, one is never choosing for all times and places but for one particular time and place. Here, allowing for all the reservations and yet the paramount need for decision, people may well decide differently, some for violence and some for non-violence. As far as anyone can tell from outside, each may make a morally good decision, or as some people prefer to put it, a morally right one. This sharply underlines the limitations of the moralist and of the use of the moral calculator. In the eventual and concrete choice between violence and non-violence, there may be deeper realities involved than purely moral ones.

The Human and Christian Significance of Non-Violence

Non-violence covers a vast range of attitudes and activities that are far from negative in their direction and implications. It is not to be confused with non-resistance at least where the search for political change is concerned. Its attitudes are those of the Sermon on the Mount and the New Testament; in not returning evil for evil; in loving one's enemies; in the generosity of spirit that goes the 'second mile'; in transcending the barriers of class, race and sex; in seeking to cooperate with the God who was in Christ reconciling all men with himself and with one another. It retains a realistic sense of the evil that men do to one another and of the demonic elements that are encased in our social and political structures. It seeks to exorcise these and to bring liberation to the captives of society and history by the means of passive resistance, active resistance and non-violent direct action—as convenient a categorisation as any.

With this New Testament inspiration it might seem to be an exclusively Christian means. Its greatest prophet and exponent, the Mahatma Gandhi, was not of course a Christian and few enough Christians now or earlier have advocated or espoused it instead of violence in crisis situations.

In less theological and more anthropological terms and in accordance with our earlier analysis, non-violence offers two great advantages over violence. As Gandhi perceived, the oppressed or enslaved class or nation must not only liberate themselves but the oppressors also. There is a mutual enslavement, one very comfortable and one very uncomfortable, one perhaps imperceptible to the outsider and the other relatively perceptible. But the oppressor is also enslaved, however comfortably and imperceptibly, by the structures which he dominates. Gandhi's hope and strategy was to achieve mutual emancipation. Only in this way he thought could the demon of violence be truly exorcised from the structures, the ambiguity considerably diminished, true liberation and reconciliation achieved. The inevitable elimination of some in the violent struggle would obviously prevent them from enjoying historical emancipation or reconciliation. And the violent struggle would almost certainly endorse the structural violence of the society, even though that structure would now be dominated by the previously oppressed. In Christian terms the redemption of the structures of society by the exorcising of the demonic would be much more likely to result from the Gandhi philosophy and strategy.

The Latin Americans have drawn attention to Christian responsibility for the salvation of history as distinct from the history of salvation. The ambiguity of history and time and the forcible attempt to overcome this ambiguity by violence we have already discussed. Again the non-violent approach provides some promise of the conquest of this ambiguity and so as soon by Christian faith, of the salvation of history. A non-violence which is really committed and creative like that of Gandhi and King enables its practitioners to oppose and filter out the negative social and historical forces which characterise the structures and the people in them, while reinforcing and developing the positive forces in all the people. At best of course this will mean a pre-dominance of the positive, constructive and good. Non-violence fosters its own ambiguities in common with all human enterprises. Its character suggests that the ambiguity of its final achievement may be less because of the inner connection of means and ends. Violence in the programme for change with its own sometimes horrific costs will almost certainly be followed by violence in the result of change, at least in maintaining the tradition and endorsing the historical force of violence as the effective means of change. The salvation of history proceeds that bit more slowly and fitfully.

Some Personal Conclusions

Let me try to draw some fairly personal and provisional conclu-sions from these rather meandering reflections:

1. I believe the final judgment on the use of violence as an appropriate moral and Christian means of political change must be made in the concrete by people concerned for and committed to rectifying the serious injustices which suggest violence. Out-siders can certainly engage in dialogue with them and raise the kinds of consideration discussed here. They may not offer any doctrinaire prohibition or endorsement.

2. The criteria for a just revolution are of use at least in restrict-ing the easy resort to violence, and demanding some code in revolutionary as in conventional warfare.

3. Part of the outsider's as well as the insider's responsibility is to be informed in the values and techniques of non-violence. Only very serious injustice might justify violence as a last resort. There is an awful lot of political change necessary and possible in so many societies, short of recourse to the last resort. On the basis of moral-calculus alone non-violence will frequently be the more appropriate means.

4. Non-violence is not just a technique; training in its tactics

and strategy as well as in its discipline and values is a first necessity. This training is extremely important—at least as important as military training—if a successful campaign is to be launched.

5. For the Christian and theologian the salvific value of non-violence in terms of emancipation from evil social and historical forces and the salvation of society and history is more readily discernible and more easily maintained than any salvific value of violence. This is true only of creative non-violence born of concern and commitment, not that of passivity and indifference. In so far as the structures may be described as 'violent', passivity and indifference endorse that violence.

6. Christian Churches, believers and theologians should consider how far they collectively and personally should opt for non-violence—not in the sanctuary or the prayer-meeting or the lecture-hall, but in real engagement with the struggle for peace and justice, freedom and fulfilment. Such an option will involve concern and commitment to the political and social goals as well as understanding and training.

7. Where that option has been fully taken up, effective moral leadership is again possible. Otherwise we are condemned to wearily repeating or more wearily listening to denunciations of violence without an incarnate annunciation of alternatives.

8. Whichever option one takes up in the concrete situation one has to accept the consequences morally and spiritually as well as materially. And at the risk of repetition I must say that not making any choice is also a choice in favour of 'no change' with all its consequent responsibilities.

The Irish Situation

The violence in Ireland at present can, as I said, be seen as part of a wider world phenomenon. It has its own peculiar Irish roots and characteristics. It is justified by its supporters in the name of political change—indeed it is excused and condemned on sometimes very similar grounds. It is excused by its Irish advocates on the grounds that the British don't understand or accept any other means at least where Ireland is concerned. The last resort argument! It is condemned by some of its opponents on the grounds that the 'barbaric' Irish don't understand or know how to use any other methods. The excuse and condemnation rest on quite inaccurate historical grounds. Ireland has a very long and successful tradition of using non-violent means to wrest concessions from the British, from O'Connell to Parnell and into the twentieth century. The British have yielded to such pressures from Emancipation through the Land Acts at the beginning of the century. It is important to set Irish violence in this historical context if one is not either to glorify it or to despair of it. It is undoubtedly true that the strong violent strand has existed in various anti-British campaigns over. the last couple of centuries. This tradition dies hard and helps to fuel at least some of the IRA violence we are now experiencing. And that violence shows no signs of simply disappearing in face of either denunciation, repression or appeal to alternative methods. Without being unnecessarily pessimistic one might say that it could last into the twenty-first century much to the shame as well as the horrific suffering of people in both islands.

Partial Insider and Shared Responsibility

We can feel free to discuss this violence to some effect because we are all partial 'insiders'. It is an Irish-British problem and we all have some personal responsibility in creating it; we share some responsibility for removing it. I should like to explore the concepts of partial insider and shared responsibility a bit more fully. It may be more helpful and honest for me to try it in a personal way and so hope to stimulate you to explore your position and responsibility. I am an Irishman. That is more noticeable in London and Cambridge than it is in Ireland and Maynooth College. I come out of a particular racial, cultural and historical, even geographical and climatic background. Part of that background is nationalist, with an inherited belief in the right of Irishmen to determine their own destiny and in the frustration of this right in the past by Englishmen. This inherited nationalism includes the acceptance of violence as sometimes necessary and sometimes successful in asserting Irish rights and overcoming English frustration. For all the further education, experience and opportunity for reflection which I have had, I cannot simply shed this background. Yet I should not be enslaved; none of us can shed our backgrounds, but they should not enslave us. They have to be put in a much wider context, greatly qualified by other aspects of the truth, but it would be dishonest to ignore the persisting reality that one's background has. I have experienced in myself the temptation to political violence, certainly to the endorsement of violence for the sake of political change in Ireland as well as in some other countries where the social evil as I encountered it was much more obvious and widespread but where I did not identify so naturally with the people involved. I am not admitting this for anybody's titillation, or my own satisfaction but to help us to come to terms with what being an insider may mean. I can identify with men of violence to some degree because of my historical background and because I know the thrust to violence in myself, faced with serious frustration and with the awful oppression of majorities and minorities of which I am aware. My historical and professional backgrounds then combine to make me want to understand the men of violence, particularly the Irish men of violence, and on both sides of the Irish divide.

That understanding leads me to sympathise with some of the frustrations which led them into violence in the first place, and to share some of the goals which they claim to seek. Beyond that I see the violence we are now witnessing as utterly inhuman and barbaric in its practice and entirely unsuitable to its aims. I find it simply unjustifiable. Denunciation however necessary is clearly not enough. The violent men have to be restrained and their potential victims protected. The law and order struggle has to go on. Repression however essential is not enough either. The sources of the frustration, the political aims of the violence have to be understood and tackled with appropriate methods. Alternatives must be provided. The insider, however partial, has to grapple with the sources of the violence and endeavour to provide alternatives to it. This is our shared responsibility. The final section of this paper will seek to examine the sources and suggest some alternatives. It is necessarily sketchy and incomplete.

Future Prospects

Northern Ireland has been an unstable society for sixty years now. It could, I fear, go on being so for quite a long time yet. And the present kind of unstability is obviously and savagely destructive. It is well documented by now how far the political structures, regional and local, were defective in providing peace, fairness, freedom and fulfilment for all the people of Northern Ireland. Some of that has been rectified in law and in practice since the present struggle began, although there is a lot of progress still to be made. And it is not adequate to defer that further progress to when and if the violence ends. But these defects do not constitute the deepest problem, although they were the immediate goal of the Civil Rights Movement, which preceded the present violence. A rather different view would see the struggle in terms of a United Ireland or a United Kingdom. And this holds enormous fascination for participants and observers of the struggle, leading to practical despair because no compromise seems possible between the two points of view. The commitment of the overwhelming mass of the people in the Republic and of the minority in the North to seek such a goal by peaceful means only, creates its own difficulties, notably the IRA response that peaceful means have never succeeded and never will. Must Irish people therefore abandon their traditional aspiration for unity? This question may be distorting the debate and encouraging the violence by failing to distinguish the many different aspects of the problem.

There are, as I mentioned earlier, several levels of structural or social justice and injustice. They have to be discerned and tackled in an orderly, effective and indeed urgent fashion in and through time. The fair distribution of goods, services and opportunities is basic. It has already received attention and legislation but that attention and legislation have to be turned into concrete reality in the houses, schools, shops, farms, factories, recreation centres in every locality in Northern Ireland. There is endless work for everybody here and very widely shared responsibility for all of us.

Equal protection of rights and liberties is closely related to fairness of distribution and essential to creating trust in Northern Ireland between the authorities and the people. A Bill of Human Rights might be a useful device in pursuing this equality and establishing this trust.

More critical still is the effective participation in shaping the destiny of the region by all the citizens. This is much more basic to democracy than particular forms of parliamentary government. Where one side is permanently excluded from power such participation is impossible.

But all this can only be properly achieved in a context of peace. The violent men are preventing the process. The fears they reinforce are impeding the people who ought to be working together for fairness, freedom and fulfilment. The fears they reinforce—for the fears were already there and are either exploited or reinforced by the violent men. To simplify drastically, the basic fear of both sides is that of absorption by the other and so of permanent loss of identity—the fear of communal death. The exorcising of that fear is the greatest challenge to that distinguishing characteristic of Christians which is meant to drive out fear—love. When the fear is finally exorcised, the violence will finally cease. And the task of Christian love is to be incarnated at all levels of activity and relationship we have discussed as essential to promoting peace through fairness, freedom and fulfilment, by developing the appropriate personal attitudes and social structures to ensure peace for our people. That love must extend to the men of violence, to understanding them, to restraining them and ultimately to converting them. This will be achieved not by the force of denunciation but by our concern and commitment to rectifying the injustices, to promoting alternative non-violent means of political change and by taking the risk of radically changing or converting ourselves. To ensure a new community in Northern Ireland, the hope of all of us, a new mankind and a new Christianity may have to come to birth in both islands.

10

Theology and Irish Divisions[1]

The Last Ten Years

I SIT down to write this paper on June 20 1978, exactly ten years after Austin Currie's occupation of a house in Caledon, County Tyrone, in protest against its unfair allocation to a Protestant rather than Catholics. This event is generally taken to be the opening of the protest campaign that developed into a decade of unfinished disturbance in Northern Ireland. Last week Amnesty International published its report criticising police methods of interrogation. This weekend a couple of policemen have been killed by the Provisional IRA, one after abduction. A priest was kidnapped in retaliation but later released. *The Sunday Times* began another of its block-buster surveys, entitled this time : Ulster 1968-78, A Decade of Despair. Mrs Thatcher, leader of the Conservative Party, reassures the Unionists in Belfast. The killings, bombings, kidnappings and torture with their allegations and counter-allegations ebb and flow; media interest waxes and wanes; but the politics seem as barren as ever and any workable solution further off than on June 20 1968.

Where does the committed Christian stand in all this? What have the Churches done? What can they do? To attend more precisely to the burden of this paper, what can theology offer to the Churches in understanding and responding to the situation?

It may seem a little late to be posing questions of this kind. And they have been posed before. The special weekend conference organised by the Irish Theological Association at Dundalk in December 1971 brought together theologians, clergy and other Christians, Protestant and Catholic, North and South, to examine possibilities and prospects of Christian reconciliation in Ireland.

The most concrete result of that meeting was the commission established by the ITA to examine the Constitution and Laws of the Republic in so far as they were discriminatory on religious grounds. The report of that commission was published in June 1972.[2]

In February 1976 the Irish Theological Association and the Institute for Religion and Theology of Great Britain and Ireland jointly organised a meeting at Maynooth on Theological Education and Irish Divisions.[3] And the 1977 Annual Conference of the Irish Theological Association discussed some aspects of the same question under the heading of its general theme 'Liberation Theology', which concluded with a paper on 'An Irish Theology of Liberation?'[4] In 1978 a Catholic priest, Father Joe McVeigh, published a pamphlet with the title *Thoughts on Liberation in Ireland*. All the while the Irish School of Ecumenics under its tireless Director, Father Michael Hurley SJ, sought to promote joint theological investigation and mutual theological understanding. Many other theologians and Christians were in public and private discussing the same issues of Christian responsibility and reconciliation in Ireland.

Meantime many more official conversations, including extensive and serious theological preparations, were taking place between the churches. The inter-Church conferences held at Ballymascanlon between 1973 and 1977 constituted the major public achievement of inter-Church dialogue in Ireland.

It would be quite unfair therefore to suggest that nothing has been attempted, that no theological concern has been manifested. A great deal has. But what has been achieved? Achievement is not easily or quickly measured in such a delicate and difficult enterprise. Among quite a number of Protestants and Catholics including theologians, mutual understanding, trust and friendship have been irrevocably established in a way that can only improve general relationships between the Churches in the years ahead. More tangible results include the joint Report of Violence published in 1976. The disappointment of some people at the progress made on such issues as inter-Church marriages, inter-Church schools, relations between law and morality and the role of the Orange Order should not obscure the shift in attitudes and communications which has occurred since 1968.

Has all this activity led to any greater theological insight into the sources, significance and final dissolution of Irish divisions? Have the Churches and their theologians been able to discern what these divisions and their troubled, sometimes murderous expression (1,838 times to date) are saying to them about the Christian mission in Ireland today? The conferences, reports and the frequent joint statements by Church leaders appealing for peace and condemning violence give evidence of a common Christian witness largely unknown in Ireland in the pre-1968 period. Is this adequate? To dismiss these efforts as no more than a minimal realisation by the Churches of their common calling or a hasty reaction to the threat to their continuing credibility may be tempting to some critics but is hardly fair or illuminating. However, as far as theological insight is concerned, that is, reflection on faith in the Irish situation, one cannot help feeling dissatisfied with the efforts and results recorded above.

So much of the theology that is discussed, taught and written in Ireland is unaware of and uninfluenced by the events of the last ten years. Has any Irish theologian critically developed in his theology in face of these events or learned from them or even felt the need to? To wring one's hands over the continuance of the divisions, the violence, the political stalemate and the limitations in inter-Church relations while ignoring the responsibilities and failures of theologians themselves would be just one more example of the Irish (human) penchant for blaming others. This paper is less concerned with blaming anybody than with trying to confront Irish divisions in faith-reflection in the hope of discerning something of the Christian call which they undoubtedly embody.

Politics and Religion in Northern Ireland

The division is notoriously a division of Protestants and Catholics. For some participants, observers and analysts Protestant and Catholic are no more than convenient labels for communities divided more in their ethnic origins, cultural heritage, political affiliation and economic power. The leaders of the Churches themselves took some such view in their joint statement of May 1973 when they said:

The conflict is not primarily religious in character. It is based rather on political and social issues with deep historical roots. Undoubtedly again for reasons that are largely historical, the political and social divisions have religious overtones. But this is far from saying that the conflict between extremists here is anything remotely resembling a religious war.[5]

I doubt if it is very fruitful to pursue the debate, still unfinished, as to how far the 'religious overtones' conceded by the Church leaders amount, as others claim, to a significant religious component in the origin and continuance of the divisions, whose violent expressions may still fall far short of a 'religious war'. At best the religious divisions in their coincidence with the ethnic, cultural, political and economic divisions contributed to the consolidation of the two communities in their mutual misunderstanding, mistrust and at times bitter hostility. Religious structures and leadership through Churches, schools, voluntary organisations and services provided much of the framework for separate social existence by the two communities. Their separate identities are preserved and fostered by myths and slogans that have some religious significance. 'A Protestant state for a Protestant people' and the ideal of 'Catholic Ireland' reveal something of that.

While the debate about the extent of the religious component in Irish divisions may be inconclusive, theologians and churchmen cannot afford to ignore the widespread belief that such a component exists. Many Irish Protestants see the Catholic Church as a political force in the country and fear that their identity and integrity would be threatened in a united Ireland with a Catholic majority. Many Catholics regard the Northern state as established precisely to protect Protestant interests, religious as well as political and economic. They interpret their experience of fifty years of Stormont rule as discriminatory against them and that at least partly on religious grounds.

Prima facie evidence for both these claims certainly exists although, in almost mirror image responses, the claims of the one would be strongly denied by the other. More important for the churches than vindicating accusations against rivals, would be a questioning of how far this religious component has been manipulated by the Churches' own adherents for political and economic reasons. Have the Churches been used, even allowed themselves to be used, by people preoccupied with power and privilege and not with the Gospel or its implications for society? More seriously, have Church leaders consciously or unconsciously fed the fires of divisiveness by misleading or dishonest claims about the Catholic threat to religious freedom or about the rights of a Catholic majority to express its moral views (as interpreted by the Catholic hierarchy) in statutory and constitutional law?

Because of such abuses, actual or threatening, many perceptive Christians, clerical, theological and lay, have called for a conscious and deliberate disengagement of Catholic and Protestant leaders from political affairs. This would involve, for Protestant clergy for example, the severing of links with the Orange Order, if not the total dismantling of the Order and the resignation of Protestant clergy from political office. For the Catholic Church it would, according to these critics, involve a disengagement from the nationalist cause by clergy and a refusal to use hierarchical power over the faithful to maintain laws against contraception and divorce which violate Protestant moral sensibilities.

Taking and keeping religion out of politics is the succinct advice of these commentators.[6] As it is presented it has obvious attractions in the face of destructive divisions. How far these attractions will influence the churchmen on either side who have the power and responsibility to take the decisions is another matter. The reluctance, even inability, of one side to understand its own position, in contrast to that of the other, as involving interference in politics has a long and complex history.

That historical stance may seem to some justified by the increased awareness of the political and social relevance of the Gospel in the political and liberation theologies developing in Europe, Latin America and elsewhere. To take one's stand on the Churches' obligation to distance themselves from politics would run directly against the thrust of some of the most significant Christian theology and praxis in the world today and relegate the Churches to the periphery of life. Yet to endorse the present (perceived) Church involvement in the Irish political situation is to further the destructive divisions which have issued in so much killing, maiming and hatred over the past decade and far beyond. It is partly the responsibility of theologians to help the Churches over this cruel dilemma.

The Churches as Truly Churches of Christ

Precisely because of the paralysis which the political situation engenders, it may be more useful to begin in Northern Ireland (as contrasted with South America or South Africa), with the Churches' own awareness of their own identity and mission as churches of Christ. Because of the strength and exclusivity of its sense of identity and mission and because it is my own Church, I shall inevitably be more aware of, understanding of and demanding of the Catholic Church. Yet part of the Irish difficulty is the inability to transcend the boundaries of Catholic or Protestant precisely at the level of Church. Indeed, the way to overcoming the dilemma posed above lies through a new understanding of Church by all the Churches, an understanding that is faithful to the theological tradition of a particular Church yet enriches and transforms it by dialogue with the traditions of other Churches.

Such dialogue was endorsed and encouraged at Vatican II in practical and theological terms. At the theological level the previous exclusivist claims of the Catholic Church were qualified by the recognition of at least the shared faith and baptism it enjoys with other Churches and of the genuine ecclesial elements which may be found in them, right up to the threshold of complete unity in the case of the Orthodox Churches. Complementary to that shift in understanding of the other Churches and perhaps more important for our purposes was the shift in self-understanding of the Catholic Church, in which the true Church of Christ is now said to subsist. The Church itself is seen first of all as symbolising and realising the presence of the divine mystery in continuity with Jesus Christ and constituted by a people, the New Israel, in continuity with the old. Its unity symbolises the ultimate unity of mankind as sons and daughters of the Father. Its message and mission are the proclaiming and realising of the fulfilment and unity of mankind. To this mystery, sign, message and mission the structures of the Church are directed. To borrow the methodical presentation of Avery Dulles, the institutional or structural model of the Church is secondary and subordinate to the models of the Church as sacrament, people, herald and servant.[7]

It would not be too much to say that Ireland, in common with the wider Christian world of the nineteenth and twentieth centuries, understood the Catholic Church almost exclusively in institutional and juridical terms. Even the Body of Christ doctrine, so closely related to the people and sacrament models, was heavily juridicised in its presentation and exclusivist in its claims.

The juridicism and exclusivism still tend to predominate in the Catholic Church as perceived in Ireland by its own members and other Christians. The power of the bishops, real or apparent, but certainly perceived, as it affects both Church life and civil affairs, reflects the dominant juridicism. Catholics must obey their bishops in social moral teaching. Leadership is given by ruling. The limitations of ecumenical relationships through wariness, mistrust or apathy are in part attributable to the old exclusivism. There is only one true Church and unity will be finally achieved only by acceptance of that Church's structure and authority. The 'integrism' of Ian Paisley responds in turn by rejecting what he sees as the deceit of ecumenism compounding the deceit of power-sharing. Both can only lead to union with Rome and with Dublin —equally abhorrent and ultimately identical.

Vatican II has indicated and the Irish situation demands a different way. If Church is primarily the locus of God's presence in continuity with his presence in Jesus Christ, and if the Protestant Churches are to be addressed as and regarded as Churches by the Catholic Church (and vice versa), then there is clear call to recognise and strive to understand that divine presence in these other Churches. For any Church to be truly Church as locus of the divine presence it must be sensitive to and aware of that presence in the Churches about it. The Protestant Churches then constitute centres of divine presence and so of divine revelation for the Catholic Church, just as the Catholic Church does for them. The faith of Irish Catholics is incomplete and impaired in so far as it does not recognise the divine revelation coming to them through the people, practices and traditions of other Irish churches. Faith-reflection or theology in Ireland must attend to this complementary locus of divine presence, revelation and truth in the contiguous Christian Churches and their traditions. More attention to these traditions in the past would have helped Catholic theologians and believers in avoiding an unbalanced juridicism by having a greater sense of the Church as God's people. The non-episcopal Churches, for example, with their greater awareness of the priesthood of the whole people and of all as full—and therefore equal—members of the Church provide an obvious source of theological enlightenment and practical guidance for the hierarchical Churches with their temptation to first and second class membership and to confining initiative, responsibility and authority to the upper levels of bishops and clergy.

The Catholic and episcopal Churches with their focal points of communion and leadership in the ordained ministry of bishops and priests and their sacramental celebrations provide a valuable theological insight into the more specific sacramental life of the Church and the concrete symbol and location of divine presence. Practical safeguards against a reduction of authority derived from Jesus Christ to arbitrary local historical decision may be more effectively provided in the episcopal Churches. And the unity of the Roman Church in which institutional elements are essential if sometimes exaggerated, provides the beginnings of the sacrament of unity of mankind in a way that local, national or ethnic Churches could never essay.

The Church as herald or proclaimer of the Word has been realised in different ways by the different post-Reformation traditions—the traditions relevant to Ireland. The Protestant tradition in general has laid more emphasis on the Bible and the preaching of the Word. Many of the developments at Vatican II derived from the biblical renaissance in the Catholic Church, in turn dependent on the inspiration and scholarship of outstanding Protestants. In Ireland where the Bible is increasingly an open book for Catholics, an enormous amount still remains to be done. By escaping narrow denominational boundaries Catholic believers and scholars do and can learn from Protestants a great deal about the written core of their tradition in the Old and New Testaments and so develop a Church more fully nurtured in the Word of God and more effectively equipped for its role as herald.

The servant Church is a notion dear to both Catholics and Protestants in Ireland. Yet historical circumstances have conspired to prevent one group from seeing the other as more than merely power-seeking and dominant in contrast to the self seen as caring and serving its own people—'its own people'—there's the rub. In most areas of service, the two traditions have confined themselves by and large to their own people as Catholics or Protestants. Such service of its own in educational, medical or other social work by one Church was perceived by the other as a means of control rather than service. And attempts to cross the boundary lines in schools or scouting, for example, were perceived as attempts at proselytising. It is time the Irish Churches honestly examined their consciences in regard to both these accusations, control and proselytising. Yet it is more than time for them to transform the self-serving picture of the servant Church and so of its servant leader, Jesus Christ, which is so readily, however mistakenly, perceptible to observers today.

The service to which the Churches are called transcends their own members and interests. It is a service to mankind. If, as the Synod of Bishops in 1971 declared, 'Action on behalf of justice and participation in the transformation of the world appear to us as a *constitutive* dimension of the preaching of the Gospel',[8] then the Churches as servants are destroying their work as heralds or preachers of the Gospel in so far as they are not engaged in the search for justice and transformation of society. Few societies need justice and transformation as urgently as that of divided Ireland. The traditional self-service will clearly not do. The service must in so far as it is of Catholic origin be available in acceptable terms to Protestants; in so far as it is of Protestant origin be equally available and acceptable to Catholics. This means that the service must not be aimed at control of one's own and proselytising of the others. It must not be threatening to the others, reinforcing the barriers, but liberating. It must be the loving service of the suffering, self-emptying servant who is prepared to die for the redemption and freedom of the other (*Phil.* 2: 4-8).

One of the recurrent emphases of contemporary theology is that on insight born of praxis. A truly Christian theology depends on the praxis of a truly servant Church. A truly servant Church in Ireland and particularly in Northern Ireland is one which attends to those beyond its own historical margins, Catholics for the Protestant Churches, Protestants for the Catholic Church. Conceived and pursued in this way the service of the Churches to society might escape the cruel dilemma of interfering in politics and so reinforcing political divisions or of being relegated to the margins of society and of real life. At least they would have taken another step in the discovery of their fuller truth as Christian Churches. In Ireland today it is not possible to be truly Church without as Catholics being open to the heritage, life and aspirations of the Protestant Churches or as Protestant being equally open to the Catholic.

As theology is a Church discipline, Irish theology must take place in the expanded Catholic and Protestant Churches where the riches and limitations of the one are the resources and concern of the other. What this means for joint theological projects, for theological education for ordinands and laity and for preaching and teaching the faith in pulpits and schools needs careful thought and whole-hearted commitment. The present isolation of staff and students in seminaries and universities certainly does not meet the needs of truly Christian Churches or Churches seeking to be truly Christian. Religious instruction in schools and the whole relationship of Church and school from experiments in joint schooling to teacher training and adult education require radical rethinking in the light of the call to all the Churches to be more truly Church of Christ. For to be truly Church of Christ is call as well as gift in Ireland today.

Given such a pattern of mutual acceptance in faith, common enrichment and joint practical service, the Churches might hope to provide some inspiration and model for the escape from historical and enslaving bonds in the areas of politics, culture and economics. Until the Churches achieve this mutual liberation and enrichment or are seen to be seriously attempting them, they have nothing really to offer in face of political, cultural and economic divisions. It is no longer a question of how far there is a religious component in the historic Irish divisions and hostilities. It is for the Churches first of all a summons to find their identities as more truly Churches of Christ in the context of neighbouring Churches as signs and realisations of God's presence and sources of fuller Christian understanding and practice. Their response to this summons will have important social repercussions so that the new question may be posed: not how far are the Churches part of the problem, but how far are they part of the solution?

Disciples of the One Christ

Further strictly inter-Church problems concerning, for example, marriage and eucharist would not automatically be resolved by the view that the Catholic or Protestant Churches in Ireland cannot be truly Churches of Christ without an understanding of and enrichment by other Christian traditions. However, all these problems would look rather different in the light of the new approach. If the problems did not yield immediate and easy solutions, they could be a challenge to deeper understanding and cooperation rather than a source of deeper misunderstanding and division.

The strictly ecclesial or churchy character of the discussions so far does not do full justice to the discipleship of Jesus Christ which all Irish Christians share as grace and responsibility, gift and call. The basic quality of this discipleship is love, love of God and neighbour which those great apostolic theologians, John and Paul, interpret critically as demand for love of neighbour. In this they are simply giving theological development to the example and teachings of Jesus as recorded in the synoptics, particularly Matthew's account of his teaching on the final judgment (*Matt.* 25).

It would be foolish to maintain that Irish Christians give clear witness to this brotherly love among themselves. The events of the last decade or even the last century seem ample evidence to the contrary unless one is to take the depersonalised or desocialised view of love, a view that is not unknown among Christians anywhere. In the depersonalised view one can affirm a certain well-wishing or benevolence towards somebody without ever doing anything for him or do something for him without ever feeling anything for him. This divorce between thinking, feeling and doing means that one might even do or feel things against him while maintaining that in some ethereal dimension one still had love for him. No doubt certain would-be Christian practitioners of violence and torture must have recourse to such distinctions. To the thoughtful understanding of Christian and non-Christian the hostility and violence of Northern Ireland are not compatible with genuine love.

The desocialised version of love permits one to have neighbourly relations in a narrowly individualist way while ignoring the hostility or conflict between institutions to which each individual belongs. To get on very well with one's Protestant or Catholic neighbours may be a necessary but it is not a sufficient condition for Christian love. The institutions to which people belong must also be animated by love. And where this is lacking, as it frequently is in Ireland, then institutional conversion is as important as personal conversion. Perhaps one aspect of the public failure of the Peace Movement was its inability in the end to generate real institutional conversion in Northern Ireland even between the Churches. Unless the Churches experience and manifest it they have no right to call on the wider cultural or class groupings to realise that institutional conversion which is necessary to their overcoming exploitation and destructive conflict.

Central to understanding the Christian quality of love is the concept of Jesus, neighbour, friend and brother. The dual basis for the loving response to each man as neighbour, friend and brother is the teaching and example of Jesus on the one hand and his sharing of himself with, even identification of himself with each person. Whatever one does to the least of these, one does to him (*Matt.* 25). The more explicit theological understanding in the writings of Paul and John reveals the meaning and depth of this identity as Jesus the word and son of the Father constitutes the medium of creation (through him all things were made), the firstborn in whom all men are restored and the head of the body of which all men are called to be members. It is in and through Christ that mankind finds the meaning and fulfilment of its existence as sons and daughters of the Father, as brothers and sisters of Jesus and of one another. The bonds that bind are familial bonds deriving from the inner trinitarian life of God himself as manifested in Jesus and conferred by the Spirit. For Christians these bonds have been consciously and explicitly identified and accepted. How far are they really identified, accepted and lived out between Protestants and Catholics in Ireland? History does not give an encouraging answer. And one may not substitute some merely individualist concept of neighbourliness for the height and depth and breadth of the love of Jesus Christ (*Eph.* 3: 18). Christian love is corporate, not individualist. It demands corporate expression not private billets doux. Catholics and Protestants in Ireland will have to find corporate and structural expression for their Christian love and in that process transcend the corporate and structured barriers that now impede and distort it. The brotherhood of Christians in Ireland which is to be sign of and summons to the realisation of a universal brotherhood must do better than the occasional unity week, prayer meeting or theological conference or common denunciation of violence. This call is particularly acute in view of the history of Irish divisions and Irish pretensions to Christianity.

In more concrete terms it is not possible to call Jesus Christ one's brother and deny the same term to the least acceptable of one's Protestant and Catholic fellow-citizens, the local priest or minister or policeman, political activist republican or unionist, UDA or IRA member. To see Christ in these or to see them as brothers in Christ will not resolve the political or economic estrangement of history. But it will put that estrangement in perspective and provide some inspiration, power and urgency in attempting to overcome it. It will reveal that overcoming as a historical and social process and not just a personal conversion. And it may break the log-jam caused by the coincidence of religious, ethnic, cultural, political and economic sources of division by removing at least the explicitly religious log. If such happy consequences should not follow or not very quickly, the Christian communities are at least engaged in an essential work of faith purification whereby they are enabled to recognise more clearly and respond more fully to the Jesus Christ who is embodied in the personal and corporate neighbour. Without such recognition and response there is not genuine Christian faith and discipleship. Without such recognition and response between Churches they are undermining, even denying the faith and discipleship on which they claim to base their identity.

Discerning the One True God

In pursuing the meaning of discipleship through love of neighbour to recognising in him, personally and corporately, the presence of Jesus Christ, one is inexorably drawn to the ultimate goal of all our seeking: the God who is Father of Jesus Christ. The divisiveness and mutual rejection which has characterised Christian communities everywhere is more than a scandal to the gentiles or unbelievers. It involves an inadequate and distorted faith and love. The inadequacy and the distortion are not filtered out by the saving presence of Jesus Christ as head of our communities, source and model of our faith. There is too much divine respect for human integrity and freedom for that to happen. The distortion gets right through as it were to the Godhead itself so that the God of Abraham and of Jesus Christ becomes domesticated and deformed into a European or American or African god, and most heinous of all into a Catholic or Protestant or Orthodox god. The deformation may have a mixture of sources, denominational, national, class. But they are all forms of self-interest, self-protection and self-aggrandisement. The Church or the nation, political or economic power, separately or in combination, enter into the constitution of our God, our supreme good, the ultimate destiny we seek—our actions if not our words will reveal this. Where our treasure is there is our heart (*Matt.* 6: 21). The criticism of some dedicated cleric as an atheist because he believed only in the Church was intended as a joke and might be more justly applied to other aspects of the lives of Christians. Yet it has to be conceded that the Church could also become an idol replacing God instead of mediating him.

In a situation such as exists in Ireland the idolatry of the denomination or particular Christian tradition is not unthinkable. And the involvement of particular Churches with other idolatrous tendencies towards nationalism/unionism, power or money as supreme good has masked and inhibited the recognition of the one true God who can shatter our beloved idols and liberate us from our comfortable slaveries. The shattering and liberating God needs to be discovered again and again in the life of the individual and the Church. Because they have tended to have divergent idolatries at least in religion and politics, the Catholic and Protestant Churches could again perform an important liberating service for each other. By seeking God from within the Irish Protestant perspective the Catholic will be confronted more easily by the limitations and deformities of his own understanding of God. The temptations to denominational and national idolatry will be more readily perceived and overcome. Protestants will find a corrective for their deforming of God in seeking him through a Catholic perspective. It is at this level of the search for God in prayer, reflection and pattern of life that the Churches may find their deepest need for one another, their most painful experience in self-surrender and their greatest mutual help. It is here above all that an Irish theology may find its distinctive task and make its most valuable contribution to the ultimate understanding and healing of Irish divisions at whatever level they exist.

New Horizons in Christian Marriage[1]

IN the conventional, transferred sense of new possibilities to be realised or new goals to be achieved, our era has abounded in new horizons in marriage as well as in other dimensions of human existence. How far these horizons have proved to be frustrating mirages and how far they have actually led to real achievement are considerations relevant to the particular dimension of marriage which concerns us here, but discussion of them would take us too far afield. How far these horizons could be described as Christian or at any rate compatible with Christianity will receive attention in the case of marriage.

The generation of new possibilities inevitably depends on people and their creative abilities. It would be unwarranted to relate the amount of human creativity in any specialised sense to actual population figures; yet the population explosion of recent times has meant a sharp increase in the units of human consciousness, experience, reflection and possible inventiveness. The media explosion has simultaneously given increased expression to such experience and reflection so that at times we seem to be unable to cope with the wealth of experience, experiment, suggestion in the diverse dimensions of human living and, in particular, in that of marriage. New horizons in human living and dying pass in rapid succession across our television screens and our own individual consciousness. Marital ideals and practices from polygamy through hippy-style communes, 'swinging partners', even to our own more numerous 'lack-of-the-due-discretion' couples, provide a dazzling array of other people's horizons when they do not entirely confuse or obscure our own.

The horizon game is more profoundly disturbing if we take seriously, as we must, the multiplicity of scientific approaches to the examination of marriage which have emerged in recent times. How much have horizons changed through the work of the biologists, the biochemists, the geneticists, from the discovery of the ovum in the 1820s to the introduction of the pill in the 1950s? And of course other health and medical developments have reduced the infant mortality rate, extended life expectancy, increased the procreative span for most women, enlarged the population enormously and created a situation in which life together for married partners may be considerably longer when life expectancy for both partners has greatly increased. (In Britain at the beginning of this century life expectancy for women was about forty-eight years, while now it is over seventy.) The further possibilities or threats which biological development offers (for example, through overcoming infertility or fertility, through test-tube babies, through genetic engineering, through safer and/or easier abortion) will also affect the horizons of marriage and continue to demand ethical clarification and a living response from Christians.

A different scientific viewpoint, that of the psychologists, has had, particularly in the aftermath of Freud, a very deep influence on Western man's view of sex, marriage and the family. Combined with anthropological and sociological studies of the different sex and marriage patterns in primitive and sophisticated societies, psychological findings and theories have at once enlarged and threatened the human basis of our Christian understanding of marriage. The stages of sexual development as outlined by Freud and refined by his successors, or the results of Kinsey's investigations into sexual habits in the United States of America, have greatly extended our knowledge and deepened our understanding. They may also have shaken our confidence in the ethical norms which we had traditionally accepted.

It is against a background of profound and continuing change in so much of the conventional wisdom on sex and marriage—and of challenge to it—that the Christian seeks his own horizon with its possibilities and goals. His response can never be simply one of flight or evasion from human developments, problems, challenges. In marriage above all he is acutely aware of the validity of the human and its development, as expressed in Creation and confirmed as well as transformed in Incarnation and Resurrection. I do not think that the theological differences between the Churches on Redemption, Justification or Sacrament would prevent agreement on the basic character of marriage as a human-created phenomenon which in the power of Jesus Christ has salvific value and divine significance. Because it is a human phenomenon it is subject to history with its ebb and flow of change, and so Christian marriage is lived and understood in the interaction between Gospel message and human development. The story of that interaction is long and complex. The different Churches give it their own nuances. However, the main structures of Christian marriage, born of that interaction, have remained constant and are agreed between the Churches, although they may differ in detail from age to age. Christian marriage is based on the exclusive and permanent union of man and woman which is formed in love and open to new life in procreation. Diversity in ecclesiology, sociology, psychology or anything else has not obscured that agreement on basic structure. The horizons opened up in our own time can, for all their exotic manifestations and finally ambiguous character, only be tested, Christian-fashion, against this foundation.

With this shared background it is possible to suggest some lines of development for the human marriages of Christians in the years ahead. If I leave aside some of the more obvious problems mentioned earlier in connection with various scientific developments, biological, psychological or sociological, this is not because I underestimate their importance or the difficulty they may pose for Christians. In a limited framework one has to choose and I choose what I consider to be the more positive possibilities opened up in our own time. These will, I believe, ultimately enlarge the Christian horizon more significantly.

One of the most seminal ideas of recent centuries has been that of democracy. From its original political setting it has found its way into industry and the economy, schooling, even the Churches and, of course, marriage and the family. At the marriage level it is still very much in a developing condition as far as relations between husband and wife, or parents and children, are concerned. The patriarchal family of long ago may have disappeared for the most part in our culture but the restrictions on wives and children in life and in law are still very real. Democracy is based on a cluster of ideas deriving from the equality of all men as human beings. It operates in group form by recognising certain basic rights of all members of the group and ensuring them a say in decisions taken on behalf of the group. Confining our attention for the moment to the couple, the democratic spirit which is now ineradicable in our society (however much it may be obscured in practice at times) demands protection for the rights of wives beyond the measure afforded by our present outdated laws. For example, equal rights in family income and property with proper protection against desertion (and any other invasion of her rights) should be a normal part of our legal system and it should not require very much time or energy to provide the necessary legislation. Similar protection of children's rights is long overdue as is only too tragically obvious.

It may seem a rather harsh approach to new horizons for Christian marriage to call for such obvious legal safeguards. Legal reform will provide the necessary framework for the democratic character which modern marriage demands and which might be better described as partnership marriage. Partnership is, of course, a frame of mind before it is a framework of law. Without the mentality the law will avail little. Without the law one is unprotected against abuses arising from lack of the correct mentality. On the positive side the partnership concept of marriage ensures the mutual respect on which true unity is built. In the spirit of partnership the couple can enter on the enterprise of building a life and a home together with growing trust and security. If the partnership must enjoy at one level the protection of the law in regard to mutual rights and duties and on a basis of strict reciprocity, it must be animated at another level by personal feelings of trust and love. The partnership quality and the personal feelings will gradually encompass new members of the family in children. Recognition of their rights and increasing participation in family councils and decisions will gradually enable them to become full partners also.

The democratic ideal of partnership derives, as I said, from the political arena. It might well return there or, at any rate, be expanded both in defence of fundamental rights of the citizens and in increase of their participation in decision-making. The partnership marriage and family require a wider context of partnership in society if they are to survive, let alone thrive. The inner dynamism of the family itself, as it reaches out to neighbour, locality and all forms of wider society, will eventually lead to frustration if such wider partnership is not guaranteed and practised.

Is all this based, fancifully perhaps, on 'secular political' ideas which can hardly have very much relevance for the Christian outside their immediate sphere of reference. Not so! Marriage for the Christian is the dynamic human reality which is shared with all men. Its Gospel structure, based on the interaction of the power and message of the Gospel with the human reality, is reinforced in its human and Christian character by the partnership concept. The equality of all men as created in the image of God, as redeemed in Christ, by whom all false historical barriers between men and women were destroyed, is realised more and more fully in the partnership marriage.

The Christian partners do not live in a religious vacuum. The health of their partnership will be related to the partnership quality of their own Christian community. A patriarchal style is no more essential to that community than it is to the marital one. In the present climate it may be no less harmful to the Christian community as a whole than to the married couples and families who constitute it. It is not a question of applying the criteria of parliamentary democracy to the Church (they may be badly enough in need of overhaul in the State). Yet a form of partnership with diverse functions but respect for certain fundamental rights and effective participation in decision-making should characterise the modern Church in which everybody is expected to be not a passive believer but an active apostle.

Partnership between the Churches is just as urgent as partnership within a particular Church. In no area is this more true in Ireland than in that of inter-Church marriage. Without genuine partnership, respect for fundamental rights and shared decision-making between the Churches in this, but also in other areas of contact and conflict, the Christian message will be continually contradicted by Christian behaviour. It is to be sincerely hoped that the deliberations about inter-Church marriages will, in a spirit of partnership, find a way to allow mutual respect and common decision-making by the Churches and by the partners to an inter-Church marriage, in the penultimate solution to this problem, which is all that can be expected in this sinful world.

The partnership of marriage then has ramifications far beyond the domestic hearth. It can and should set the style and the standard for the various forms of social life, secular and religious. To the Christian this is scarcely surprising. At the heart of all social life in the Judaeo-Christian tradition lies the Covenant, primarily between God and his people. This divine-human partnership which reached its climax in Jesus Christ forms the basis for the fraternal covenant or partnership which has been established between all men and which receives its visible expression in the Church. In illustrating the structure and character of this covenant-partnership, human marriage has played a key-role from the teaching of the prophets down to St Paul. A partnership marriage not only expresses the covenanted or graced relationship which exists between the particular couple, it offers a model and a challenge to the Church itself and to all forms of human society.

For all that, partnership remains a cold word in face of the ideals which many people set themselves and in some degree achieve in marriage. It contains, I believe, essential truth about marriage and human society generally which we ignore at our peril. The next approach to marriage, or horizon for marriage, if you prefer, that I wish to outline, gets over some of the coldness of partnership without disappearing into the vapours of the over-used 'love'. The approach is that of friendship. In friendship, the business air of recognition of rights, distribution of function, participation in decision and collaboration in implementation, which one expects in partnership, yields to a feeling of sympathy and affection in which there is a sharing of attitudes and personal interests born of mutual understanding and appreciation. One of the best and most heart-rending tributes I heard a bereaved young husband make simply stated, 'Peg and I weren't just husband and wife, we were friends.' In the rush from the patriarchal contract to the romantic idyll, marriage and its commentators may have missed the critical stage of friendship.

Friendship is a matter of choice, of continuing choice, based on mutually attractive qualities and nourished by shared interests and activities. It transforms partnership by its warmth but, more importantly, it provides the basis for stability and development to a marriage relationship that may have begun in infatuation or in that 'being swept off one's feet' feeling which can die so quickly when one finally gets back to earth in marriage. For the

young and in love one of the questions they might ask before
they commit themselves in marriage is 'Are we friends as well
as in love or, at least, do we see ourselves as capable of the more
durable if less exciting relationship of friendship?' When the
inevitable disagreements come, the intensity of that first love may
well intensify the resentment felt at disagreement, unless it is
balanced by a deep appreciation of and trust in each other, an
appreciation having some of the elements of detachment as well
as those of attachment.

In courtship and in marriage-growth the qualities of friendship
will be important to the relationship. This may become more
evident still in old age when children have grown up and left
the home and when perhaps older friends and relatives are
passing away or, at any rate, not so easily accessible. The very
openness of the friendship-marriage will enable it to overcome
the frightening isolation which many 'nuclear' marriages now
experience, particularly in large urban areas. The children themselves pose friendship problems. One may choose one's marriage-
partner as one chooses one's friends but one has no choice in one's
children or in one's parents. The biological and psychological
bonds which form the basis of the parent-child relation must be
developed gradually not only in terms of partnership as outlined
above, but also in terms of friendship, if a genuine adult relationship is finally to emerge. With this goal and the effort and
know-how to seek it, much of the generation gap would be eased
and finally overcome. Old age would become more fulfilling for
parents, and their children would be themselves much more
mature adults and be increasingly able to enjoy their parents'
company to the very end of their lives. How much richer would
family life become in this way, threatened as it now so often is
by lack of shared interests, activities, communication, and dependent either on sheer sense of duty or inarticulate loyalty, either
of which could be hurtful and even· destructive. With the goal
of friendship in front of them, parents are also less liable to
indulge their children uncritically or possess them selfishly.

The friendship-marriage embodies and reflects the attitude of
him who does not now call us servants but friends (*John* 15: 15).
The Covenant with Israel has always rested on God's loving
choice, tender care and fidelity towards his people. While Lord
of Creation and of the Gentiles, his bonds with Israel were of

the personal friendship kind. The fullness of that friendship became apparent in Jesus Christ, particularly in its bearing with and overcoming dissent, indeed rejection.

Those professed friends of Christ who form the Churches must look within and without to see what bonds of friendship bind them together. In any Church, difference and dissent is inevitable and has potential for enrichment. Too often it turns sour and destructive because the dissenters have not learned to express dissent with respect and affection. They have not learned the lesson of the friendship-family where very deep differences must sometimes be faced and can be overcome on the basis of trust and respect developed through the years.

Failures in friendly trust and respect within the individual Churches tend to be repeated on a larger scale between the Churches. We have many fine examples of how inter-Church friendships, if one may use such an awkward phrase, have flourished in face of all kinds of difficulty. Yet again the topic of inter-Church marriages underlines the difficulties facing growing friendship between members of the different Churches, particularly among the young. Without such friendship can we ever have normal relationships between the different communities in Ireland? And where such friendship is lacking, perhaps prevented or discouraged, what kind of Christian witness is being given to people who so easily hide behind barriers of class or race or religion to exclude from any real sharing the friends who are offered to them in Christ? The friendship-marriage, particularly between Christians from different Churches, must act as judgment on and challenge to all such ecclesial and social failure.

Beyond partnership and friendship (but not submerging them) marriage has been characterised for Christians (and for all men) as 'two in one flesh'. The 'flesh' in Hebrew tradition whence we get the phrase, is not simply the physical body but the total bodily person. So the full and typical expression of marriage unity is sexual intercourse. The intimacy of such expression hardly needs emphasising. However, it is only in more recent times that we have begun to understand the full personal quality of it, to appreciate the layers of significance and communication (unfortunately, sometimes lack of communication) which it can bear. And yet it can only express as much real care as the relationship in its partnership and friendship dimensions has really achieved, although it is expression of promise and commitment as well as of achievement. The love which conquers all, overcomes all difficulties and for the newly-married might seem readily accessible in the joys of intercourse, has to be worked at and for. Despite its gift-like character it remains a continuing and demanding task. The celebration in one flesh rejoices in the mutual gift and prepares for the common task. In its own structure it is essentially covenantal and can be the clearest human manifestation of God's covenantal love for his people. The *communio* of marriage illustrates again the communion to which all men are called in Christ. The particular marriage, its family life, its activity in the believing community and its contribution to the wider society should in word and deed extend that communion of humanity and sanctity we call God's kingdom.

Living love is always creative; it seeks to transcend itself, to expand out from its present confines to new centres or objects of that love. The loving communion of marriage is specifically directed in its creativity to the highest form of human creativity: the conception, bearing and rearing of further human beings, new centres of partnership, friendship and love. The gift of children through birth or adoption begins a new stage in the husband and wife relationship which can enrich them and the wider community, but will make increasing, if also enriching, demands on their resources and those of the community. Perhaps enough has already been said about the parent-child relationship —as it ought to develop in terms of partnership and friendship animated by love. Yet the horizon of parenthood may in practice be very unsatisfactory for the majority of parents and children. Too many fathers, for instance, may opt out of parenthood altogether because of their involvement in the job. Too many parents may exclude themselves—or be excluded—from any effective participation in the child's development, i.e. education, once schooling starts. The now extended process of adolescence may develop into complete breakdown in communication, giving no scope for partnership or friendship. A great deal more attention should be paid to the stages of development in parenthood as in childhood, and parents should be drawn more effectively into the education of their children, which in turn should bear many more of the marks of partnership between school and home, between teachers, parents and children. The destruction of the distinction between bond and free, to which St Paul called attention, might require a little application in our educational system.

Christianity might well be interpreted or misinterpreted as a horizon game; one more utopian ideology which inspires its adherents with aspirations which are doomed to eventual frustration. Indeed many romantic couples float into marriage on a wave of feeling only to founder on the first rock of difficulty. The difficulties, even fatalities in marriage, are notorious. How far the increasing divorce rate all over the world indicates greater marital unhappiness today than in earlier times when divorce was not so readily available, may be open to debate. At all events failed marriages are widespread and obvious. And it should be unchristian to shrug them off with more promises, with the Utopia this time displaced to the next life. The Christian takes suffering and failure seriously in this life. He knows that he is committed to fighting it, by seeking first of all to prevent it and, where that does not work, to overcome or at least alleviate it. His Master spent too much of his precious little time dealing with the ordinary this-worldly sufferings of his contemporaries for any Christian to suppose that he can substitute a stony promise even of eternal life for genuine loving care and service of the suffering. The same Master's account of the final assessment of his disciples (*Matt.* 25) does not augur well for any self-styled Christian who passes the wounded by on the other side. Consciousness of and compassion for the wounded in marriage have grown apace in recent times. There remains an immense amount to be done in research, in providing trained personnel, in attracting voluntary workers, in financing social services which bear directly on marriage difficulties from case-work to home visitation to housing. The long-promised reforms in this area will not, I hope, be further delayed.

Prevention is naturally better than cure. We do have some achievement by voluntary bodies organised by the Churches to provide pre-marriage education. But their own members would admit that they are reaching too few too late. For the rest, we have promises but no legislative or administrative action to help to prepare the vast majority of our younger people for marriage. The inadequate or—worse—divided witness of the Churches cannot provide sufficient impetus or inspiration to ensure that the resources of society as a whole are harnessed to this essential educational and remedial work. If the new horizons of Christian marriage are not to be a continuous judgment on Christian Churches, some very energetic and cooperative initiatives are urgently required.

The historical horizons now opening up to human and Christian marriage are full of exciting challenges. They will meet their measure of failure in every individual marriage. Their final significance does not however rest on the rate of empirical success achieved, on the actual number of marriages which attain a high or, at least, satisfactory degree of partnership, friendship and loving communion, important as that is. For the historical horizon derives its ultimate meaning and significance from the Easter horizon revealed by the Risen Christ. And it is to that ultimate horizon that the Christian finally hopes to attain. The happiest of marriages is broken by death or it would be if we had not the promise of new and fuller life in resurrection. Here there may be no giving or taking in marriage but this new and fuller life is the charity which will in St Paul's words abide, the charity or love which receives its most intimate human expression in authentic marriage. To highlight that further horizon, particularly in the area of sexual loving, Jesus and the Churches have recognised the special call of celibacy for the sake of the Kingdom. It is the complement and not the rival of marriage, endorsing marriage's historical horizons which it does not precisely share, but joining with marriage to relate all our living and loving to the horizon that is beyond all our earthly horizons of family, society or Church, and yet encompasses them all.

12

Scandal[1]

The Moral Theology Tradition

IN the manual tradition of moral theology scandal had a well-defined meaning taken over from Aquinas and with undoubted roots in the New Testament, for example in Matthew 18: 6ff, Romans 14: 15 and Corinthians 8: 9. The tradition persists practically unchanged in more recent and renewed works such as Bernard Häring's *The Law of Christ II* and Karl Hormann's *Lexikon der Christlichen Moral.*

The common definition: *factum vel dictum minus rectum praebens (alteri) occasionem ruinae,* envisaged scandal as an external act or word which, either because it was wrong in itself or appeared wrong in the circumstances, could lead another into sin, his spiritual ruin. The distinctions between direct and indirect dealt with the intention of the scandal-giver; if he intended the sin of the other it was direct; if he merely foresaw and permitted it was indirect. Direct scandal was always wrong, but indirect, by an action good in itself, could be justified in certain circumstances on the criteria of the act of double effect.

This was the background to the Church's pastoral and canonical practice in assessing the damage caused by scandal, forbidding it and punishing it.

Despite its biblical roots and historical respectability this approach to scandal was very inadequate. It did not at all do justice to the full biblical tradition, particularly that of the New Testament. It took little account of the psychological and socio-logical implications, positive and negative. It belonged to a tradition of moral analysis that was too juridical in form and negative in expression without sufficient attention to the real character of evil in the world. The tradition was too much concerned with individual actions without recognising historical process in which individual actions belonged. And it considered only individual agents and not groups or communities as subjects of moral activity. Any re-appraisal of scandal demands a return to the fuller New Testament concept and its discussion in the larger anthropological context in which theology, including moral theology, works today.

The New Testament Message

It is legitimate here to take for granted the Old Testament linguistic background to *skandalon* and its cognates in the Septuagint and the New Testament. The twofold idea of a trap or snare (originally, stick setting it off) and an obstacle in the way, which one might fall over, and their transferred religious usage offer an obvious starting-point for the use of the term by Jesus in the Synoptics as well as by Paul and John. And although close linguistic analysis of the kind provided by Stahlin helps a great deal with the New Testament understanding of the term *skandalon,* the reality is richer than the usage of any particular term reveals.

The reality is concerned primarily and predominantly with the strange ways of God with men. That his ways are not conventional human ways is revealed most strikingly and paradoxically in the climactic way of the incarnation, in the Logos made flesh, in the man Jesus who was the Son of God. To complete his historical relationship with men, God adopted not merely human ways, but humanity itself in Jesus the Christ. Yet that foundation stone proved the real stone of stumbling to destruction for those of his own who were unwilling to receive him (*Rom.* 9: 33; 1 *Pet.* 2: 8). The primary scandal of the New Testament is Jesus himself as Simeon recognised at the outset when he described him as set for the fall (ptósin) and resurrection of many in Israel (*Luke* 2: 34).

In his behaviour and preaching Jesus became increasingly an offence, a scandal to the Jewish people and particularly their religious leaders. His association with sinners, his freedom with the traditions of men, his attitude to the Sabbath and above all his messianic claims proved such a stumbling block that not only was he not accepted in faith as he strove to be but he was rejected, hated and finally put to death. Even some of his own disciples were scandalised at his Eucharistic promises and walked no more with him (*John* 6: 61, 66). John the Baptist had his doubts and questions (*Matt.* 11: 2-6). The chosen band of faithful with their leader Peter were scandalised at the prospect of his suffering and death (*Matt.* 16: 22f) and on its occasion abandoned him in fear and faithlessness (*Mark* 14: 27; *Matt.* 26: 31).

The scandal of Jesus provoked the decision of faith or unfaith. Only in faith could he be accepted in his true Messiahship. Those who were unwilling or unable to accept his message, ways and person refused thereby God's saving offer. Instead of faith in Jesus they settled for self-justification through the works of the law (*Rom.* 9: 31f). The most loving gift which Yahweh had to offer his own people, his Son, was rejected by many as the prophets had been before him. The owner of the vineyard could do no more for his people than he had done and they reacted by killing his son (*Mark* 12: 1ff). To the scandal, for his contemporaries, of Jesus' life was added the scandal of his death. For Paul the scandal of the Cross became the crucial point of faith-decision for Jew and Gentile alike (1 *Cor.* 1: 23 etc.).

The Scandal of God's Ways with Men

The New Testament data with their Old Testament background take us to the heart of scandal—the scandal of God's ways with men. The saving grace offered above all in Jesus Christ is the *Krisis,* the judgment, the critical point of decision for belief and unbelief. It goes to the heart of human existence itself in final eschatological terms, final fulfilment or final destruction. Scandal is not primarily a question for morality or ethics but a question for faith. Man's ultimate destiny is at stake.

The scandal of Jesus and of the Cross require further and deeper reflection by theologians and the Church. This New Testament sense has never been entirely lost although it played very little role in moral theology. The belief that the Church or the Christian must never be entirely conformed to this world but must somehow be a sign of contradiction (in Simeon's other term *Luke* 2: 34) has always been recognised, however ambiguously it may have operated in practice. The contradiction or discontinuity can too easily become a self-righteous defensive reaction against the God-given signs of the times and lead Church and Christian to rejection of the wider divine call embodied in current history, in defence of narrower ecclesiastical interests. The mistakes of the Sadducees and Pharisees are not a first century phenomenon only. Discerning the signs of the times and responding to the divine call beyond its present fixed horizons are permanent tasks for Church and Christian. Failure to do so is to be scandalised afresh at the message and power of Jesus. It is a failure in faith, the primary attribute of Christians. The community of the Church as well as the individual Christian may be guilty of this failure and fail to share in the blessing of him who is not scandalised in Jesus (*Matt.* 11 : 6). Conformity and non-conformity to the sinful world are hereby translated into the call to discern and tread the pilgrim way of faith in hope and love. Undiscerning or blind self-indulgent and self-protective (*Matt.* 15) non-conformity in face of a particular civilisation is no more an act of faith than an undiscerning self-indulgent conformity. At the theological and pastoral level the work of listening to and responding to the true call of God as embodied in the world in which we live must continue unremittingly. Mistakes in acceptance and rejection are always possible and, as the scandals Jesus predicted, inevitably occur. The challenge of the mistakes is to repentance and a deeper commitment in faith, not to put up the barriers and exclude the world and its God. The more practical applications of this summons to the Church to confront the scandal of his Word in his world will require much fuller consideration.

The Paradox of Love and Evil

It is necessary however to pursue more deeply the mystery of the scandal of Jesus Christ and of the Cross. It is part of our accepted wisdom as well as a lesson taught us in so many words in John's First Epistle (1 *John* 4) that to love we must first of all be loved. The more we are loved, the greater capacity we have for love, the more we will love in return. Yet this does not seem to have happened in the case of God's final gift of love, his own Son, the very personification of loving. His love undoubtedly attracted in faith the love of many sinners and ordinary folk.

It also provoked hatred and rejection to the point of murder. While he is the paradigm case, Jesus is not alone in human history in this respect. In our own time we have witnessed the assassination of Gandhi and Martin Luther King, the execution of Franz Jägerstätter and Dietrich Bonhoeffer among countless others.

Love at a certain intensity seems to intensify and reveal the deeper evil in man. It is as if, to adapt Eliot's words, we can bear only a little loving. More systematically it means that we have to take more seriously the forces of evil in the world and the fact that the intensification of loving in a particular individual or community provokes its counterpart in the intensification of evil or hatred. Perhaps this is part of the background to the exorcism stories in the New Testament as it certainly seems to be part of the divisiveness which Jesus introduced into the world 'bringing not peace but the sword' and setting father against son, mother against daughter (*Matt.* 10 : 34par.). It would also throw light on the evil which the followers of Gandhi and Martin Luther King called forth from the servants of the establishment which they opposed.

In endeavouring to understand the New Testament meaning of scandal as a test or crisis point we have to pay more attention to the evil which is structured into our world. Traditional moral theology tended to analyse scandal and human behaviour in general without sufficient awareness of this evil and of the ambiguity which it creates in all of us, Christian and non-Christian, Church and world. Given such an awareness it is more necessary to follow the path of Jesus Christ in faith and hope irrespective of the scandal it causes and the evil it provokes. But it is salutary to recall that the ambiguity also affects Church and Christian and that the evil inherent in them may in their reaction to genuine love and prophetic action be intensified to the point of rejecting a further manifestation of Jesus within or without the confines of the visible Church.

The further reaches of the mystery of the scandal of Jesus extend to the favourite Pauline presentation of it in terms of the scandal of the Cross. The elimination of Jesus the blasphemous scandaliser on the Cross seemed to guarantee to the unbelieving the triumph of hatred over love to the believing and the just execution of a disturber and criminal. Both were confounded in the Resurrection. When hatred had done its worst, reached its peak and removed the scandalous threat, it had in fact undermined itself. The love even unto dying triumphed over dying in the

Resurrection. The worst that hatred could achieve proved the gateway to the ultimate triumph of love. The believers were confounded in their brief infidelity and restored in their faith. To the unbelievers the very criminal execution itself could only seem scandalous and foolish as a basis for the preaching of God's achievement of salvation and reconciliation. The scandal of his death was all the more potent for those who had never known him in life. Paul's insistence on the scandal of it as the paradoxical giving of new life to all men by God revealed the crisis point for faith in God's ways, a faith that transcended any self-domination or self-justification by man. The test of fidelity to this achievement must be the embodiment of the scandal of the Cross in Christian living with all the risks that entails for misunderstanding, derision and rejection.

Warning Against Scandal

A further aspect of the puzzling scandal of Jesus Christ was his concern to avoid scandal in paying the temple tax, for example (*Matt.* 17: 27). His condemnation of those through whom scandals would come, inevitable though they be, was developed in his admonition to sacrifice eye or limb should it be an occasion of scandal (*Matt.* 18: 8par). He was not a deliberate provoker of the scandal which concerned him, the lapsing from faith into final destruction. This teaching, together with Paul's concern in his letters to the Romans (14, 15) and Corinthians (1 *Cor.* 8, 9) about sacrificing one's freedom to avoid actions that might be the occasion of another's lapse, provided the background to the theological tradition. However, it was divorced in this tradition both from the scandal of Jesus himself, and from an awareness of the wider evil, and it was impoverished by its neglect of the eschatological faith risk which informed the treatment by Jesus and Paul.

Pastoral Implications

It is time to draw some tentative pastoral conclusions from this attempt to reestablish a true theological basis for the understanding and judgment of scandal.

The Church itself, in word and more particularly in deed, in its life and structures, must manifest to all men the scandal of Jesus Christ as a call to faith. It will seek to do this in a manner calculated to draw men to Christ by attending to the genuine signs and characteristics of Jesus which the particular civilisation embodies. And it must do so, conscious of the risk of intensification of evil and rejection which this may entail. Its identification with the poor and neglected rather than a courting of the rich and powerful is a useful criterion in assessing the true scandal of the Church. Its own structures and activities as a community dedicated to truth, freedom and justice for all its members and ultimately for mankind will prevent the scandal of human weakness from obscuring the scandal of divine love. In the prevention of participation by so many members in Church life, in the inadequacy of structures for communication and judgment, in the preference for power rather than truth or justice, in the need for a new life-style for clergy, religious and laity, the scandal of man's ways in the Church is frequently manifested. The indefectibility of the Church based on the divine promise should not make it complacent about the urgent call of continually displacing the scandal of human weakness to reveal the true scandal of Jesus Christ.

Response to Scandal

However, the scandal of human weakness will always be part of the Church as a whole. The ambiguity of human endeavour always presupposes the fearful reality of evil at the heart of our best endeavour. So the Church has to provide room for creative experiment and prophetic word and action that may to human weakness appear scandalous in the primary Christian sense. Its response to such experiment and prophecy must be one of faith, seeking to understand and discriminate between the gracious God-given and the sinful man-laden. It must be one of patience because, Gamaliel-fashion, the Church should let the community through time arrive at a considered judgment. It must be one of love because the experimenter and the prophet need the loving support of the community if they are not to be isolated socially and psychologically and be distorted in their role into cranks and eccentrics.

Assessment in faith and response in love are not easy and may not always seem adequate to the truth of Christ or the life of the community. The temptation to turn them into a juridical sentence with or without a due process may be irresistible. Such a process and sentence may indeed be sometimes demanded but it should be on the very rare occasion when faith and love have seemed to fail utterly in keeping the agent in genuine communication with the community of the Church. And such process must be directed to restoring that communication as quickly as possible. For the process to achieve this, the community as a whole must share in it in a representative capacity: one-man or arbitrary exercises of authority only compound the scandal.

Where the human weakness has no creative pretensions the faith and love response still remains primary. How far such human weakness constitutes scandal depends very much on the actual person involved, his circumstances and those of the possibly scandalised as well as their capacity to discriminate in faith and love in response. And this is the lead that should first of all be given to them. Again the judicial procedure is a last resort but must bear all the marks of fairness in seeking a reconciliation in faith and love.

The traditional moral theological treatment of scandal with its canonical counterpart clearly does not reflect the thrust of the New Testament teaching. It ignores the true challenge of scandal in theological terms as a summons to faith and love. It does not provide for truly creative Christian experiments or genuine prophetic voices and the difficulties in assessing these. In areas as diverse as doctrinal development, the life-style of religious communities or priests, prayer movements, liberation movements, inter-Church worship and communion, inter-Church marriages, inter-Church schooling, and the pastoral and sacramental care of the divorced and homosexual, room for growth through experimentation must be maintained against any self-righteous cries of 'scandal'.

In responding to the scandal of human weakness the same faith in discrimination and love in support is required of the individual Christian and the Christian community. This is more likely to ensure the maturity in Christ to which all Christians are summoned than easy recourse to moral and canonical condemnation, necessary though these may be as a very last resort.

13

Theology as Sociobiography

IN much of this book moral reflection and analysis has focused on the interaction between the personal and the social. The autobiographical dimension of theology with its emphasis on personal conversion and development takes account of the social context in which the individual becomes a person. That social context has a life of its own. That life has a theological significance in providing the agenda as well as the resources for faith and theological reflection. Charting this social life as inspiration and source of theology is the task of this post-script on 'theology as sociobiography'.

The title, awkward as it sounds, helps in relation to the Introduction, to maintain the tension between the personal and social which so many of the intervening chapters reflect. And it provides a convenient framework for examining how far the themes presented here come out of the recent social context in which the author had to work and are illuminated by it. Such examination, I believe, fosters a more critical understanding of theological interests and positions while at the same time it can produce genuine theological insight in its own right.

The first problem facing the theologian who undertakes this project of examining theologically his 'sociobiography' is the plurality of social contexts in which he lives. The possibility and the difficulty of differentiating and structuring these overlapping social contexts and communities have already been considered.[1] For the immediate purpose it will be certainly simpler and perhaps sufficient to look at the three general contexts and communities in which the theologian moves—the ecclesial, the academic and the secular-civic.

These contexts and communities are not finally distinct and separate. In so far as the theologian is and must be a man of faith, he lives and works within the community of faith, the Church or *ecclesia*. Is so far as he is a member of a university he lives and works with his colleagues in other disciplines not only in the academic community but in the wider secular community which the academic community serves. Even without the mediation of a university the theologian belongs to linguistic, cultural and political communities which are properly described as secular but which enter into the very questions he asks and the answers he essays as a Christian believer engaged in critical reflection on his faith. While the ecclesial, academic and secular-civic communities suggest a helpful framework for our discussion, they overlap and interact in multiple and subtle ways which will not, indeed cannot, be fully conceptualised.

In discussing the immediate social contexts of the themes treated in this book, I am primarily concerned with the contexts contemporary with the work produced here. Such contemporary contexts have a history, a past and a future. What they have been enters into their structure here and now in a constitutive way. What they will be is already transforming that structure. Yet to retain this discussion within manageable boundaries the significant features of the present have to be selected in the light of both their past historical genesis and their potential for further genesis or development in the future. Such selection is a matter of judgment based on information, personal experience and social influence. The very interpretation of social context for our purposes is already socially influenced. The inescapable if justifiable character of such an interpretative circle presents one of the most searching questions on method with which theologians—and not only theologians but philosophers, social scientists and other academic colleagues—are still grappling.[2] The final answer to this question does not seem to lie with intellectual analysis alone, powerful assistance as this may provide. However much may be achieved in exposing superficial and crude certainties or in the exclusion of paralysing scepticism, some faith or hope, which may be justified in various ways but not finally demonstrated, remains basic to this as to other intellectual enterprises. Theology shares its weaknesses as well as its strengths with sciences, human and physical, more revered because regarded as more rigorous in our own day.

The critical value of examining the social context of one's

theology does not necessarily include a solution to the fundamental interpretative or hermeneutical problem. It does however expose that problem more directly in alerting people to the social forces at work both directly in the theology itself and more subtly in the very selection of social forces which are considered to be worth analysing as influential in one's theology. The final methodical and methodological justification of my particular selection cannot be fully and properly undertaken here. Some practical justification may emerge in the results achieved.

I. The Ecclesial Context and Community

The Church in which these papers were composed and presented is the Roman Catholic Church in the middle to late 1970s. To be more precise still, while a number of the papers have been presented outside Ireland, the Roman Catholic Church in Ireland of this period constitutes the immediate context in terms of both challenge and resources. The distinction and the interaction between the universal Church and the local Church illustrate both the general problem of overlapping communities and contexts and an aspect of Church which was vigorously recovered at Vatican II. It is the post-Vatican II Church which concerns us. By the mid-seventies, however, the euphoria and excitement of the mid-sixties and early seventies had been moderated at least to the point of tolerable coexistence for all but the most agitated. Yet it was difficult to say how far a renewed, vital and unified community had emerged from the 'growing pains' of the previous decade. It was in that ill-defined and still uneasy state of the Church, universal and local, that this exercise in theology took place between 1974 and 1978.

In selecting the significant ecclesial influences from that period I will naturally be influenced by my own preoccupations as a moral theologian. Such distinctiveness belongs in part to discussion of the academic context. The moral theologian should be considered here primarily as a theologian, a critical investigator and exponent of the Church's faith from within the Church community.

The context and condition of the Church community influences his work no less than that of the dogmatic theologian, in so far as such distinctions are intelligible and defensible at all. That context and condition should be evaluated not only in doctrinal terms but also in moral terms. To such evaluation the moral theologian should pay particular attention.

A cluster of fresh doctrinal insights in the current understanding of the Church paved the way for developments in its moral condition which have deeply affected theology. The doctrine of the Church, its structure, its relationships and its mission as outlined in the documents of Vatican II on the Church, Revelation, Ecumenism, the Church in the Modern World, and Religious Freedom, to take the more obvious sources, transformed the image, attitudes and activities of the Church from those of a relatively closed and independent organisation to those of a relatively open and inter-dependent community.

The call to all the members of the Church to join in its tasks of understanding, preaching and living the saving word of God creates a new learning situation within the Church. The further openness to other Christian Churches and to the world at once complicates and enriches the learning potential. It is in such a context and condition that the theological expansion of the sixties occurred. Despite the vagaries of the intervening history, that context, condition and expansion are still effective today. The relationship between Church and theology which emerged during and after Vatican II has, with inevitable qualifications, persisted.

In many ways the outstanding characteristic of the interaction between community and theology since Vatican II has been freedom. The influence of theological developments on the teaching of Vatican II, the style of that teaching with a pastoral and dialogical rather than definitive bias and the content of this teaching as it bore on the Church's internal and external relations, encouraged a sense of freedom, exploration and discovery in theological work which had been unknown for a long time.

Such freedom brought a refreshing honesty and openness in theological writing. Writing between the lines or with one eye over one's shoulder no longer seemed necessary or acceptable. Theology became alive and exciting. Interest was intense. Conferences flourished. Publications multiplied. Stars were born.

Much that was said and written was ephemeral, sloppy and cliché-ridden. Yet there was a genuine dedication to the truth, a vigorous and honest quest for it, quite an amount of valuable and durable achievement and some truly creative and pioneering work. Purged of the dross, the durable and creative achievements continue to enrich the Church. Such achievements are by no means at an end. They may even be in their intitial stages although without the heady excitement and inevitable illusions of new beginnings.

Freedom in theological thinking and writing means freedom to look at issues freshly and differently, to depart if necessary from the prevailing viewpoint and inevitably to make mistakes. Honesty means reporting how one sees it, differently, perhaps erroneously. The result for theology was not only authenticity and creativity but diversity. In a Church accustomed for so long to a consistent, even rigid single line in most issues, diversity was perceived as threatening as well as enriching. As the early euphoria died away the diversity produced conflict and dissent, most dramatically exposed in the disputes over the Tridentine Mass and contraception (issues in themselves peripheral to the Church's central message and mission).

The diversity and dissent on a range of issues but particularly on contraception had consequences for theology and moral theology, for theologians and moral theologians, which have not yet been fully worked out morally and intellectually or integrated into a deeper understanding of theology's ecclesial context. In the sociobiographical terms relevant here it is necessary to recognise the unfinished character of this crisis and development and at the same time draw up a provisional balance-sheet of the profit and loss to theology in the Church which has accrued from the disputes.

Focusing on the example of contraception as a critical one, particularly for theologians of the Church and of morality, one can discern a general source of dissent and conflict which derives from the explicit teaching of Vatican II and to which I have already referred. The Decree on Ecumenism states (par. 11):

> When comparing doctrines with one another, they (Catholic theologians) should remember that in Catholic doctrines there exists an order or 'hierarchy' of truths, since they vary in their relation to the foundation of the Christian faith.

In the debates and dissent experienced within the Church over the last decade little attention has been given to this principle.

Does this imply that the adversaries take the principle of 'hierarchy of truths' as applicable only to inter-Church and not to intra-Church discussion? If so how is such exclusiveness justified? Surely how 'truths . . . vary in their relation to the foundation of the Christian faith' matters enormously to the manner and matter of disputes within the Church as well as to debates between the Churches.

Perhaps the rejection of the principle turns on a failure to find criteria for variation in centrality or primary relationships to the foundation of the Christian faith. Even if no totally satisfactory criteria could be found, there are sufficient guidelines in scripture, tradition, creeds, councils and catechisms to be able to distinguish teaching on the Creation, Incarnation, Redemption and Resurrection from that on Religious Freedom, for example. Indeed it was on such a basis, however implicit, that Vatican II was able to issue its decree on Religious Freedom in a way that significantly departed from papal and Church teaching over the previous century, without creating a crisis for any discernible minority.

Are the other issues in dispute more clearly and closely related to the centre and foundations of the faith and so incapable of the same detached discussion? On the basis of the centrality of certain saving truths as witnessed in scripture and tradition, it is difficult to see how contraception has such a close relationship. Using a negative criterion one might ask if the recognition of contraception as morally good or evil makes a serious difference to one's basic belief in God, Jesus Christ and the Church. This is not an argument for accepting or rejecting contraception. It is simply a device to see whether on the basis of conciliar principle of the hierarchy of truths, now widely accepted in ecumenical dialogue and theological work, it is possible to find agreement on the secondary and subordinate character of certain issues and so put the debate about them into a certain perspective, prevent it in other words from getting out of proportion and becoming a basis for mutual, if implicit, excommunication.

Two obvious difficulties about the application of the principle to controversial issues immediately arise. It is clearly in the interest of those advocating change to describe a certain issue as secondary in relation to the foundations of Christian faith. It is equally in the interest of those opposing change to see the same issue as closely related to the central truths. The conflict of interest, especially if it is not acknowledged, may be more difficult to resolve than the conflict of truth but they will be closely related. The interest may have psychological and sociological aspects in terms of self-protection, self-aggrandisement or self-indulgence. Few disputants can entirely escape these. However the interest may and usually will also have a theological dimension in terms of the meaning of Church authority and the range of Christian freedom.

People who did not have or could not find a satisfactory moral argument for or against contraception tended to take their stance on the basis of either authority or freedom. In asserting the subordinate character of a particular issue in dispute such as contraception, one is regarded by opponents not so much as removing destructive tension and promoting reasonable and charitable debate but as undermining legitimate authority and encouraging illegitimate freedom. The counter-charge is that of distorting the true nature of authority and unduly restricting freedom. When a particular issue, however subordinate, becomes entangled with the deeper issues of authority and freedom the principle of hierarchy of truths is very difficult to apply. Until some more satisfactory understanding of the relationship between authority and freedom in the search for and maintenance of Christian truth than the preconciliar rigidity or post-conciliar confusion provide, the principle of a hierarchy of truths cannot be properly applied. Meantime however it has a value as a goal to be sought and as a limited influence on the dissensions occurring.

The dissent which surrounded the encyclical *Humanae Vitae,* dealing with contraception, stimulated further study into the limits of dissent within the Church. The doctrine of religious assent to papal and other authoritative statements which Vatican II had endorsed as it emerged from the tradition was examined in terms of the right to public as well as private dissent.[3] This led to a further exploration of the relationship between the role of the pope and bishops as teaching authority and the role of the theologians. That exploration is still far from complete. Yet so far it has yielded positive results in terms of the grounding of papal-episcopal teaching authority in scripture, tradition and the faith of the believing community. Theological responsibility and freedom have the same foundations but perform different tasks of exploring and developing the faith-understanding of the community as well as expounding and guaranteeing it. In fulfilling these tasks freedom is clearly essential but it is freedom in and for the total ecclesial community and it must be in conjunction with, if sometimes in tension with, the more pastoral teaching responsibility of the pope and bishops as the focal points of unity in the Church as a whole.[4] The old simple juridical model is no longer adequate to the Church in its discovery and presentation of the saving truth of Christ any more than it is in the living of that truth. As you cannot make people good by legislation or juridical orders, neither can you discern and decide the truth by legislation. A satisfactory alternative to the juridical model has yet to be developed. Progress can be reported.

Part of the progress as far as moral theology is concerned is an emphasis on presentation of Christian understanding in prophetic rather than juridical terms. The documents of Vatican II tended to propose rather than impose truth. Dogmatic definitions with previous sometimes juridical associations were avoided. The style was predominantly pastoral; the method that of appeal. This was even more evident in the recent social encyclicals with their prophetic presentation of the great social problems of mankind and their appeal to all men of goodwill to join in solving them. It is a style singularly apt for the presentation of Christian truth, particularly moral truth, as truth to be lived. It is to be hoped that it will influence this presentation not only in questions of social morality but also of personal morality.

The great danger about the imposition of moral truth in juridical fashion is not that it will provoke dissent and disobedience. Frequently in today's climate it will. More profoundly it impoverishes moral truth and moral living by not offering the truth as having a validity in itself which must be personally and so critically appropriated before it can issue in truly personal and so moral activity. Without that personal, critical appropriation, the moral agent simply obeys the directive of a superior. This is valuable and necessary at times but as a way of life it makes the actual truth irrelevant and reduces all virtues to the virtue of obedience to the great impoverishment of moral life and development.[5] For these reasons the encyclical *Humanae Vitae* might have been better composed and recommended as an appeal to the truth than as a demand for obedience. One of the consoling results of the reception which greeted it might be a return to the manner of teaching adopted by the social encyclicals.

There were less consoling consequences for Church and theology after *Humanae Vitae* and other disputes. Although the earlier freedom has not disappeared and even a healthier self-criticism in the exercise of that freedom has emerged, there has been a definite reduction in the ease and honesty of communication within the Church. This can be verified in various ways. The gaps opened between bishops and theologians or clergy and laity or at least between defenders and critics of *Humanae Vitae* have persisted but are for the most part not discussed. There is almost a conspiracy of silence, certainly of non-communication on this issue. If this bespoke a charitable willingness to respect and live with difference or even a tiredness and resignation for the moment at the failure to achieve consensus, it would not be unhealthy. It does however more frequently bespeak a dishonesty all round which is not at all healthy. Some bishops, theologians, priests and laity do not fully agree with *Humanae Vitae*, yet go along with it in public out of a mistaken loyalty, or unwillingness to rock the boat, or personal interest and convenience. Some who do accept it may be unwilling to defend it in certain circumstances as unpopular or may unconsciously but dishonestly re-interpret it to try to combine fidelity to papal teaching with concern for the actual problems of their people. Defenders of the encyclical may be black-balled by critics in various circles. More effectively, because of the Church's power structure, critics, however committed in their faith and discreet in their criticism, are treated as suspect and disloyal, and excluded from opportunities and positions in the Church in which they might usefully contribute.[6] The honesty and so the freedom which erupted in the Church fifteen years ago have been badly battered although they have by no means disappeared. One of the most urgent tasks of the Church for theology is to renew that honesty and freedom coupled with the trust and tolerance they imply. Without these values theology will not thrive and the life and mission of the Church will continue to suffer.

In discussing the ecclesial context of moral theology as an aspect of recent sociobiography one is in danger of exaggerating the difficulties and limitations of the present in contrast with a romantic exaggeration of the period during and just after the

Council. That is not the intention here. As far as moral theology is concerned the enrichment which the Council promised is of course far from realised but the resources, stimulus and freedom to carry on the task of renewal exist in sufficient measure within the Catholic Church. The improved relationship with other Churches extends those Christian resources still further as this book has frequently indicated. And the openness to the wide world, formulated at the Council and endorsed so effectively by Pope and Church since, particularly in social morality, offers the moral theologian enormous scope and exciting challenge. The scope and challenge, the opportunities and the difficulties provided by his ecclesial context apply no more to the moral theologian in Ireland than to his colleagues elsewhere. Some particular aspects of his situation have emerged in earlier chapters.

II. *The Academic Context and Community*

With the exception of some mainland European countries, Roman Catholic theology teachers did not, prior to Vatican II, regard themselves primarily as academics or members of the academic and university community. Some still do not. However there has been a marked change, particularly in English-speaking countries, above all perhaps in the United States. The theologian as academic, as a professional in his own right within the Church and on equal terms with others in the academic world has become the norm rather than the exception.

The interest in theology and prestige of certain theologians at the time of Council and its own dependence on and promotion of theological work, affected the ecclesial status of theology. That status in the conciliar and post-conciliar documents was recognised as of a university level where standards and structures should be as far as possible the wider civil university context of the particular country or region (*Normae Quaedam*). These standards included of course (legitimate) academic freedom and university autonomy which also characterise theological activity. In this spirit the *Index of Prohibited Books* was abolished, the Holy Office with its inquisitorial traditions revamped as the Congregation for the Faith and the ruling on previous censorship of books relaxed. The International Commission for Theology established in 1967 seemed to set the seal on official Church encouragement to the emergence of theologians as a distinctive and duly autonomous body of academics within the Church.

Theologians themselves quickly adapted to the new academic context. Apart from the multiplication of conferences and publications, scholarly organisations in theology developed or were founded for the first time. In Ireland two significant departures occurred with the establishment of the Irish Theological Association in 1966 and of the Irish Federation of University Teachers in 1964. The Irish Theological Association was the first professional body of its kind in Ireland.[7] Despite some episcopal hesitations and attempts at restriction in its first years, it rapidly developed a life and style of its own. It helped to break the isolation experienced by individual theology teachers, especially in seminary conditions, and to mould an identity and confidence in theological work. Members of more specialised disciplines met as scripture scholars organised into the Irish Biblical Association. In a less formal manner there were regular meetings of the moral theologians. Contact with similar theological organisations elsewhere and membership of international organisations helped theologians throughout the Church to share problems and insights and to develop an *esprit de corps* which was notably absent in earlier times.

The new values which characterised the work of such organisations and of individual theologians were first of all the values of the wider academic community. In that respect the foundation of the Irish Federation of University Teachers and the active participation of theologians from Maynooth in it from the beginning had an important impact on Irish theological life. At the further critical stage of its development from a loose federation of associations of academics in the individual university colleges into a unified and legally recognised union with the right in law to negotiate on behalf of its members, it had a theologian as Chairman of Council and President of the Federation. And the Federation itself developed links with university teacher organisations in Northern Ireland, Great Britain and Europe through the A.U.T. (Association of University Teachers, Britain) and I.A.U.P.L. (International Association of University Professors and Lecturers in Europe).

This acceptance into the wider academic community posed and poses difficulties for the theologian. How can he combine his academic integrity with his Church loyalty or in somewhat different terms his academic vocation to the pursuit and presentation of truth with his ecclesial and pastoral responsibility for the building up of the Church community? It would be a mistake to fudge these difficulties by underplaying either his academic or his ecclesial calling or the potential tension between them. The Catholic theologians I know and respect in Ireland and elsewhere take fully seriously their academic and their ecclesial responsibilities. Indeed part of the self-identification of the Catholic theologian is his belonging to the Catholic Church. And he frequently experiences the tension involved. The resolution of that tension in a creative way rather than its dissolution by compromise may depend rather less than is sometimes believed on exclusively theological insights dealing with authority and freedom already discussed and a bit more on the wisdom and practice of the academic community in which the theologian now increasingly finds himself.

Romanticising the academic community or the university as composed of totally dedicated scholars who escape personal ambition, prejudice, jealousy and all manner of weakness in the dedicated and collaborative search for truth is nonsense. It is a human community with all of humanity's weaknesses. It has its careerists and opportunists, its politicians and power-seekers, not entirely unlike that other human community, the Church. What both also share, and in a distinctive fashion, is a commitment to truth that provides a goal for their organisation and a standard for their performance. While that is a necessary but not a sufficient condition for the existence and definition of the Church, it is so pre-eminently the condition for the existence and work of the university that it may be regarded as sufficient. Other aspects of university life are implications of that commitment in teaching, research and examining or necessary adjuncts to its efficient discharge in organisation and administration.

The commitment to truth that should characterise the academic in his research and teaching implies or demands a personal stance of undeniably moral quality. His personal honesty and integrity are critical to both aspects of his work. The threats to that honesty and integrity are manifold in origin and form. The desire for a quiet life, the prospect of promotion, the demands of prestige among one's colleagues or in the wider society, the quick and easy buck, the pressures of family life, the laziness and carelessness all are heir to—all these can and do so easily erode the honesty and integrity to which academics aspire. The fact that within the academic community there remain ideals to be achieved and standards by which to be judged provides support for and challenge to theologians also. The humility which true and continuous learning involves, the openness and tolerance of others and their viewpoints combined with critical skill in assessing one's own and others' achievements, the respect for those with whom one thoughtfully disagrees, may be only partially realised among academics including theologians, but again they constitute a permanent challenge.

In social terms the academic community is collegial and collaborative. It is not possible to become a mathematician or a literary critic, a biologist or a historian without being initiated into the (sub) community of the appropriate discipline. Initiation involves assimilation of and to an established body of knowledge, a set of skills and attitudes, a group of fellow-workers. It means entering a living tradition from which one at first is dominantly recipient but to which one eventually and increasingly contributes. The contribution may not be at the level of new knowledge. Skills and attitudes have to be developed also. The knowledge has to be shared with fresh initiates and the general public. The tradition and its community has to be strengthened, purified and organised in diverse ways. The frontier men in any discipline are dependent on a living, learning community of colleagues and students which has roots in the broader academic community with its traditions, skills and standards, and finally in the general cultural and civic community whose interest in learning provides the stimulus and the resources for such development. The discipline of theology has its own specific characteristics but the general picture of its collegial character corresponds quite closely to that of other disciplines as outlined here.

Collegiality and collaboration with colleagues—this is not the only social dimension integral to academic work. The achievements of former colleagues, recent and remote, affect the strength of the discipline and enter into its identity. History plays a crucial role in understanding what and where any discipline is now, if only to predict and protect what and where it may be in the future. And the future bears immediately on the organisation and orientation of every scholarly discipline, even one self-consciously preoccupied with the past. What future archaeologists will make of one's current interpretations of the evidence, what future evidence might be sought, what further techniques might be developed for the more exact understanding of the evidence available, these are all questions which the archaeologist cannot evade. That his and other historical work can so easily enter into man's wider self-understanding is part of the established wisdom of university life, from the Greeks and the medievals to the new universities. Theology hardly needs to learn that lesson. But it should never be allowed to forget it. The dialogue with the past, the extension of the community through tradition, is essential to academic work even when the dominant orientation is towards the future.

Another immediate future orientation is to the initiates, the students, the new generations. Without a new generation the community and tradition peter out. Without effective teaching there is no new generation. The tension between research and teaching which can be very real for particular individuals and institutions should not be allowed to obscure the necessity of either or their essential interrelation. Without a research element the particular faculty or department is not really engaged at the frontier of the discipline or involved in the growth process which keeps the tradition alive. So it cannot really introduce its students directly to the living reality of a discipline on the move which should at least distinguish university initiation and education. With the challenge of the new generation and of its continuing integration the research-minded, in the human sciences certainly, may lose touch with questions and energies necessary to their continuing development. Theology needs the cutting edge of frontier work as well as the integration of new generations in its pursuit of its particular truth. And it can do this more comfortably and consistently in the collegial context of sister-disciplines at university, than in the isolation of special institutes or seminaries.

The collegiality and collaboration may not be confined to the discipline. The overall academic community with its diversity of disciplines can or should reinforce the attitudes and skills that all academic work requires. The interdisciplinary contact can or should be enriching in method and matter for many disparate disciplines. More significantly still, the fragmentation that specialisation involves, which has sometimes a disorientating effect on personal and social life generally, may be partially healed in a unified learning community. It is not feasible to discuss profitably such a complex and apparently intractable problem here. For our purposes it is important to recognise that the fragmentation is not a 'two cultures' problem. It enters deeply into the scientific world and into particular scientific disciplines.

Theology is no less affected and has to seek its own way of keeping its growing specialisations at least in communication with one another if not in manageable unity. It could have its own contribution to offer in helping to cope with fragmentation, if no longer as pretender to queenship. The poor widow with her mite is a more apt image here. At the level of the individual academic there is an ultimately unifying quality about Christian faith even in its implicit forms which theology can discern, investigate and expound. The celebration of the liturgy can be seen, in theological reflection, as an expression and promotion of community in a way that is responsive to the apparently irresistible centrifugal thrust of academic specialisation. The truths and attitudes with which theology is concerned might at least throw some light on how the fissiparous forces which affect academic life today can be overcome and also give some help with this.

These truths and attitudes should also illuminate, in academic life as elsewhere, the curious mixture of pain and joy which affects human endeavour. The pain and joy of learning are a parable of all human activity. Perhaps a critical test of the academic is how vulnerable he is to the real pain of learning, how far he can surrender and be self-emptying in the face of truth that in the end is as much given as achieved. Equally testing is how far he can rest in the accomplishment—even, as the medievals might see it, find joy in the question, how far is there a contemplative side to his work.

The brief and cryptic allusions of the last couple of paragraphs are not intended to introduce an element of mystification into academic work, to give theology some kind of divine right to be in the university, still less to resurrect its ancient hegemony or make a plea for a Catholic university. They are simply another aspect of a complex sociobiography which in academic terms has engaged me more deeply with academic life in Ireland and elsewhere and so has prompted me to explore what theology has to learn from the academic community as a whole and what it may have to offer in return. Adequate treatment of either aspect would require a volume of its own.

The social dimension of the academic (and theological) community does not stop at the portals of the university or formal educational establishment. Academics, including theologians, have to take more seriously the wider social context in which their particular commitment to truth has to be organised and realised. Despite their dependence on society for resources and their provision of society's professionals, it is doubtful if the universities have worked out an adequate theoretical basis for their relationship to the society in which they live or if they display by and large a satisfactory practical involvement. In this matter theologians may have to look elsewhere for guidelines and even provide some of their own.

III. The Civic Context and Community

Much of this book has already revealed the impact of civic and secular issues on theological work, from the concerns of ecology to the politics of Northern Ireland. The difficulty of structuring the context of society as a whole in which theology is carried on, by which it is influenced and to whose problem it must respond merited a separate chapter. In this postscript I may be forgiven (even applauded), if I confine myself to some brief reflections on the changing civic and secular situation as it bears on theology.

The *apertura al mondo* which Vatican II and such documents as The Church in the Modern World signalled had its counterparts in the other Christian Churches. The slogan that the world writes the agenda for the Church and theology,[8] had its own difficulties but it did recall and underline the continuing mission of the Church to make the achievements and problems, joys and sorrows of the world its own, as part of the gift and task given by the creating and redeeming God of Jesus Christ.

For the theologian and particularly the moral theologian, the accelerating discovery of social issues has affected his priorities and methods in a way which is still incomplete and confusing. The prospect of a unified method of moral analysis which will allow him to deal effectively and concretely with local strikes, violence for political change, violation of human rights, racial and sex discrimination, educational deprivation and economic exploitation, population growth and endemic starvation, to mention a few typical problems, is still remote. But at least the difficulty and the need have been noted. Just as confusing for the Christian theologian is the systematic relationship between such moral analysis, the commitment it requires and his faith in Jesus Christ. Relating the personal and the social, the secular and the Christian in a critical and convincing way, constitutes the continuing quest of the moral theologians.

The civic and secular context in which they pursue their quest shares the ambiguity of the ecclesial and academic contexts. It is gift and threat, potentially enriching and potentially destructive. A pre-conciliar mistake was to view this worldly context as exclusively or at least dominantly threatening. A post-conciliar temptation incipient in *Gaudium et Spes* and much more developed in some secular theologies was to view it as at least dominantly gift. The ineradicable ambiguity, the persistent evil as well as good, which characterises all human realities, ecclesial and academic as well as secular/civic has to be taken fully seriously as the earlier chapter on 'Scandal' suggested.

For the theologian generalisations about the good and evil of the modern world are also dangerous. The danger may be at least reduced if one avoids rather vacuous and certainly unverifiable generalisations about modern man as 'man come of age' or about modern civilisation such as 'the contraceptive mentality'. The most one can hope for is some shaft of light or half-light that illuminates uneasily and uncertainly both some fragile achievement or gift which bespeaks a richer future if it persists and some destructive tendency which seriously threatens the future if not checked. The further determination of gift and threat here derives from their influence on theology as experienced by a particular theologian. Due to pressure of space only a couple of instances will be chosen as illustrations.

The 'man come of age' slogan might in the light of all mankind's self-destruction of which we have daily evidence, be derided as tragically ironic. And no doubt the cruel fate which transforms the fresh if partial insight into a slogan and so into a cliché has already rendered it useless and opaque to all but the most uncritical. The technological achievement which many wielders of· the slogan saw as its justification has already rebounded in nature and society and confirmed the inherent ambiguity of all historical progress. Yet a shaft of half-light has uncovered an aspiration and revealed a possibility of enormous theological and moral significance. Mankind may not yet have come of age. It may in the simple idealistic categories of some optimists never do so. Yet the thrust towards adulthood and maturity in directing and developing one's own life by integrating the resources available to one in responsible and responsive action in society and history, provides a prospect and a challenge which may never be adequately realised but can never again be fully obscured or denied. Mankind in community and individual terms is called to be determiner of its own destiny, shaper and subject of its own history.[9] For theologians and moralists, with their insistence on human responsibility for historical activity and eternal salvation, this may seem at first old hat. Yet it provokes very searching questions on how far man's assumption in history for his own destiny is compatible with much of the past and present God-talk. Will the growing emergence of mankind in this fashion do irretrievable damage, psychologically and sociologically, to belief in and dependence on God? Can you separate such psychological and sociological conditioning or liberation from the philosophical and theological?

Such psychological and sociological influences are already observable in questioning and rejection of faith. Even if the questioning is wholesome and the rejection unjustified, how far can this mind-set of taking responsibility for one's life and beliefs be accommodated in a Church so rigidly structured and so juridically active as the Catholic Church appears to so many? Faith may survive without or in spite of the Church. But theology, educational principle and common sense combine in recognising that faith in the God of Jesus Christ can only be realised and kept alive by initiation into the tradition of belief and into the community in which that belief is preserved and embodied. However, the initiation into and existence within that tradition and community will come under severe strain unless they can adapt and grow to meet the thrust to maturity which people now experience. As the community's frontiersmen, theologians have a particular responsibility critically to discern and embody this thrust in themselves and so enable the community to transcend its present top-heavy structures and paternalistic and sometimes repressive attitudes. So much can the Church and theology benefit from the gift of secular insight and practice.

The 'contraceptive mentality' slogan is even more opaque and misleading, and ill-suited to exposing the basic evil tendency it was seeking to curb. That evil tendency takes many forms and has received many descriptions from concerned Christians and non-Christians. I wish to fasten on one aspect and description of it here as illustrative of the persisting evil in the world which can affect theology and the Church as much as academic and civil life. The two adjectives which occur to me as summarising so much of that evil (although again not without their ambiguity and so related good) are 'disposable' and 'dispensable'. In a civilisation dominated by economic considerations which in turn have been dominated by growth and profitability, disposable goods from cars to cups become a way of life and an attitude of mind. The way of life and attitude of mind could not stop at artefacts. Nature was there to be disposed of and so were ideas, cultural achievements, human relationships, individual people, even whole classes, races and societies. The disposal of or dispensing with ideas and cultural achievements was initially a matter of ignoring and then a matter of ignorance. The fashionable theologies which at times displaced the historical achievement of the Church's greatest minds in the lecture hall or publication by treating previous theological work as disposable in that fashion, cut themselves off from its roots and created the conditions for their displacement in turn. Disposable theology was in, so the latest theology was quickly out. To seek to be always in fashion even in theology is to be always just out. The difficult, painful and sometimes boring demands of a serious theology for writer and reader, lecturer and student were not welcome to people seeking instant returns and continuing kicks. The frustration of the search for enduring satisfaction in continuously changing instant returns may cure some addicts but so much destruction is wreaked meantime.

More serious, for theology also, is not the disposability of ideas or intellectual work but of people. Of course the gates of Auschwitz no longer clang in our ears and Gulag is remote from our control and our thoughts except when the latest dissident is on trial or the latest volume of Solzhenitsyn is in the Sunday papers. But the disposing of and dispensing with people goes on all round us. It enters into the shape of our society through our treatment of prisoners, homosexuals, handicapped, itinerants, isolated and old and all the others on the margins. They are our responsibility. Our resources, priorities, attitudes, actions and omissions can decide how they are treated and live. In a less direct and effective but still true sense, the deprived in other parts of the world are also our responsibility and are disposed of and dispensed with by our ignorance, apathy and selfishness.

In moral theology and in the Church this disposability is recognised and condemned in a range of issues individual, social and sexual. The evils of disposable fetuses or races or marriages are frequent cause for moral condemnation and increasingly a source of moral response. The moral understanding which comes to surface here needs further and deeper exploration. It also needs less selectivity in its articulation and action. Too many people suffer the fate of disposability at the hands of Christians, even Christian leaders and even with the Church itself. Priests and religious who resign and are refused an outlet for their theological or other educational skills and for their Christian commitment are obvious examples of disposable people as far as the Church is concerned. Others have their rights violated and so, denied access to the appropriate procedures, are refused protection, they are disposed of or dispensed with. The disposal of dissidents if not to labour camps at least to obscurity still occurs in a Church which ought to be a countersign in itself to the disposability it condemns elsewhere. Theology and theologians, particularly moral theologians, must become increasingly conscious of the thrust to disposal of people for profit, power or convenience which forms such a frightening feature of our age. They must discern and resist this in Church, in university and in civil society. From the growing awareness of human rights and of the need for their protection which the secular-civic context now provides, they can interpret for the Church the lessons, the structures and the laws which it also needs if it is to avoid the permanent temptation to dispose of the unwanted and inconvenient.

Sociobiography is too grand a name for the crude outlines of contexts and communities which I have attempted here. Even given my restricted focus of impact on theology I might have dealt with a great many other forms and contexts. Some of these have surfaced in earlier chapters. The rest were chosen for reasons personal as well as social. Sociobiography and autobiography are inextricable. Both are equally influential in theological work. That influence is difficult to discern and even more difficult to articulate.

Much of it may never be discerned or articulated at all, at least by the particular theologian. His attempts to do so will help protect his theology from self-deception and self-interest. The attempts must go on. Autobiography, sociobiography and theology remain unfinished tasks.

Notes

Introduction
(pp. 1–13)
1. Cf. J. Navone, *Theology as Story*, London 1977; J. B. Metz, *Glaube in Geschichte u. Gesellschaft*, Mainz 1977, particularly pp. 181–203.

Chapter One
(pp. 14–39)
1. Cf. S. Fagan, *Has Sin Changed?*, Dublin 1978; J. F. Gustafson, *Protestant and Roman Catholic Ethics*, Chicago: London 1978, pp. 1–12.
2. For more developed treatment of fundamental option and appropriate literature, cf. author's article on this topic in *New Catholic Encyclopedia*, vol. XVI (supplement), Washington 1976. For the idea of character as central to moral thinking cf. S. Hauerwas, *Character and the Christian Life*, San Antonio 1975.
3. *S. Theol.* I–II q.94, a.4, c. Cf. John E. Naus, S.J., *The Nature of the Practical Intellect according to St Thomas Aquinas*, Rome 1959, particularly pp. 35–68.
4. The best accounts of this development available in English are by Richard McCormick, S.J., cf. 'Notes on Moral Theology', *Theological Studies* XXXIX, March 1978; *Theological Studies* XXXVI/1, March 1975; 'Ambiguity in Moral Choice' (Marquette Lecture) 1973. A very extensive bibliography on both sides of the debate is also provided.
5. A useful history of Catholic teaching from biblical times to the present day is provided in G. F. Maxwell, *Slavery and the Catholic Church*, Chichester (Canada) and London 1975.
6. Cf. R. Aubert, *Pie IX*, Paris 1952.
7. J. T. Noonan, *The Scholastic Analysis of Usury*, Cambridge, Mass. 1957; *Contraception*, Cambridge, Mass. 1965.
8. Cf. author's article, 'Conscience' in J. P. Mackey, ed., *Morals, Law and Authority*, Dublin 1969.

9. In an interesting way this problem is bringing Catholic and Reformed moral theologians together, cf. P. Baelz, *Ethics and Belief*, London 1977; J. M. Gustafson, *Can Ethics be Christian?*, Chicago 1975; V. McNamara, 'Religion and Morality', *Irish Theological Quarterly*, April 1977.

10. A helpful comment on the priority of moral practice over moral principle may be found in G. F. Dorr, 'Principles of Pluralism', *Studies*, LXVII/265–6, Spring/Summer 1978, pp. 14–27.

11. Some insight into these difficulties is provided by F. Böckle in *Fundamental-moral*, Munich 1977, pp. 48–92, and in the diverse writings of Karl Rahner, cf. *Foundations of Christian Belief*, pp. 24–115.

12. Cf. J. M. Gustafson, op. cit., pp. 117–49.

13. Cf. J. L. Segundo, *The Liberation of Theology*, Dublin 1977, pp. 7–34; A. Furro, *The Militant Gospel*, London 1977, pp. 305–425.

14. For more extended treatment of the ideas outlined here cf. author's 'The Natural Law and the Law of Christ', *Invitation and Response*, Dublin 1972; 'Moral Theology Renewed', *Irish Ecclesiastical Record*, December 1965.

15. Cf. J. Sobrino, *Christology at the Crossroads*, London 1978. The special significance of Jesus' faith for fundamental moral theology is treated pp. 108–39.

16. Cf. C. Curran, 'Pluralism in Catholic Moral Theology', *Ongoing Revision in Moral Theology*, Notre Dame 1975, pp. 37–65.

17. Cf. J. B. Metz, 'Redemption and Emancipation', *Cross Currents*, XXVII/3, p. 321 (this article was first published as 'Erlosung u. Emanzipation' in *Glaube in Geschichte u. Gesellschaft*, Mainz 1977.

Chapter Two
(pp. 40–57)

1. From R. W. A. McKinney, ed., *Creation, Christ and Culture, Studies in Honour of T. F. Torrance*, Edinburgh 1976.

2. The basis of these developments is contained in the first document issued by Vatican II *Constitutio de Sacra Liturgia*, cf. Abbott/Gallagher, eds., *The Documents of Vatican II*, London 1966, pp. 137–77.

3. A useful account of the early developments of the movement in the Catholic Church is contained in Edward D. O'Connor, C.S.C., *The Pentecostal Movement in the Catholic Church*, Ave Maria Press, 1971. Since then a flood of literature has appeared: the most prestigious, because of his office, the book by Cardinal L. J. Suenens,

A New Pentecost?, London 1975. A thoughtful symposium on the Prayer and Renewal Movement in the Catholic Church appears in *La Vie Spirituelle*, juillet-août 1975, No. 609 T 129. For the older movement outside the Roman Catholic Church, cf. W. J. Hollenweger, *The Pentecostals*, London 1972.

4. In liturgical affairs a certain resistance to the developments has been associated with groups upholding the Latin and Tridentine form of the Mass. The charismatic prayer movement has also had its critics and opponents, but as it has not official status it does not cause the same difficulties.

5. Again there is a vast literature but quite a helpful recent collection of essays is to be found in Gene Outka and John P. Reeder, Jr, *Religion and Morality*, New York 1973. Some of my own thoughts on this wider issue are developed in my recent book, *Gift and Call*, Dublin 1975, particularly chs. 1, 4 and 12.

6. Typical manuals in common usage at that time were Nolden-Schmitt, *Summa Theologiae Moralis*, I–III, Barcelona 1951, or M. Zalba, *Theologiae Moralis Compendium*, I–II, Madrid 1958.

7. The various catechisms such as the Maynooth Catechism dealt with the matter in these terms and a fairly comprehensive account of the theology on which they were based is to be found in the article by A. Fonck, 'Prière', *Dictionaire de Théologie Catholique*, XIII/I, Paris 1936, pp. 169–244.

8. This point is made by Fonck, op. cit. I find it difficult to accept very sharply distinguished and contrasting typologies in the classic study of Friedrich Heiler, *Prayer*, London 1932, particularly the total contrast between what he calls mystical and prophetic prayer. I would largely agree with criticisms of him by M. Nedoncelle, *The Nature and Use of Prayer*, London 1964, pp. 106–11.

9. For a description of the manual tradition and criticism of it cf. author's 'Moral Theology: The Need for Renewal' in *Moral Theology Renewed*, ed. E. McDonagh, Dublin 1965, pp. 13–30.

10. For this section cf. Nolden-Schmitt, op. cit. II, pp. 132–47; M. Zalba, op. cit. I, pp. 531–62.

11. Two of the great pioneers of this work were: Fritz Tillman, in *Handbuch der Katholischen Sittenlehre* I–IV, particularly his own volume Bd. III, *Die Idee der Nachfolge Christi*, first published in 1933 and in 4th ed., Dusseldorf 1953; and Bernard Häring, *The Law of Christ* I–III (Eng. trs.), Cork 1961–7. For some account of the background to these developments cf. author's 'Moral Theology: The Need for Renewal', op. cit.

12. An attempt to provide such an 'ontological' anthropology is found

in the author's 'The Law of Christ and the Natural Law', *Duty and Discernment*, London 1975.

13. I have developed this point elsewhere in the essay, 'Liturgy and Christian Living' in *The Christian in the World* ed. B. Devlin, Dublin 1968.

14. S. Tugwell, *Did you receive the Spirit?*, London 1972.

15. P. Hocken, *You, He Made Alive*, London 1972. Cf. M. Thornton, *Prayer, a New Encounter*, London 1972.

16. The best 'insider' account of this is probably Francis MacNutt, *Healing*, Ave Maria Press 1975.

17. These reservations are based on limited personal experience of the movement itself and so should not be exaggerated. Yet the history of not entirely dissimilar movements in the past would suggest that they may not be without some basis. P. Baelz, *Prayer and Providence*, London 1968, would, together with some of the more classical treatments such as St Thomas Aquinas, *Summa Contra Gentes*, Bk III, provide useful balance on this matter. R. A. Knox, *Enthusiasm*, Oxford 1950, still provides a very valuable historical counterbalance to other temptations of such a movement.

18. This is the point of departure of my recent book *Gift and Call*, Dublin 1975. What follows is, in the analysis of morality, largely based on that work.

19. Ibid., particularly chs. 4, 10.

20. Although I was helped by them at the time, I do not find very satisfactory as theological analyses the earlier attempts to deal with this challenge of prayer in a secular culture, by J. Danielou, *Prayer as a Political Problem*, London 1967, and D. Rhymes, *Prayer in the Secular City*, London 1967.

21. The interesting work of M. Nedoncelle already cited does move from an analysis of prayer between men to prayer between men and God. But this is an entirely different approach from the one used here although it could have some useful connecting points.

22. This is obviously related to Rudolf Otto's *The Idea of the Holy*, London 1968. For more useful comments cf. John P. Reeder, Jr, 'The Relation of the Moral and the Numinous in Otto's Notion of the Holy' in Outka and Reeder (eds.) op. cit.

23. Whatever its ultimate theological limitations, John Robinson's *Honest to God*, London 1963, and the ensuing debate did clearly find echoes of recognition among many Christians.

24. This problem was given considerable recent attention in Roman Catholic theology in the discussion of 'anonymous Christianity' associated in particular with Karl Rahner.

25. As I have noted before (op. cit.) there is still no fully satisfactory moral analysis of the relationships between groups.
26. Cf. my 'Human Violence: A Question of Ethics or Salvation', ch. 10, op. cit., for a fuller discussion of this question.

Chapter Three
(pp. 58–75)
1. From *In Libertatem Vocati Estis, Miscellanea Bernard Häring*, Rome 1977.
2. Cf. my *Invitation and Response. Essays in Christian Moral Theology*, Dublin 1972.
3. Cf. ch. 2 supra.

Chapter Four
(pp. 76–89)
1. Based on a lecture given at Cambridge University, March 1978.

Chapter Five
(pp. 90–100)
1. Based on a lecture given at Oxford University, March 1978.

Chapter Six
(pp. 101–111)
1. Based on a lecture given to the Irish Theological Association, November 1974.

Chapter Seven
(pp. 112–118)
1. Based on a lecture given to the Social Study Conference, August 1978 at Creeslough, Ireland.

Chapter Eight
(pp. 119–137)
1. Translations of this article appeared in the European (non-English) language editions of *Concilium*, December 1975. Later, in 1976, the article was published in the *Irish Theological Quarterly*.
2. The Shorter Oxford English Dictionary defines it as 'the scientific study of the practical or industrial arts' but admits the transferred sense of 'practical arts collectively'. The extended sense which I adopt can be readily understood from such works as Melvin Kranzberg and Carroll W. Purcell (eds.) *Technology in Western Civilisation*, Oxford University Press 1967, cf. Peter F. Drucker,

Technology, Management and Society, London 1970, chs. 3, 4, 5, 7, 11.

3. Drucker, op. cit., would suggest a date 7,000 years ago for what he calls the 'irrigation revolution', p. 110.

4. Cf. Kranzberg and Purcell, op. cit.; Drucker, op. cit.; Moorman, ed., *Science and Technology in Europe,* London 1968.

5. Cf. E. G. Mesthene, 'Technology and Values' in K. Vaux, ed., *Who Shall Live?*, Philadelphia 1970, pp. 55ff.

6. Drucker, 'The First Technological Revolution', op. cit., pp. 110ff.

7. The literature is so extensive by now and in all languages that it is not even useful to attempt a representative selection.

8. Drucker, op. cit. pp. 47ff.

9. This is akin to the title of a valuable book by Jacques Ellul, *The Technological Revolution,* New York 1964.

10. Ward and Dubos *Only One Earth,* London 1972, is a classic example from the very wide literature available.

11. Cf. *A Blueprint for Survival* by the Editors of *The Ecologist,* London 1972. This draws extensively on *Man's Impact on the Global Environment: The Study of Critical Environmental Problems,* MIT Press, a very authoritative study by a group of leading American scientists, and on Meadows et al., *The Limits to Growth, A Report for the Club of Rome's Project on the Predicament of Mankind,* London 1972, which is much more debated as to its methodology and conclusions.

12. *A Blueprint,* pp. 23–4.

13. Cf. Ward and Dubos, op. cit., etc.

14. I. Illich, *Energy and Equity,* London 1974.

15. Cf. 'The Triple Revolution', a letter to President Lyndon B. Johnson, 22 March 1964, reprinted in E. Fromm, ed., *Socialist Humanism,* London 1967, pp. 409ff.

16. Cf. for example, H. Marcuse, *One Dimensional Man,* London 1964.

17. I. Illich, *Medical Nemesis,* London 1975.

18. Cf. *A Blueprint:* A. S. Nash, 'Food, Population and Man's Environment' in R. H. Preston, *Technology and Social Justice,* London 1971.

19. Cf. H. Marcuse, 'The Triple Revolution', op. cit., M. Neil, 'The Phenomenon of Technology: Liberation or Alienation of Man' in E. Fromm ed., op. cit.

20. Cf. my *Gift and Call,* Dublin 1975.

21. I have a more detailed discussion of this in *Gift and Call,* ch. 3: The Moral Subject.

22. Cf. A useful discussion of values in social ethics which highlights

liberty and equality in a similar way by R. S. Downie, *Roles and Values*, London 1971, pp. 25–55.
23. Cf. J. Rawls, *A Theory of Justice*, Cambridge, Mass. 1971, particularly chs. 1, 2, 5.
24. A good example of this is given by J. V. Taylor, *Enough is Enough*, London 1975, p. 89.
25. E. F. Schumacker, in his influential work *Small is Beautiful*, London 1972, and other articles such as 'What is happening to Intermediate Technology', *Frontier*, vol. 9, no. 11, Summer 1972, stresses the subordination of economics and technology to people and their needs.
26. B.B.C. broadcast, June 1975.
27. Cf. Meadows et al., *The Limits to Growth* and subsequent debate.
28. M. Mesarovic and E. Pestel, *Mankind at the Turning Point. The Second Report to the Club of Rome*, London 1975, takes advantage of the criticisms of *The Limits to Growth*, has a more realistic attitude to relation between growth, stability and development, and proposes a more flexible model for dealing with the problems.
29. Cf. *A Blueprint, Mankind at the Turning Point*.
30. In an otherwise valuable article, 'Removing the Rubbish', *Encounter*, vol. XLII, no. 4, April 1974, John Passmore unjustly concludes that Christian theology cannot adequately meet the ecological call to 'stewardship and cooperation'. This article forms the last chapter of his book, *Man's Responsibility for Nature*, London 1974.
31. This is to some extent the philosophy of *A Blueprint*.

Chapter Nine
(pp. 138–152)
1. Based on a lecture given at King's College, London University, March 1977 and subsequently published in *The Furrow*, February 1978.

Chapter Ten
(pp. 153–167)
1. Based on a lecture given at Bristol University, March 1978.
2. Cf. *The Furrow*, June 1972.
3. Cf. *The Furrow*, March 1976.
4. D. Lane, ed., *Liberation Theology: an Irish Dialogue*, Dublin 1977.
5. Cf. J. Darby, *Conflict in Northern Ireland*, Dublin 1976, p. 114.
6. One of the most forcible and penetrating of these commentators is Richard Hanson, formerly Church of Ireland Bishop of Clogher and now Professor in the Faculty of Theology, University of Manchester.

7. Cf. A. Dulles, *Models of the Church*, Dublin 1975.
8. Cf. 'Justice in the World', par. 6, p. 514, in J. Gremillon, *The Gospel of Peace and Justice*, New York 1975.

Chapter Eleven
(pp. 168–178)
1. From M. Hurley, ed., *Beyond Tolerance*, London 1975.

Chapter Twelve
(pp. 179–187)
1. From *Concilium* 7, New York 1977.

Chapter Thirteen
(pp. 188–208)
1. See above, ch. 6: Secularity, Christianity and Society.
2. Contemporary philosophical and theological discussions of these difficulties have not been adequately considered by moral theologians yet. Cf. ch. 1: The Quest for Moral Theology, pp. 14–39 above, and notes 11 and 12.
3. Cf. C. Curran, ed., *Contraception; Authority and Dissent*, New York 1968.
4. Cf. A. Dulles, *The Resilient Church*, Dublin 1978, ch. 5: Doctrinal Authority for a Pilgrim Church, pp. 93–112.
5. Cf. F. Böckle, 'Faith and Deeds' in Tracy, Küng, Metz, ed., *Towards Vatican III*, Dublin 1978, pp. 113–14.
6. Allegations of this kind of treatment are frequent but not always easy to substantiate or document, partly because one cannot be sure how far other reasons may have been partly or wholly responsible for exclusion. However cf. the exclusion of Philip Land, S.J., from the World Population Conference in 1974 (cf. P. Hebblethwaite, *The Runaway Church*, London 1975, p. 217), the experiences of Charles Curran (*Ongoing Revision in Moral Theology*, Notre Dame 1975, pp. 260–294), and the comment in The Tablet Notebook on the need to preserve the anonymity of a moral theological contributor on the tenth anniversary of *Humanae Vitae* in order to protect him in his chair (*The Tablet*, 29 July 1978, p. 733).

On the general problem of dishonesty in the Church on disagreement about contraception and other issues of particular concern in the Irish situation cf G. Daly, 'Christian Response to Religious Pluralism', *Studies* LXVII/265–6, Spring/Summer 1978, p. 73.
7. Apart from its strictly academic achievements at conferences and in publications, the Irish Theological Association has made notable

contributions to the self-understanding of theology in Ireland, with its two reports on Theology and the University, in 1972 and 1977.

8. This slogan is usually associated with the World Council of Churches in the mid-sixties and, in particular, the Uppsala Assembly of 1967. For a critical reaction cf. A. Dulles, op. cit., pp. 84ff.

9. For a more developed discussion of this cf. the author's 'An Irish Theology of Liberation?' in D. Lane, ed., *Liberation Theology— An Irish Dialogue,* Dublin 1977, pp. 86–102.